Palash Krishna Mehrotra was born in Bombay in 1975. He was educated at St Stephen's College, Delhi, where he did his B.A. in philosophy, and won the Radhakrishnan Scholarship to read for a PPE at Balliol College, Oxford.

His debut collection of stories, *Eunuch Park: Fifteen Stories of Love and Destruction*, was shortlisted for the Shakti Bhatt First Book Prize and the Hindu Prize for Fiction. His first book of non-fiction, *The Butterfly Generation: A Personal Journey Into the Passions and Follies of India's Technicolor Youth*, was a finalist for the Crossword Book Award. He is also the editor of an anthology, *Recess: The Penguin Book of Schooldays*.

He was Contributing Editor at *Rolling Stone India* and writes a fortnightly column for *Mail Today Sunday*, *DailyO* and *Daily Mail Online*.

He lives in New Delhi and Dehradun.

HOUSE SPIRIT

drinking in India

Stories • Essays • Poems

EDITED BY
PALASH KRISHNA
MEHROTRA

SPEAKING
TIGER

SPEAKING TIGER PUBLISHING PVT. LTD
4381/4, Ansari Road, Daryaganj
New Delhi 110002

First published by Speaking Tiger in paperback 2016

Introduction copyright © Palash Krishna Mehrotra 2016
Stories, Essays, Poems copyright © Individual contributors 2016
Anthology copyright © Speaking Tiger 2016

ISBN: 978-93-85755-87-3
eISBN: 978-93-85755-92-7

10 9 8 7 6 5 4 3 2 1

The moral right of the authors has been asserted.

Typeset in Adobe Garamond Pro by SÜRYA, New Delhi
Printed at Thomson Press India Ltd.

For Rory White

COPYRIGHT ACKNOWLEGEMENTS

The Publishers acknowledge with thanks permission from the authors and publishers to reproduce the following:

A shorter version of 'Fear and Loathing in Ahmedabad: Drinking in Prohibition Gujarat' by Soumya Bhattacharya first appeared in *The Hindustan Times*, 18 July 2009.

'Hanging on Like Death' first appeared in the short story collection *Difficult Pleasures* by Anjum Hasan, Penguin Viking, 2012.

'Government Country: Poems' by Adil Jussawalla is excerpted from *Trying to Say Goodbye*, Almost Island Books, Mumbai, 2011, reprinted 2012, 2015. 'A Glass Too Many' is excerpted from *Maps for a Mortal Moon*, Aleph Book Company, 2014.

'Dancing With Men' by Palash Krishna Mehrotra is excerpted from *Eunuch Park: Fifteen Stories of Love and Destruction*, Penguin Books India, 2009.

'First Infinities' by Vijay Nambisan is excerpted from *First Infinities*, Poetrywala, 2015.

'Ten Feet Tall', 'Wastrel Song', 'Denial', 'Unknown' and 'The Morning After' (under the title 'Bar Music') by Manohar Shetty, were first published in *Living Room*, HarperCollins Publishers India, 2014. 'Taverna' was first published in *The Baffler*, MIT and in *Body Language*, Poetrywala, Mumbai.

'On An Odyssey Through Toddy Shops' by Samanth Subramaniam is excerpted from *Following Fish: Travels Around the Indian Coast*, Penguin Viking, 2010.

'The Alcoholic at Dawn' by Jeet Thayil is excerpted from *Collected Poems*, Aleph Book Company, 2015. 'Delirium' is excerpted from his forthcoming novel, a work in progress.

'Chilling Out at the Deluxe Bar' and 'The Highways of Mofussiluru' are excerpted from Zac O'Yeah's *Mr Majestic! The Tout of Bengaluru* originally published in hardback by Hachette in 2012 and in paperback by Pan, an imprint of PanMacmillan India, in 2015.

CONTENTS

'Now that we are a republic, and there is no "pub" in it, let us hope we will not become a relic.'

—C.K. Daphthary, former Attorney General of India, on Probhibition being reimposed in Bombay in 1949

Friends, you must forgive me, for I am somewhat drunk.

As the flask goes round, give me just a sip—
Not full to the top, just enough to wet my lip,
For I am somewhat drunk.

If I speak rude words, blame it on the drink;
You too may call me names, or whatever else you think,
For I am somewhat drunk.

What can I do, if I try to walk I stumble,
Don't be cross with me, please don't grumble,
For I am somewhat drunk.

The Friday prayer is always there, it won't run away;
I'll come along with you, if for a while you'll stay,
For I am somewhat drunk.

Meer can be as touchy as hell when it is his whim;
He's made of fragile glass, take no liberty with him,
For he is somewhat drunk.

—Meer Taqi Meer
(translated by Khushwant Singh)

INTRODUCTION

'Pure Premium Drinking Experience'

Our attitude to drinking is the same as it is to sex. We don't do it. But, like sex, we do it all the time. And some states, it seems, do it more than others.

Advertising for liquor brands is banned. I remember a commercial for 8 PM (originally a whisky brand) apple juice. The man has a sip and crazy things happen to him. The tag line goes—'8 PM apple juice. Kuchh bhi ho sakta hai' (Anything can happen). Possibly the most potent apple juice ever concocted. Fermented maybe?

The states with solid drinking reputations are Uttarakhand, Punjab and Kerala. I realized this when I emerged back into the 'real' world after spending several years in Dehradun, drinking 8 PM whisky. My first port of call was Bombay. I went to a party and drank too much. A friend turned to me and said, 'What's with the drinking, Palash? Uttarakhand, eh?' In Delhi, I went to a doctor with a stomach bug. He asked me if I drank. I said yes. How much? I told him. It was way above the NHS recommended daily intake. He asked me where I was from. When I said Dehradun, his eyes lit up. 'Ah. We've had this problem with boys from Uttarakhand.'

Punjab is the Ireland of India. Drinking is more than acceptable. In fact, in Punjab, it's those who don't drink who are considered suspect. Prices are among the lowest in the country. It was Punjab after all that gave the world the Patiala peg.

Kerala, the state of melancholic Mallus, is also my favourite place to drink. I love dives (more on this in a bit) and Kerala has plenty. Apart from the local tipple, toddy, Kerala loves its brandy. This came as a pleasant surprise. Coming from the north, I associated brandy with older people. My grandmother always has a shot before she goes to bed. But in Kerala, everyone drinks 'braandee'. Here's how you do it: bite into a boiled egg and a piece of bitter gourd pickle, raise your pinky finger and wash it down with half a glass of Honeybee mixed with water. Have another bite; drain the glass. Now you're a man. In Anup Kutty's story 'Police Uncle', set in Kerala, a character adds brandy to everything he drinks: '"Does brandy mix well with toddy?" I ask him. He loves mixing brandy with everything—beer, whisky… even pure ethanol. Once we got so hammered on a concoction of beer and brandy that I was talking to imaginary people by the pond.'

~

For many Indians, drinking is taboo at home. Which is why the quarter bottle remains a runaway bestseller. It's something that can be consumed quickly and discarded. We drink everywhere—on trains, outside liquor vends, in our cars, but rarely at home. It's important to maintain appearances. In Allahabad, my hometown, people hire cycle rickshaws by the half hour. The rickshaw puller's brief is to keep pedalling until the booze runs out. People also drink standing behind the beer shop. They blend into the darkness of the night, and sip their beer surrounded by the stench of sewage.

The car drinkers come in two categories. Those who drink and drive at the same time, and those who park outside a tandoori chicken joint and open a bottle. I have a school friend in Allahabad who cannot drink at home, not because his wife minds, but because he lives with his father, mother and elder brother and they would throw a fit. On Sundays, he takes his wife and kid for a drive, and drinks while he's driving. It's three pleasures in one, he told me, 'Drinking pleasure, wifely pleasure and driving pleasure.'

I was once with another friend who likes to drink while he's driving. I was frightened out of my wits. I invited him to my place. Why not sit and enjoy a drink? He had a ready explanation. 'I get too high if I have my rum sitting down. Driving keeps me sane.'

We like our liquor so much that we drink on trains too, even though it's prohibited. You can be fined for smoking on a train, but you'll rarely be penalized for drinking. In our tipple tradition, drinking is always done on an empty stomach, before dinner. In the old days, when Rajdhanis had chair cars, the attendants would come around with soda and soft drinks an hour before dinner was served. You chose your mixer, tipped the bearer and settled down into the cocktail hour on a running train.

Then there are the efficient, organized types who board the train having done their homework. This man will start getting restless by six in the evening. He will look at his watch every few minutes. At seven, he will cast guilty glances at fellow passengers, then stick his hand into his duffle bag and pull out a Bisleri bottle containing a yellowish liquid that looks like Morarji Cola but is actually whisky mixed with water. Since he's well prepared he will, in all probability, also be armed with a ten-rupee packet of Haldiram's bhujiya. A sip of Bagpiper. A mouthful of bhujiya. Sip again. Feeling sociable? Good time to call home. 'Beta, how was your exam? Aaj ghar pe khana kya bana hai?'

On long-distance trains, you don't even have to carry your liquor. There's a system in place. On the Rajdhani to Guwahati, they will get you as many quarters of McDowells No.1 whisky as you want, though at a slight mark-up. All you need to do is ask the right attendant. A regular on the route gave me some sound advice. 'Don't pay a rupee more than two hundred. The tip is included in the price'

I like to drink in dives. Home is boring and familiar. Delhi bars are overpriced and I cannot stand fawning waiters who keep refilling your glass even though the previous beer is far from over.

But Delhi doesn't have dive bars. Bombay and Bangalore have many, and, of late, so does Dehradun. My local in Dehradun, Meedos, is splendid. It's dingy, and dank, and by seven in the evening it's packed with grim-faced men. Surly waiters bang wet glasses and beer on your table and walk away. It's very matter of fact. By eight, people are abusing their bosses; by nine, they are building castles in the air; by ten, they are headed home to their inquisitive wives. And dinner.

~

The Gujarati writer Pavankumar Jain says in 'Confidence Trickster':

> For many years though I drank hooch on certain fixed days of the year:
>
> January 26—India's Republic Day
> August 15—India's Independence Day
> October 2—Gandhiji's birth anniversary
> The various voting days when municipal, state and parliamentary elections were held.
>
> On these designated dry days, I had an uncontrollable urge to drink. The illicit liquor addas were the only places I could wet my parched throat.

It's May 2009. It's the fourth dry day in seven days. I am walking the railway tracks in Delhi's Jal Vihar with two rickshaw pullers in rags looking for a drink. There are slums on either side, children play and pee on the tracks, every third shanty doubles as a makeshift bar.

No one knows why it's a dry day. We have had three days of elections, one day of drinking and again—no booze. One rickshaw puller insists it's Guru Purab. Another claims it's counting day. It will be weeks before I find out that it was actually Buddha Purnima.

But here in Jal Vihar, in the middle of this filthy slum, you can buy anything you want: Royal Stag, McDowells, country liquor. Dozens of tipplers—many of them middle class—are wandering around with bottles of Zingaro beer. My men take me to their preferred joint—a small room with a fridge full of strong beer, buckets full of tamper-proof IMFL quarters, jerry cans full of country liquor. We sit and drink, and as so often happens after drinking, we talk.

The men I am with don't spend too much time on their drinks. By middle-class standards I don't spend too much time finishing a glass either, but these guys are fast. I have no intention of competing with them. The quarters are downed in one go. I sip on my Zingaro.

It's nice though. Unlike Bombay, Delhi doesn't have any watering holes for the working class. We have ridiculous dingy overpriced pubs with depressing wrought-iron furniture. These illegal slum bars are different. Class barriers break down and people talk to each other, like they would in most bars around the world. We talk the IPL and politics. No one seems to like Advani here. The general consensus is that if Advani came to power there would be more terrorism, more riots. One of my mates has had too much already. He is writhing on the floor, a mad little ball of energy, a malfunctioning robot with nothing on his mind. He is carried out gently and left near the tracks outside.

My other rickshaw-puller friend is talking now, his tongue greased by alcohol. He used to be a cook. He can cook everything from Chinese to South Indian. I ask him why he is pulling rickshaws for a living when he has kitchen skills. He says he has been fired. By whom and why? He points vaguely across the railway tracks and says, Nafisa Ali. Why did she fire you? Because I used to drink and beat my wife. My wife is still there. Living in that house. But they wouldn't let me enter until I apologized to my wife and promised to quit drinking.

Our man is livid. He downs two more quarters and explains his position: 'A man never apologizes to his woman. The day he does so he is finished as a man. I will not do so till the day I die.' I nod my head in agreement.

He could be making all this up. But his stories paint him in such poor light I am inclined to believe him. He is certainly not boasting. He says he doesn't like Madam but her husband, Major Sahab, is a good man. Sahab drinks Scotch from America while memsahib drinks vodka.

Things are getting heavy by now. Writhing Robot has recovered sufficiently to pick himself up from the railway tracks and walk back into the barroom. I say we should get going. I need to buy a bottle of whisky. It's only available in quarters. My cohorts insist it's unsafe for me to carry the bottles out of the slum. There are cops outside on the road who are interested in making a quick buck. They offer to stuff their pockets with the quarters and escort me to an autorickshaw. It's a deal.

Outside it's dark. There is a railway engine parked on one of the tracks, hooting away like a lonesome bull. It groans and whistles and hisses smoke. There are more people milling about. The men with

my whisky are weaving in and out of the crowd, nimbly, swiftly; they
have been doing this all their lives. I catch up with them. I ask them
to return the bottles to me. I'll take a chance with the cops. What
prevents them from vanishing into the strange darkness, leaving me
not high and very dry?

They empty out their pockets on the tracks. The bottles are on the
ground. There is more honking and hooting. I look up. The engine
on the parallel track is still stationary. It just seems to be making more
noise than it should. Somebody screams, Watch out. All of us turn
around. There is a train right behind us. I dive to the side and crouch
under a protruding corrugated iron roof. Nafisa's ex-cook and Writhing
Robot dive too but not before they have collected the whisky. Twenty
seconds later the train passes.

I grab the bottles and make for the exit with the cook. Writhing
Robot is doing funny things by now. His speech is slurred so I can't
make out what he's saying. One minute he is on the tracks on his
back, legs in the air like an upturned beetle. The next he is standing,
legs wide apart, railing against the world from his imaginary soap box.

~

While the liquor industry has expanded, and new foreign brands enter
the market every month, little has changed on the ground for the
Indian tippler. Thekas, as liquor shops are called in the north, remain
poky holes where one passes money through a grilled window to buy
a bottle. These thekas are prehistoric mafia-owned dens. They stock
what they want, sell what they want, at the price they deem proper.
You jostle for space—cash in hand, elbow your fellow tipplers and
finally get your request across, only to find that your brand is not in
stock. If you do manage to get a brand of your choice, chances are that
you will pay a mark-up of ten rupees or more, on the printed MRP.

There is a politician-liquor mafia nexus. It's this mafia that decides
what you drink and how much you pay for it. In Dehradun, Indian
rum disappeared from liquor vend shelves for several months in
2015. The only rum available was Bacardi. In UP, for many years,
the mark-up on liquor was openly called the 'Mayawati tax'. She is

even supposed to have lost one state election because of this—it had become an 'issue' for the price-conscious Indian voter. Sometimes the mark-up was as much as Rs 40. I too remember having arguments with vend owners, with fellow tipplers irately pitching in. This, one soon realized, was a waste of time, because everyone in town was selling at higher than the listed price.

Ponty Chadha controlled the liquor business in Noida and Uttarakhand. The man had an efficient private police, an extra-legal excise army. This private police had its own hierarchy and its job was to prevent smuggling of liquor from other states, to make sure that truckloads of cheaper liquor from, say, Punjab didn't flood Ponty's territory. In a way, he was doing the excise department's job for them. In reality, he was protecting his own territory. While the man on the street had to shell out way above the legitimate price, Ponty fuelled the money back into his liquor business and launched his own brands. Raffles rum was one of them. Raffles did reasonably well, and managed to take some market share away from the old classics like Celebration, Old Monk and Sikkim. Because he had a monopoly over liquor vends, Ponty made sure that Raffles rum was easily available, often at the cost of other brands.

Much of this corruption is because the government maintains a tight grip on the liquor business. It's far too lucrative and politicians want their share of the pie. It's the state government that auctions liquor vends, mostly to their cronies, every financial year. One gentleman in Dehradun made so much money from his liquor vends that he pulled out of liquor retail and reinvested his cash in coaching centres—the new beer.

Government control of the liquor business has its roots in colonial times. As Sumanta Banerjee writes in his essay 'Alcoholics Unanimous':

> In 1790, it [the British administration] took over the right of collecting duties on spirits from the Bengali zamindars on the moral ground that 'the immoderate use of spirituous liquors and drugs....had become prevalent among many of the lower orders of people owing to the very inconsiderable price at which they were manufactured and sold.' Intent on increasing its revenue through

a centralized system, the government first granted licenses to local entrepreneurs to set up distilleries in large towns and fixed high rates of taxes and high prices of liquor.

Apart from revenue, the other reason for the British administration's interference was its racist belief that alcohol bred criminal tendencies in the 'lower orders'. In 1863, Calcutta's Police Commissioner claimed that 'a very large proportion of all crime is caused by drunkenness... (and that) liquor shops are frequented by every class of criminals...In Calcutta no house can be licensed, and no person can obtain a license to sell liquor without any (police) sanction...'

As Banerjee points out, 'while medical practitioners tend to attribute almost every physical ailment to consumption of liquor, the police are obsessed with linking every crime with booze.' This belief holds as true today as it did in colonial times. Abhinav Kumar, a serving IPS officer, writes in his essay 'The Theka':

> From a police viewpoint, a theka was the epicentre of the forces of crime and disorder. It had to be monitored with a hawk's eye and dealt with a firm hand... The theka and the police have a symbiotic relationship. Each needs the other for different reasons. The proprietor of a theka keeps the police in good humour so that the countless daily violations of our cumbersome excise laws go unnoticed and are not acted upon. The police need the theka to serve as a lightning rod for young drinkers, who in their opinion are the demographic most likely to cause trouble, as compared to law-abiding teetotallers.

In an interesting aside, Kumar talks about the ecosystem that forms around a theka: 'A shop selling snacks, masala peanuts mostly, a paan shop, with a side alley or a backyard to enable the excessively inebriated to relieve themselves in a manner of their choosing.' Pavankumar Jain mentions this too, albeit in a different time—Prohibition-era Bombay:

> The entrance of this hooch joint was covered with a dirty cloth curtain. Outside the joint, hawkers sold hard boiled eggs, pieces of fried fish and boiled chana. Over the years, these two markers—the dirty cloth curtain on the door, and the hawkers selling fish or chana

close by, always helped me locate a hooch joint, even in areas totally unfamiliar to me.

While the link between alcohol and criminality is debatable, there has always been a connection between whoring and drinking. In nineteenth-century Calcutta, taverns stretched from Lalbazar in the White Town, to the south, near the dockyard in Khidirpur. The Lalbazar taverns provided the European sailors and soldiers with arrack, while 'the Khidirpur grog house-cum-bordellos offered them an equally hot spread of women from all parts of the world...These women came in search of fortune, but unlike their more fortunate sisters (who found husbands among the city's European residents), ended up as barmaids-turned-dockyard prostitutes,' says Sumanta Banerjee.

~

Cheap whisky that's in the price range of Rs 240 and Rs 700 is the one I'm most familiar with. At the lower end are Aristocrat, Bagpiper and Diplomat, at the higher, Peter Scot. In socialist India, the high life was associated with a prestigious government job, like being a diplomat. We also had the aspirational Director's Special, aspirational because in socialist India there was hardly any private sector and so very few directors of companies. Then comes McDowells No. 1 and its premium version, Platinum. The former is a 'blockbuster', as it is called in the trade, the whisky that is adulterated the most. Which is why it now comes in a tamper-proof golden carry bag.

There's Officers Choice Prestige Whisky ('with caramel colour added') which claims to be the drink of honest upright officers (even though the brand historically targeted daily-wage earners), and Radico's 8 PM, which was the first to break from aspirational names like Diplomat, appealing instead to the time in the evening when middle-class India sits down to have a drink. And finally, there's Peter Scot, which used to be the favourite drink of High Court lawyers but has now slid down the snob chart. I'm not even going near Blenders Pride and the world that lies beyond. To me it's like China—a country that I've heard a lot about but never visited. I hope to do so one day.

Purists say that Indian whisky is not whisky. According to the Scotch Whisky Association's annual report of 2013:

> There is no compulsory definition of whisky in India, and the Indian voluntary standard does not require whisky to be distilled from cereals or to be matured. Very little Indian 'whisky' qualifies as whisky in the EU owing to the use of molasses or neutral alcohol, limited maturation (if any) and the use of flavourings. Such spirits are, of course, considerably cheaper to produce than genuine whisky.

This though hasn't stopped us from drinking it. Royal Stag clocked sales of fifteen million cases last year, while Imperial Blue sold twelve million cases. Imperial Blue's packaging claims that the whisky's 'smoothness' is appreciated by 'whisky connoisseurs worldwide'. The copywriting on the McDowell's No. 1 bottle claims, 'Somewhere in the world, it's always No. 1 time.' So, as you sit down to a peg of McDowell's in Bhopal, someone is doing the same in Detroit and Zurich. Okay, not. But the claim is not entirely unfounded. Imperial Blue is exported to a dozen African countries. In fact, Pernod Ricard exports Royal Stag, Imperial Blue and Blenders Pride to East Asia, the Middle East and Africa—so it *is* always No. 1 time somewhere in the world. According to the UK-based magazine and portal *The Spirits Business*, Kishore Chhabria sold 255 million litres of his Officer's Choice whisky in 2014, displacing Smirnoff as the world's largest spirits brand by volume. Officer's Choice had already surpassed Johnnie Walker as the world's largest selling whisky in 2013.

There is an entire lost world of copywriting on these bottles, which underlines the gap between ambition and reality. Lost because the target consumer can hardly even read the fine print; most cut to the chase and throw away the bulky packaging outside the liquor vend. Imperial Blue has spawned an entire breed of imitators in the sub-Rs 400 market: Officer's Choice Blue, Dennis and my favourite, White & Blue. Now W&B is not as simple as it sounds: 'White signifies purity and perfection. Blue symbolizes masculinity, wisdom and royalty.' W&B, 'a heavenly blend', is 'a fusion of both'. Its 'captivating nuances come from the choicest composition of the blend giving it a smoky aroma and a mellow taste of pure royal lifestyle.'

The royal theme continues in Royal Challenge, described as 'a richly rewarding symphony of subtle notes'. It is another matter that the ubiquitous RC has emerged as the graft whisky of India; you give a bottle of RC as a bribe for a job quickly done on the sly.

If Officer's Choice targeted the blue-collar worker, their premium grain variant OC Blue is meant for bleeding heart yuppies-with-a-conscience. Their marketing mantra is spelt out on their website: 'The equity of Officer's Choice Blue is centered around the value of righteousness. The brand connects to the target audience of young, modern and progressive consumers by asking them to take a stand against social wrongs and is brought alive through the clarion call of "Raise Your Voice".'

Most of these whiskies also flaunt a range of dubious awards they have won, for some reason mostly in Brussels, or something called the 'World Beverage Competition, USA'. The Belgians are obviously big connoisseurs of Indian whisky, the EU guidelines on whisky notwithstanding.

The copywriting is always miles ahead of the whisky itself. Blue Patrol Reserve is a 'skilfully crafted Elite master blend that is rich in aroma and flavour resulting in a pure Premium Dinking Experience... Cherish the Bliss of Elixir!!!'

McDowells No. 1 Platinum claims to have been crafted by 'Our master blender based in Glasgow'. The writing on the bottle breaks down its appreciation of the whisky into three categories. Aroma: 'Classic peat skillfully embedded on silky layers of rich malt and matured oak wood which gets well rounded with a sweet touch of vanilla, honey and complex spring flowers.' Taste: 'Complex yet distinct peat, matured oak wood and malt, with vanilla on the edges, makes the whisky very smooth and palate warming; enriched almond, clove and cinnamon at the end gives the whisky a distinguished character.' Finish: 'Warm peat and lingering malt which is luxuriously smooth and gratifying.'

The distinguished kings of the IMFL market are Solan No. 1 ('A blend of oakwood matured malts and select Indian grain spirits'), and Blenders Pride, which has always bothered me because I feel somewhere in its name, I don't know exactly where, there's a missing apostrophe. The master blenders in question here, the label tells us, were Messrs Patrick Joseph Loots and Abbey Stephens, who 'decided to roll out one particular cask of whisky from the cool cellars of the distillery and expose it to the warmth of the setting sun at regular intervals. The delicate sweetness and aromatic flavour of the blend is testimony to the spectacular success of the experiment.' It's not clear where this event took place, in Scotland or at their manufacturing plant in Rajasthan. This is where I prefer Brihans, a socialist-era classic. The bottle says that it is 'Blended by 'whisky' experts.' At least they got the punctuation mark right.

Every evening at 8 p.m., like millions of fellow Indians, I down some molasses with swadeshi pride and hiccup through the crackernoise in my belly. I never forget to read the copywriting on the bottle. For I know the indelible, imperial, royal truth: whisky is always in the words.

~

Why do we start drinking? What does the first sip taste like? As with sex, the first time is often not the most memorable. In his essay, 'Some Pathologies', Amit Chaudhuri writes:

> I began drinking beer when I was sixteen years old because it seemed to go well with playing the guitar and being a young man. Opening the can with an inaugural pop gave much satisfaction; I poured, and admired the surplus of froth on the top; I liked the mild bitter cold taste. After five sips, I grew bored of the increasing tepidity. Finishing a glass was hard work, requiring diligence and commitment.

In Gautam Bhatia's story, 'Aristocrat', eight eleven-year-olds gather at a friend's place to have their first...gulp:

> The eight of us from Class 7, Section B, who sat there knew from the deathly drawing room silence that we were all there for a calculated and risky adventure... A tray with eight glasses and a Golden Eagle was placed on the centre table, along with six lemonades and potato chips. Samir poured out the equivalent of a peg in each glass. And waited. For a long while I just sat staring at the glass, thinking

dark thoughts… Horrible thoughts. But I guess some things had to be done.

Pavankumar Jain has his first drink—a teaspoon of feni—in the library of Bombay's St Xavier's College. The librarian, it turns out, likes his feni, and drinks on the job:

> I gulped down a teaspoonful of it. It had an unbearably strong and unfamiliar smell. Very bitter. A somewhat burning sensation in the throat, causing short spasms of dry cough. What? Nothing happened. Why does the librarian sip this useless stuff? Anyway, that was my initiation ritual, deeksha if you may, to enter the adult world.

For the first-timer, Henry Derozio, in an essay he wrote in 1824, has some impeccable advice:

> Persevere with resolution in so good a cause. Your heads are weak; time and custom will strengthen them. The porters of Baghdad begin when children to carry mimic burdens. As their years and strength increase, so do the loads which they voluntarily impose upon themselves… Let a single bottle be the starting post and drink an additional glass at the end of every week; by the 1st of April 1825, you will drink one bottle and fifty-two glasses per diem. There are about eight good glasses to the bottle.

Like the porters of Baghdad, Mayank Shekhar ('Booze, Bollywood, Bombay & I') began mimicking his burden at the age of five, but with dire consequences:

> It kinda became clear to me that more often than not it was the villain who drank lots—ideally in his 'aiyashi ka den', surrounded by gora guests and hot dancers. Inspired by one of those scenes, I once raised my glass of water to my brother, and said, 'Let's have a drink'—slurring it in a leery way that only Prem Chopra could. Recall Kevin Arnold's elder brother from the TV show *The Wonder Years*? Yeah that *was* my brother. He blackmailed me about revealing this 'let's have a drink' line to my parents for at least a couple of years. Whenever he needed to arm-twist me to get anything done, he'd pull out the code word, 'SLO (Secret Leaked Out)' and I would quickly fall in line.'

Shekhar, who would grow up to be an astute film critic, was a classic victim of reel life influencing real life:

> You only had to be a half-indulgent uncle/aunty type to walk up and gently request, 'Beta, kuch poem ya gaana sunao,' and I would begin to stagger and sway with an imagined booze bottle in my hand, singing aloud, *'Jaha char yar mil jaye wahi raat ho gulzar. Jaha char yar....'* I'm not sure what my neighbourhood uncle/aunty types thought of me (or rather of my parents), but there was just no stopping beyond this point, *'Khel risky tha, whisky ne kiya beda paar. Jaha char yar...'* The feedback I got for my performance was that I was really good at this. And so, when my mama (mom's brother) was getting married, I had begun preparing steps for the grand brass-band act to the track, *'De daru, de daru. Oh mere bhaiya, de daru',* from *Karma* (1986).

Drinking in Hindi cinema is an act loaded with symbolism. As we see in Sidharth Bhatia's 'Permit Room', you don't just pour yourself a drink or have a beer in the normal course of things:

> Depending on the context it is placed in, drinking can signify evil, moral depravity or a slide into a personal hell. It can also be used to evoke laughter, since it makes the drinker do funny and stupid things. If the on-screen character lifting that glass to the mouth is a woman, the viewer gets a frisson of excitement, because it is almost certain she is a good girl gone astray. Rarely is drinking casual, a lifestyle choice with no subtext or in-your-face moralizing. Whenever a bottle is picked up and poured into a glass (usually in close up), the viewer knows there is a message in it.

Bhatia finds some evidence of 'normal' drinking in the 1939 film *Brandy ki Botal*, where a man goes in search of a bottle of brandy. Along the way, he encounters all sorts of drinkers, including regular drinkers (as opposed to alcoholics). But even this film was made when films with a reformist agenda were all the rage. There was a message in this brandy ki botal: Don't drink.

Kanika Gahlaut ('When Nights Turn into Decades') divides drinkers into three types:

The binge drinkers. They let go. And then next morning, they are in control again.

The sliding drinkers—you see them fall slowly and steadily into the arms of the seductive booze, unable to come up again, the intellect slowly wasting away.

The hangers on: drinking for them is not the purpose. They feed off the energy of other drinkers, going with the flow.

Clearly, Derozio belonged to the first category. In his essay 'On Drunkenness' quoted from above, which Rosinka Chaudhuri describes as 'a passionate vindication of the state of drunkenness', Derozio boasts that he has arrived at 'such a state of comparative beatitude' that he can drink 'any given quantity' of alcohol at night and yet 'rise the next morning as fresh as any one-pint man in the universe.' In fact, he wouldn't mind drinking more—it's the tropical climate that gets in the way: 'The nights are unfortunately too short in this country to admit of any serious debauchery.' But drinking too much is bound to cause a hangover—and a headache. This doesn't seem to bother Derozio. Pain and pleasure follow each other. It's in the natural course of things: 'If two men ride upon one horse,' says the sage Sancho, 'one *must* ride behind.'

Ritwik Ghatak would perhaps occupy the second category. About Ghatak, Sandip Roy writes in 'Whisky Nation':

Ghatak was an alcoholic who started with branded liquor and ended with country booze that rotted his liver and even consigned him to an asylum. He looked like an old broken man when he died but he was only fifty-one. In his 1974 film *Jukti Takko Aar Gappo*, Nilkantha, the washed-up intellectual played by Ghatak himself, lies in an alcoholic stupor while his wife removes everything from his phonograph to his books from around him, afraid that he will otherwise sell them for another drink. The raw intensity of Ghatak, with a burn as intense as that cheap whisky, scared me as much as the refined baritone of Satyajit Ray, as smooth as a smoky single malt, soothed me.

Those who drink and those who don't, often eye each other with suspicion. Amit Chaudhuri might have the very occasional glass of wine, but most times not even that:

> This is seen by the people I encounter socially not only to be inexplicable but suspect. For, to deliberately reject pleasure is sinister... Once you're discovered, you are looked upon as the last surviving human being might be by the new colonies of body snatchers: with hostility and accusation. They nod and smile when you refuse the glass, but the eyes say, '*What?* You *look* just like one of us'.

Fellow Calcuttan, Derozio, could be one of these body snatchers, looking askance at Chaudhuri:

> The whole moral beauty, the very pith and marrow of what Philosopher Square would call 'the eternal fitness of things' in conviviality, consists in simultaneous and contemporaneous intoxication; and nothing is so complete a wet blanket to all good fellowship as the unique and unaccommodating sobriety of an individual.

One suspects that if Chaudhuri and Derozio met at a party today they'd give each other a polite miss.

~

Most liquor vends are still hole-in-the-wall affairs where chances of being groped are higher than in a crowded lurching bus. This is where the Average Indian Male goes to buy real booze, i.e. Indian whisky. But what about the women? In the big cities where liquor shops have opened inside malls, women find it easier to buy alcohol. In cities like Bangalore, you can even order online. Gahlaut again:

> For a whole new generation of women, the easy access to alcohol has been like crossing the final bastion to be equal with men: the right to waste shitloads of money on LITs in one evening. Or to bunk work to drink martinis with a colleague and heap abuses on the patriarchal system at the workplace.

Not in small towns. Let alone buying alcohol, once in Allahabad, the bartender in a hotel bar told my mother that he wouldn't even serve her. Small town bars are frequented exclusively by men. I describe one such bar in my story, 'Dancing With Men':

> I hit the floor and start dancing on my own. I move around trying to penetrate the privacy of these male couples. One of them moves a step back, allowing me to join in. Now there are three of us. The man spreads his legs, throws his head back. I go down on my knees, slide and land under his crotch. My gaping mouth almost kisses the man's bulge. I can smell the smell. I can hear myself singing 'kajra re, kajra re, tere kale, kale naina.' We reverse roles. The man twirls around like a girl while I thrust my pelvis at him... And so the night continues—men dancing in perfect harmony. There is some pushing and some shoving, a bit of aggro but not real, more like role-playing. With no girls around, the men have nothing to fight over. We make the best of whatever we have been given: a floor, a DJ, each other.

In this conservative climate where women are not supposed to drink, it comes as a pleasant surprise to find that women are an intrinsic part of the liquor trade, and they have been so for a long time. As Sumanta Banerjee discovers:

> Although alcohol had primarily been considered a man's drink, curiously enough it was a woman who was one of the earliest tavern owners in Calcutta. Her name was Demingo Ash (probably a European or Eurasian). She obtained a license from the East India Company administration to run a shop selling arrack, combining hotel accommodation, sometime around 1710.

Pavankumar Jain describes going to an 'Aunty bar' in Prohibition-era Bombay:

> In those days of Prohibition, he took me to a nearby illicit country liquor bar. It was a dingy dark room, part of someone's house. The room had a few tables and chairs and was crowded. An old woman, the owner of the house, served the drinks.

Arunabh Saikia ('The Bootlegger and the Bandicoot') goes to meet one of these old ladies in the Sansi colony of Majnu Ka Tila, in north Delhi. Shanti Devi is rumoured to be Delhi's oldest bootlegger: 'She remembers the chronology of the Gandhis' (or the Nehrus, if you may) deaths—'first badmash Sanjay, then Indira and then Rajiv.' She remembers Rajiv Gandhi's blood-soaked shoes—the Lotto sneakers he was wearing when he was blown up by a suicide bomber: 'We had taken the 212 to attend the cremation. He had big feet, I cried when I saw his shoes—the blood was still fresh.' She gives young Saikia an earful when he corrects her dates—Indira died in 1984, not 1987: 'What do you know? You were not even a thought then.'

~

Alcohol has the effect of calming frayed nerves. A drink, some say, 'takes the edge off'. Like music, it soothes the savage beast. But it can also do the opposite. It can bring out the beast within. It amplifies and exaggerates your grouse. Your mind is a cauldron of slights, imagined or otherwise. When you reach for the bottle, you might also reach for your gun. A simple disagreement can become a matter of life and death. A reasonable person becomes intractable. Voices and tempers rise; the lurking violence within becomes an ugly reality without. Gahlaut writes about this:

> In homes in neighbouring areas—for instance the village near west Delhi from which my father's family hails—villages which have had to suddenly deal with urbanization, and the social problems it brings, alcohol is every family's dirty secret.
>
> Alcohol is not a manifestation of empowerment here—as it is for the gay boys who climbed atop a bar and gyrated to music at a Rohit Bal after party—but a tool of fear.
>
> It is the fear we felt as children when we heard that the head of a family in the village, in an alcohol fuelled rage, shot dead his entire family before turning the gun on himself.

Jairaj Singh too talks about his father's cousins 'who upon drinking could very easily pull out guns from the cabinets, ready to declare war over an argument or a misunderstanding.'

~

'I had learnt my alphabet of drinking so well,' Pavankumar Jain says, 'that I could repeat it forward and backward umpteen times, without halting once to breathe in between.' What do you do when you've exhausted yourself with this repetitive back and forth? You stop reciting the alphabet. You call an end to your drinking career. It's time to retire.

Gahlaut decided on premature retirement. The golden handshake followed by way of pretty butterflies:

> Well, the point is this—I no longer drink. I am forty. After twenty years of drinking—which has been respectable enough to land me a piece in this anthology—I find myself going further and further away from the bottle. The birds and the butterflies have always been here, I just never saw them in my drinking years. I was too busy—busy tripping into the house past midnight, hoping no one would notice the swaying walk or the car parked wrong, to crash on the bed, head spinning.

Manohar Shetty stopped on his own, without any external help. Having shunned the local bar, Alcoholics Anonymous is not the substitute club he chooses to join: 'I've never had the humility to go to an AA meeting. My mind has never functioned in that fashion, of seeking a remedy outside for my own misdeeds. Indeed the more a boozer is harangued and chastised, the more he will drink.' Nambisan, on the other hand, endorses AA with some conviction: 'This is my lasting impression of AA: It is a wonderful thing, and the Twelve Steps are a programme which even teetotallers would do well to follow.'

Vijay Nambisan takes the rehab route. Of course, rehabs come in all shapes and sizes. According to Elton John, his old pal Billy Joel checks into the wrong kind of rehab—the ones with television. At the age of forty-three, Elton himself went to one where he had to make his own bed and swab the floor. It had no TV. Nambisan's rehab is the sort Sir Elton might have relished.

Drink works for some and not for others. In his poem 'Taverna', Shetty writes about a man who practices yoga daily and hasn't touched a drop in his life, and yet dies at forty-four of cardiac arrest.

Sitting in Goodluck taverna, the poet observes 74-year-old Eddie, who drinks from sunset to midnight every day and yet 'He goes home on his/ Moped without/ Troubling the potholes/ Or the pigs and sleeps/ The sleep of the just.'

~

This anthology almost did not happen. I failed to meet Renuka Chatterjee, my editor, for the first meeting at a bar in Delhi's Habitat Centre. I picked up the phone when she called to say that she'd already reached. I lied that I was on my way. The truth was that I was in bed, still recovering from the previous day's hangover. Renuka asked if I was okay with fish tikka, that she'd order it in the meanwhile. I said, 'Go ahead. Be there in twenty minutes'. My intentions were good. I slipped back into sleep and woke up the next day. Renuka finished the fish tikka and returned home.

There were other delays too. Some writers backed out. One potential contributor got prickly about the fact that I'd called her up to solicit a piece on drinking. 'Palash, I really don't drink that much,' she said firmly, before planting the receiver back on the instrument. Others got writer's block.

Pavankumar Jain passed away in the middle of writing his piece. Jain was painstakingly meticulous about recording detail. No detail was too small not to be recorded. His unfinished handwritten manuscript mentions the last time he worked on the essay which appears here: 'Wednesday, 25/09/2013. 3.26 a.m.' One contributor checked into rehab while writing his essay on rehab. When Vijay Nambisan returned he thought the anthology must already have been published. He was pleasantly surprised to find that it was still maturing in my cellar. Nambisan writes a piece here, moving and chilling by turns, called 'Rehab Diary'.

So, gentle reader, here it is: the first anthology about drinking in India. I hope it tastes all the better because of the delays—it's seven years vatted, like Old Monk.

PALASH KRISHNA MEHROTRA
Dehradun
February 2016

PART ONE

Stories & Poems

ARISTOCRAT

Gautam Bhatia

I started drinking at eleven. Not 11 a.m., eleven years, when in Class 7. Right in the middle of Inorganic Chemistry when Arora Sir was writing an equation on the blackboard, Samir, fearless Samir, tapped me lightly on the shoulder and said, 'My place, after school. There's beer in the fridge.' To give real meaning to the proposition, he added, 'My parents are away.'

Beer. The guy really said beer. It was as good as suggesting that we take our English Ma'am, Mrs G, into the bushes to play with her breasts. Really, it was unthinkable. But Samir was best at the unthinkable. He started every sentence with 'arrey bhanchod', and ended with some English cuss word like bastard or asshole. The guy was really mature at an early age. So when he suggested beer, I knew it wouldn't be some fake stuff like American root beer, or lemonade or something. You had to hand it to him. He had guts.

At the time we lived in an old yellowing government bungalow set in its own garden compound, thick-walled and perpetually peeling and staining with the monsoons. The grass, when it was green, was really green, when yellow, it was as good as dead. It was the same everywhere, in every house down the full length of the street, the whole neighborhood. Exactly like that. I don't know why, but there was a sameness to everything, a kind of colourless homogeneity where nothing stood out. Houses were yellow, Ambassadors cream, shirts white, boundary walls red. Pa's suit was grey, always grey, shoes black, like every father's. The only time he took them off was early morning when he pulled up his pant legs to rub his soles in the dewy grass in the garden. His sole rub was the first sign of winter.

There were only three customary privileges to adulthood denied to us at that age: sex, drink and driving. I had already seen Kavita naked in the swimming pool change room, so sex was out of the way. I had driven Ajay's Ambassador, even though during the drive it had remained parked in the driveway. All that remained finally was the taste of liquor on the tongue. Luckily, in a co-ed school, signs of adulthood were everywhere. Raj carried a condom packet in his Sanskrit book, which he carelessly dropped in front of the girls in Assembly, then took his time picking it up; with a clear wink at Meera he would issue an apology, 'Oh sorry, I think I'll need that tonight.' My best friend Prakash had tasted rum at the age of nine; his father was the owner of Punjab Distilleries. Kabir even had an empty bottle of Vat 69 in his school bag. At eleven, I was still a liquor virgin.

In the morning, with barely any breakfast, Pa was always in his rose patch quickly and quietly away from the house, standing alone in his corner garden examining some new variety like Montezuma's Revenge or Tequila Gold, or something else from his Rose and Garden Hybrids *book. He was always in his grey suit, red striped tie, held down by a silver clasp. I could see the shiny cuff links sticking out of his coat sleeve, glinting in the sunshine. His hair had begun to turn white near his ears but the rest was black, perfectly in place. It outlined his Vaselined face in an unwavering curve—like one of those styles you select from a barber shop catalogue. The centre parting was so exact, as if he had used the instruments out of my geometry box to bisect his head into equal halves. I bet if you counted the hairs on the right they would be equal to those on the left. He always pruned and plucked his exotic rose bushes, with special shears he picked up from a garden shop near Hampstead Heath, whose monthly journal arrived regularly and lay on the cane table on the verandah, with the Queen Elizabeth stamps on the envelope. Even if the other letters were not picked up, the rose journal was, and carefully catalogued in the study bookshelf. A few days later paper clips were tagged to its pages, and within a few weeks, new rose varieties would arrive, lining the side of the garden, like new students waiting to join class. He for his part, tenderly examined each leaf, each new hybrid every morning, till the driver brought the Ambassador to the front porch and held open the rear door. Then reluctantly, he would pull himself away.*

The cycles outside Samir's house were far too numerous to indicate that this was to be an exclusive afternoon of beer tasting. Samir had tapped many shoulders. The eight of us from Class 7, Section B, who sat there knew from the deathly drawing room silence that we were all there for a calculated and risky adventure. Things could go terribly wrong; as they often did when the illicit met with the conventions of middle-class life. And Anil's supreme confidence and exaggerated gestures made me even more uncomfortable. A tray with eight glasses and a bottle of Golden Eagle beer was placed on the centre table, along with six lemonades and potato chips. Samir poured out the equivalent of a peg in each glass. And waited. For a long while I just sat staring at the glass, thinking dark thoughts, seeing myself lying dead on the cold stone floor, choked on the awful stuff. Pa standing by and saying, 'Well, he asked for it!' I saw my body moved to the morgue, then tossed half-burnt into the Jamuna. Relatives talking, 'He was so young', 'Such promise', 'bad influence…' Ma wailing in the back. Horrible thoughts. But I guess some things had to be done.

The verandah was really the best part of the house. You could sit there morning or evening dozing semi-conscious, slurping tea, doing absolutely nothing. Towards the side, and linking to the verandah was a high English sort of porch, held up on columns, and framed along one side by a green painted jaffrey, fluffed white with jasmine. A filtered shadowy light fell on the ground around the porch and disguised the white heat of the summer day and the hiss of grass burning in the afternoon sun. At lunch time Pa arrived there in the Ambassador, like some colonial governor on an inspection. The driver always emerged first, white suited and capped, in almost military performance. Pa waited in the back for the door to open fully and the driver's actions to come to a complete halt, before he lowered his John Dixon shoe, right one first, on to the polished floor, then pushing his full frame out, paused for a moment to straighten suit and tie, before click-clacking up the verandah for lunch.

Samir downed his own beer in one swig, as if he had been drinking all his life. Which he probably had. 'Chalo bastards, bottoms up.' Except me, everyone drank. Almost twenty millilitres of beer taken straight up—the equivalent of a mouthful. The shock was too much.

Rajesh came close to fainting. I could see his eyes well up with tears, as if this was some sort of family betrayal, then closing, into a semi-consciousness that was expected of so much hard liquor in one go. For a long while I couldn't get myself to lift the glass. The yeasty smell was making me sick. I could see Samir's eyes slowly mocking me, his mouth turned up at the corners in a leer of contempt. Before he got a chance to make some remark like, 'Arrey bhanchod, do you want a straw', I blocked my nose with my left hand and took a swig large enough to fill the mouth. The liquid swirled around all foamy and gassy, like a cold wave on a hot Goa beach, sending those bitter pukey fumes through the roof of my mouth. The bloody thing rose through every pore of my skin, like a sudden rush. For a moment the body accepted the invasion; hell, it had no choice, but no sooner had the message reached the brain, than I shot the glass back on the table, and spat out the mouthful with a retch so loud as to rid the body of the poison, once and for all. But it was too late. Some of the beer had already made its way to the stomach; and I began to feel sad and rotten all at once. I knew I was doomed, though I felt nothing, no sense of playful drunkenness. By that time, Rajesh's neck had fallen to one side, so I too pretended to be under the influence. In *Sholay*, Gabbar had rolled his eyes, like black marbles loose in their sockets. Mine also rolled in slavish imitation. Gabbar had trouble standing still. I discovered a close match in my step…

Ma was different. She even made the servants feel like real people, almost equal in some way. She talked to the cook about his wife's illness, looking genuinely pained as he described the boils on her stomach, then pulling out her portable medicine chest, a Parle biscuit box, she would hand out foils of tablets like prashad in a temple. And she offered advice in the most amiable way: Make sure you give her milk twice a day. If you don't have enough just take it from the fridge, okay? She was a woman of smell and taste. For her, things were real only if they could be absorbed by all the senses. She ran a sort of informal jamming and pickle unit at home. Raw mangoes were sliced before summer set in, tons of lemons were piled into glass jars of oil spiced with homegrown herbs and chilies. What can't be made at home is not worth having, she would say. To check if the achaar was ready, she just walked out into the front verandah where the glass vats were lined up, raised her sleeve to the shoulder, and dipped her whole arm into the gooey oily mess. Then yanking out a nimboo, she chewed and churned and spat, resetting the achaar clock till the next exam.

The call came barely ten minutes after I returned. It was made swiftly and to the home of every participant in the beer tasting: Your son has been drinking out of our liquor cabinet. Just like that—cold hard and direct. It was difficult to believe that things so good could go so wrong, so quickly. Away on a long weekend to Dehradun, Samir's mother had decided to cut short her trip and return home, for whatever reason. I don't know, maybe she had a premonition. But her sudden appearance had obviously ruffled Samir enough to quickly share the blame with the whole fraternity. Who could blame him. I would have done the same. *All of Class 7, Section B, had raided the liquor cabinet.* Pa spoke little, but when something needed to be communicated he spoke even less. His open bedroom door, usually shut, was an indication that he wanted to say something, something serious. He emerged from the bedroom, calm and cool and expressionless as ever, just like the motel manager in *Psycho*, and placed his right hand on the back of my neck. I thought this was it. Just like *Psycho*, he was going to do it in the shower. With his hand firmly on my neck, he directed me past the bedroom, through another door, into the bathroom.

Like any civil service officer, Pa brought his work home. All those cardboard files tied with ribbons full of schemes for rural water supply and split irrigation in some village. Whenever he was in the mood, which was all the time, he shut himself in the study, poring over the files, shaking his head over the mounting piles of mismatched papers full of laborious writing and signatures and jottings in the margins. He held his Parker pen in his delicate fingers, long and lean and neat, and carefully, deliberately and with the microscopic scan of a jeweller inked the documents as if they were rare parchments for a museum display. He sank the full weight of his concentration into the smudge of words and Asoka insignias and rubber stamps all displayed on yellow green sheets. A gentleman with a gentleman's job. The IAS was a service without end, a job whose satisfaction was in the act of doing. I don't think he ever found out if the money made it to the irrigation scheme, or if the villages ever got their water. He couldn't care less. The civil service had certain standards, and he was only out to uphold them.

I stood shivering in the bath tub, clad only in my underwear. He had lined up the beer bottles along its rim, first one, then three, then six, a bartender just before the opening of the bar. But instead of polishing glasses and wiping tables, he had serious parental intent written in his moves. He placed an empty beer mug near my shivering hand, and poured a full bottle of Golden Eagle into the glass. Then he pulled up his shaving stool near me, and with a flick of the eye, motioned to me to start drinking. I looked at his face, then at the beer mug, back to his face, but he held his unflinching gaze, a look so completely impassive, without contempt, without malice, without emotion, merely a carpenter looking to use one of the implements of his trade. Whenever he got like this—usually during report card signing or the time when at the age of eight I had locked Sita in the trunk of the car during hide-and-seek—there was little to do but follow his signals, without apology or visible remorse. So I brought the glass to my lips, lifting it with both hands, and drank the yellow liquid, bitter and foul tasting. Unable to deflect his gaze, I continued slowly, gulp upon difficult gulp, filling my insides with liquid and foam and air, and wetting face and neck as the overflow worked its way down my neck and chest into the underwear. There was no chance of altering his unwavering cold stance. More than half a bottle had made its way into my stomach. I returned the almost empty mug to the rim of the bath tub, and looked to him for some relief, some pity. None came. He opened the second bottle and refilled the glass, remaining as impassive and disconnected as the laundry stand before which he sat. I picked up the glass.

On Saturdays, those summer half days, when the officers from the ministry met after lunch at the Officer's Club on Raisina Road, he was at the Gymkhana Club pool. It was a weekly ritual he maintained since he joined the IAS, wherever he was posted, he swam, in Mirzapur, in Lucknow, even when district magistrate in Nainital. He swam, not the languid shallow strokes of a weekend enthusiast, or a casual flapping of a water splasher. No, he swam in deft strides, slicing the water with such precision—not a movement out of line—it was as if a highly charged battery-powered machine had been released. People moved swiftly out of his path, lest they drown in the sharp cone of his water glide. Some left the pool altogether to watch from the sidelines, too humbled to be seen in competition with such perfection. Sometimes when I came out to take books from the library, word would get out that he was there in the pool, and I'd walk across the lawn to have a look. There he was, all alone in the sharp afternoon light, a fish amongst a set of clumsy alligators. I knew he had seen me, but he never looked up, never acknowledged that I was there. But it was the only time I saw him outside his suit.

Oddly, the second bottle went down easier. The beer swilled and expanded in my mouth, but before I had a chance to think of what I was doing, it had made its way down my throat and into a stomach that felt light and ready for more. So more came. I realized if I took it in short gulps and with my eyes shut it became a mere counting game. One, two, three, gulp, one, two, three, gulp, numbers raced along till the mug was empty. It was much harder if I thought of it as a challenge, and kept my eyes focused on the yellow foam that floated below my nose in the round glass, like staring down the barrel of a beer gun. The idea was not to think about what you were doing, and it happened easier. Of course, I didn't want to gloat, but I could sense the demolition of this second mug as a form of personal triumph, as if I had outwitted him at his own game. From the corner of my eye I could see he was a bit surprised, but didn't really want to show it. He never really wanted to show anything anyway, that was his nature. Without looking at him I placed the empty mug on the rim of the bath tub, and heard the sound of more beer being poured.

When you opened the door to Pa's study, he always looked up startled. A Japanese chime had been installed at the door to give him a warning. Instead of glaring at you he'd look blankly up from his reading, as if waiting for the intrusion to pass. He hated anyone touching his books, and he regarded each one sitting snug on the shelf with such love and possession, as if nothing else mattered. But Ma made us touch and taste everything. She was a tap of emotion always on full flow. In the evening after dinner, she held on to the two of us on the sofa, me on one side, Sita on the other, her eyes glued to some senti movie like The Sound of Music *or* Ben Hur *or something. She always sobbed quietly through the whole movie, never once dabbing her eyes or feeling ashamed that a grown woman should be seen crying. She just let the stream run down her red lipsticked lips, feeling bad as hell for Julie Andrews and the raw deal she got. Every movie made her cry.* My Fair Lady, Laurel and Hardy, *everything. Even documentaries of Nehru.*

The third bottle went down slower, air pockets had formed in my food pipe and the gulps alternated with reflux. I had to stop. Through the corner of my eye, I watched as Pa remained resolute as ever to complete his task. On the ledge stood another three bottles, cold and glistering with dew. It was a sight so repulsive, I began to feel ill just looking at them. Then without warning, even before I could take another sip, my body buckled. It heaved and convulsed, a wave of nausea swept inside, as if an internal earthquake of ten on the Richter scale was causing a stomach Tsunami. All the contents of my stomach propelled out of my mouth in a yellow stream, a massive dam burst; spraying and washing along the walls of the bath tub. I lost my balance and was on all fours with giddiness and fear, waiting for a reaction, any reaction. But it wasn't forthcoming.

In the evening with the first sound of the car crunching on red gravel the house turned quiet, and as you heard the tyres hiss to a halt on the porch, the house drifted into a prolonged silence. Radios were turned down, the servants stopped their chatter, kitchen dishes made no sound. For a few minutes even bird noises ceased. In the dark verandah he strode, straight from the car, there he sat, after placing his briefcase on the side chair, on one of those lazy cane recliners, looking out without focus at nothing at all, just watching the garden and rose bushes and the distant trees, watching evening turn to night, and the black night slowly devouring the sky. Seated rigid, fully suited all the while till the bushes and the bougainvillea hedges and the grass began to look black and the only flicker of light came from a copper lantern that hung at the edge of the verandah. Barely a dim glow, enough to smudge the side of his face in its yellow light and to let everyone know that he was still there, and to leave him alone.

I tried to convey to him that I had had enough. I hoped my expression said that I was now truly unsteady on my feet and may collapse any moment. Even though under his unrelenting gaze, I was actually steady as ever. But I felt cold. I had been there on all fours soaked in my own liquid—part beer, part piss and vomit—it slaked the skin and clung to me, a damp fog. He merely popped open the fourth bottle and waited. Coated in my own stomach slime, I slowly stood up. Tears welled up, through the unfocused haze, I saw only the metal sink hole of the tub slowly swallowing the trickle of bile and beer. I couldn't look at him, though I could hear the sound of another bottle being emptied into the mug. For a few minutes more he sat on his stool, looking away; then he walked out.

He lay in the deep end of the pool, till morning. Mrs Chandra was always the first one there, beginning her laps at six in the morning before the pool filled up with children. She screamed when she saw the flayed posture, the wide open eyes and the muscular body sprawled on the blue tile twelve feet below. A tiny trail of bubbles and vomit was making its way to the surface, leftovers of a meal. At the time the security guard had been asleep on one of the deck chairs. She woke him up and the two rushed to the deep end. With a pool cleaning pole, the guard poked and prodded the body lightly and it rose up surprisingly quickly to the surface. For a second it burst sharply through the water and gave Mrs Chandra another chance to shriek. We saw him only at ten, lying out there on the tiled floor in the shade of a plastic umbrella next to a hastily put-up sign: 'Pool Closed for the Day'. He was draped in a big towel. The club doctor had examined him, and officially pronounced him 'Dead' giving the cause of death as 'Asphyxiation'. It was a kind way of saying that he had choked on a full bottle of Aristocrat, emptied into his stomach the night before and which had surfaced into his throat and lungs to choke him; but official reports especially for senior government officers are always guarded. Throughout the funeral Ma remained oddly quiet and tearless as if already reconciled to a grief that was expected. At home as the car pulled in to the driveway, she leaned across the front seat and asked me to open the glove compartment where a small bottle of Aristocrat Red lay under the car registration. From under the front seat, she fished out an empty one litre bottle of the same brand. Her face betrayed neither surprise nor emotion. It was merely the work of a housewife ensuring proper clean up after an event. At home, from his study she removed two more bottles and a glass, tucked between files and handkerchiefs. She then explored the rose garden, asking the mali to dig up the bushes carefully and to save anything he discovered in the soil. Close to two dozen empty Aristocrats appeared from the roots. She found more behind the cupboard, the shoe racks, three full bottles in the locked desk drawer, two in the garage. One even in the air-conditioning vent. One by one, they were emptied in the bathroom sink, carefully washed and dried, then lined in neat rows in the verandah. From Small to Large, like members of a family posing for an official portrait, empty, but lidded and with labels, That night, the night after he died, she sat there alone, in his chair, as he always did, watching the garden in silence.

DELIRIUM

Jeet Thayil

There was no gentle build-up, a glass of wine one evening, two the next, and so on, exponentially into the dark. He went all out from moment one. He bought himself a quarter bottle of whisky, a nip bottle, the professional's measure, and he put a slug in his coffee first thing in the morning and got to work: he went from teetotal to alcoholic in one sip. It was possible, no, it was highly likely that if he kept at the booze he would stop working, but this morning, whisky taken, he was high in the visionary company. Of lust or art. All was courtship. He banged out two self-portraits, one after the other, before lunch, without so much as breaking a sweat. They were variations on a theme, painted on pages of ghetto porn, all glossy flesh tones and harsh lighting. He gave himself an egg-shaped head and leaden eyelids; put bits of white paint around the eyes and mouth, the only white on the canvas, as it turned out; made the body and head big blocks of burnt umber and sienna; and left only one area unpainted, the heart, and—this was when he knew he was in the presence of God and all his angels—it just so happened that the heart occurred on a high-res image of an ebony vagina, slippery and liver-coloured, absolutely perfect; all he did was pencil in a few quick lines to suggest the heart's rubbery tubing. No viewer would make out what the background was, not unless he told them, which he would, to get a little buzz going in the right places and push the price up by a digit or two. The second portrait was faster and stranger, a humanoid blob of multi-coloured oil spatters. And the two finished pictures put him in such a good mood that he took Goody to Koshy's for lunch. Before leaving, in the bathroom, he killed the rest of the quarter and brushed his teeth again.

They were at a table by the window, Xavier taking big gulps of iced tea, saying, 'Remember that waiter, the one in the café on Greek Street, who refused to serve you because he said you were too young? And we had to show him your passport? We drank all day and they gave us buy-back shots and I left the keys on the bar and had to climb in through the window to get into the apartment?'—Xavier looked around him at the photos on the wall, mostly shots of old Bangalore, when you could walk the length of the promenade in a leisurely half hour and there was no traffic except the occasional Model-T import; sepia full frontals of the Town Hall, the Parade Ground and the Victoria Hotel; royals and other notables, and the inevitable picture of the Mysore Maharaja, unresplendent in his crooked turban—'Climbed in the living room window and opened the door for you and we fell asleep fully dressed. I woke up in the middle of the night because you had me in a choke hold, and all I'd done was snore.'

'It was a snore heard around the world. You were so drunk. I had a nightmare in which you were trying to kill me.'

'So you thought you'd kill me instead?'

'It was me or you.'

'Anyway, the first time you left me, in New York, I went back to London and tried to find that bar. I went up and down Greek Street and all around Soho. I thought if I got drunk enough you'd come and save me.'

'You're a silly man.'

'I never did find the bar. But I sent you e-mails and postcards and I didn't paint. I wrote sorrowful separation poems. I felt sorry for myself and drank too much. I thought you might turn up and surprise me.'

'You surprised me, I had no idea you were such an ardent lover.'

~

There was a figure beside them, a squat toadlike man in starched white kurta-pyjamas, gold ballpoint prominent in his breast pocket. It was not Xavier he was looking at, but Goody. His hands were folded in namaste. Xavier had no idea who he was, until Goody said, Mr Cherian, how nice to see you. Newton, you remember Mr. Cherian, from the party the other day? Xavier remembered: it was the Lipton man.

'May I join you?'

Xavier said, 'My pleasure. What are you drinking?'

Cherian called for a waiter and demanded beer.

'For everyone,' he said. 'Beeru.'

Even Goody was smiling agreeably. And why not? A glass of beer, a smallish glass of frothy lager, what possible harm could issue from so blameless a beverage? When it came, and was poured, glorious honey-bright refreshment, Xavier emptied his prettily sweating tankard and poured another, and only then did Goody's face register some—what?—not coldness exactly, but discomfort. And then there were more people by the table, Keith and Vincent and other AA boys.

'I can see it's working for you,' Keith said, 'not going to meetings, I mean. Helping you stay clean and sober.'

Vincent said, 'Watch out, mister, keep talking that way and the man might go for your throat.'

Xavier said, 'I'm sorry, as I said before and say again, I'm sorry and I'm sorry.'

Goody said, 'Did you attack him? My god.'

And the swadeshi Cherian said, 'Are you fellows from AA? You don't look like it, if you don't mind me saying so.'

'We should go.'

'Maybe I'll go with you,' said Cherian, but he didn't get up from his seat. And it was Xavier who went with them to the door, to shake hands and make a last apology to Vincent.

'I mean it, forgive me, I'm not okay in the head.'

'I hope I'm never so desperate I have to resort to violence.'

'You're right, you're right.'

'Yeah, well, looks like you got other problems, bro. Looks like the fat man's got his eye on your girlfriend.'

Cherian was kissing her hand.

'And she doesn't mind, does she?'

~

Goody was smiling, and, dear god, did she just bat her eyelashes at him? Xavier hadn't seen that move in years. He went back to the table. Goody was saying, I mean, I enjoy beer, though really it doesn't have much effect on me—other than to make me affectionate, that is. And then she laughed. The smarmy swadeshi still had her hand in his and she made no effort to take it away. Of course, it was entirely possible that she had a thing for ugly men. Xavier was no prize in the prettiness department. Maybe she had a thing for ugliness in all forms, human, divine, artistic. Maybe it was time to give in and give up and confront the ghost that walked with him every fucking where. It called for urgent measures, of whisky, if not beeru, winu, rumma. Xavier summoned the waiter and ordered a double Black & White with ice. He said to Goody, *Tu mettrais l'univers entier dans ta ruelle, femme impure!*

'If that's French for I'm a complete fucking alcoholic and I can't wait to flush my life down the loo, you can say it again.'

'*L'ennui rend ton âme cruelle.*'

'I say,' said Cherian. 'Who needs the French anyway? India is standing on her own two feet, *mon ami.*'

'Two feet,' said Xavier.

'If you haven't noticed,' Cherian said, 'Incredible new India, shining at last.'

Xavier stared coldly at the man. When he spoke it was in a voice Goody did not recognize.

'What new India, mister pants on fire? This is the same old India: old older oldest, as fucked up as she ever was, just wearing shiny whore make-up is all.'

~

Their voices had risen above the general Koshy's din, no small feat, considering the level of noise in the restaurant. But Xavier was beyond caring, and besides, bad behaviour seemed to have its rewards. Cherian, being the oily Malayali he was, decided it was not a good idea to be caught in the middle of a public marital spat. He scuttled off, mumbling something about being late for a lunch appointment. With his two hands, Xavier held his whisky up to the dim electric light. It was the color of smudge. Thank you, oh lord, for your small mercy, he said, and swallowed the drink and ordered another. He was glowing in the flowing, high and visionary. Goody left without another word, though she took her time gathering her things. Was she expecting mollification and coddlement? Not today, he was not in the market for Molly or Coddle; he was in for the conspicuous consumption of *Choice Old Scotch Whisky* from the twin barrels of the inestimable Dr James Buchanan and his company of highland terriers. But there was a balance to be struck, a window of chance and opportunity before the booze reinstated its depressive temperament. He needed to be back at work. Because he had had an idea, a real idea, a flash of lightning type IDEA. He lifted up the new whisky and said to the deserted table, Emperor Buchanan, to your incomparable malts and grains. Then he paid the bill and left a good tip and walked home, stopping to buy wine at a shop on Infantry Road, cheap red wine for a cheap red day. The shop owner's daughter gave him a calendar on the house, saying, it's our honour, sir, to serve you. I saw your picture in the newspaper. You can pay later if you don't have money. She gave him his change and said, in Hindi, sir, thank you, we also have free home delivery. He said, good, good, now stop calling me sir. What's your name? Dharini, she said. Dharini, he replied, it's a pleasure indeed to make your acquaintance.

~

He hung the calendar on a bare wall near his easel. It was the usual devotional scene, an array of gods in fleshy human poses. He poured himself a short glass of red and noted the absence of The Goody and tossed off the monumental mixed media nude that had been flashing in his head all day, hips so big they were a landscape of their own, boulder breasts, tree trunk legs, small delicate lovely head. He used a marker to draw a faint outline, then filled the canvas with paint, two colours, no more. Then he used the marker again. He found a piece of gold fabric in a closet, heavy gold inlaid with cheap gemstones, which he shaped into a necklace and placed on the nude's neck, and she took on the unmistakable contours of the giantess of his youth, a figure from a poem he'd once read that had filled his erotic life for weeks, the idea of living in the valleys and crevices of a big brown woman devoid of speech but full of tenderness. He was blazing. And he was thinking of Koshy's, that there was time for one last drink before they closed for the day, that they'd still be serving dinner, the waiters in a hurry to count their tips and be gone. The giantess was done. Anyone could see that he hadn't put much into it, had in fact tossed it off quickly, the necklace positioned slightly wrong, the colour dull, unfinished skin tones against flat yellow. But it didn't matter: The power was in the line, the curve of hip, the Greek serenity of her lips and eyes. The giantess was done, and so was he; time for a swig of red and out into the night.

~

He took a rickshaw and told the man to wait. At Koshy's, candles had been lit and there was music. Was it jazz, opera, heavy metal? It was impossible to tell, the sound was so muddy; or was the mud in his head? John, eradu whisky kodu, he told the old waiter, who replied in English. Sir, we are closing, do you want food? Closing time. Dread words calculated to put The Fear into any man. He called for two whiskies, then made it three, and told John to line them up on the table. Where was Goody? He should have checked her closets to see if she'd taken her clothes. No, it would take her a day or two to move everything out: art, books, toiletries, all kinds of pots and pans. Where were Keith and Vincent, his AA buddies? Where were all his friends? He went to a table by the window where a couple of middle-aged men worked on their rum and Thums Up. 'Do you think I could possibly'—Why did he get so plummy and English when he had a drop or two taken? He'd lived in Paris almost as long as he'd lived in London, but when he was drunk, or even just drinking, it was always the English who won—'possibly borrow a cigarette from you?' One of them held out a damp pack of Classic Milds and he took one. Then he went to his table and smoked, suddenly unwilling to drink, unaccountably reluctant to reach for the waiting whisky. He took a deep drag of the cigarette and held the smoke in his lungs. He actually felt the nicotine kick in, and still the drinks stood on the table, and still he didn't want them. He'd smoked too quickly, which put a pint of nausea in his head. Where were his friends? Here, of course, here they were, all three of them. He drank two, one after the other, and someone joined him.

'Mr. Koshy, the younger. How good to see you, dear boy.'

'Mr. Xavier, how are you? Looking a little the worse for wear, I'm sorry to say.'

'I'd offer you a drink, but I know you'd refuse. You would, right?'

'With pleasure.'

'Well, here's to you and your odd sobriety.'

Xavier downed his third and last whisky, and felt the heat percolate downward into his kundalini, felt the serpent goddess begin her ascent up his spine and just as quickly die; suddenly bereft, he raised his hand for the waiter.

'We're closed, at least to you. Go home, Newton, for god's sake, do yourself a favour, go home and make up to your lovely lady.'

'I think I've just seen everything, a merchant refusing to sell his merchandise. This is marvellously noble and all, but aren't you shooting yourself in the foot, old boy?'

'You have the trembles, did you know that?'

'Give me a drink, merchant, or give me the bill.'

'Your money's no good here, go home.'

But he didn't go home. He stepped out of Koshy's and found the rickshaw still waiting and took it to Dewar's, a bar hidden under flyover construction in one of the city's oldest cantonments, and there they let him buy a half bottle and sit at a table for as long as he liked. A boy put a menu and a bowl of peanuts in front of him and pulled the shutters to and lit a candle in a saucer. Police, he said, turning out the lights. What a toy town. After eleven, you drank with the lights off because the guardians of the law preferred to shake down drinkers than do some honest work. How do you tell the difference between a cop and a crook? he asked the boy.

'Ji?'

Cigarette kodu, Xavier said. The menu was a collage of old Hindi movie posters, and there was the old Dev Anand-Zeenat Aman hit *Hare Krishna Hare Rama* showing bell-bottomed lovers with the Himalayas behind them. Goody, he thought, I miss you, come home. There was already so much to tell her, the three paintings of the day and the fact that he was feeling better, almost normal, in fact. Maybe the drink had calmed him down and cured the hypomania. Was she gone with the oily Cherian to his sprawling bungalow where she would sip daytime cocktails with the city's VIP set? The boy put a pack of cigarettes on the table. Eyevathu rupiah, he said. When had he become a smoker, Xavier asked himself? Already it seemed as if he had been in this life forever, his days measured in whisky and nicotine, and he was dreading the hangover that was surely coming. But he was afraid to stop, because there was the possibility that the craziness would return. When there was about an inch of whisky left in the bottle he put it in his pocket and checked his wristwatch: it was only three, no, it was ten past three. He blew the candle out and in the sudden darkness the words came to him unbidden. He said: lift your face up to the sky and unbeffudle yourself, Commander Xavier. A great and complex task awaits you. Lift your face free of its infirmity and find her, for she is rescue from the disaster that awaits. Lift up, Saint Xavier, lift up. But when he opened the door of the bar and stepped out into the street, his legs didn't obey him and he had to bend from the waist to keep from falling over. He stopped on the main road, still bent over, but there was nothing moving at that time of night, and then, unable to walk any further, he sat heavily on the concrete bench of a bus-stop and felt the bottle shatter in his pocket and a painless jab in his hip. He picked the broken glass out of his trousers, trying to catch whatever was available for salvage, a small handful of whisky that he transferred to his mouth. His eyes closed and he thought he heard a bird, a small bird somewhere close. Just then, the sky began to lighten on a stretch of dug-up road, great shards of concrete pointing upwards like glass. No wonder there had been no rickshaws: there was no road. He limped onward, his pants wet with blood and whisky, until he came to a junction dominated by a Kannada film poster. And then, as if all of Xavier's travels had brought him to this pre-dawn meeting, he saw a man whose long hair was wet with lakewater. He was still naked from the waist down and on his wrist was the pink rakhee. The dead man said, Why did you not ask yourself the obvious question?

'As in, who but a crazy man would find himself in conversation with a dead one?'

'No, that question is not obvious, it is only uninteresting. The important question is, what does it mean when a drowned man is found without his trousers?'

'Ah,' Xavier said, as if he were about to sneeze. 'Forgive me, I don't mean to tremble so, but I can't seem to stop.'

'It means he was robbed and murdered. It means he did not drown himself as the police claim. It means he must choose someone in whom he can place his trust, some one person who will know the truth even if he is unable to act on it.'

Without warning, the tears came to Xavier's eyes.

'I'm not that person,' he said. 'I'm not worthy.'

'Yes you are. Everything is necessary, none of this will be wasted.'

'And.'

'I am Santosh, state footballer of Kerala, lover of life, now sadly expired: drowned by rascals. There is no peace in death, only unease and restless dreams.'

Then the dead man clasped Xavier to his wet black shirt and kissed him on both cheeks. As he walked away, he turned back once to point in the direction of a bridge. 'Go that way, you'll know where you are.'

~

Xavier limped toward the bridge, which, as it turned out, was a flyover, and beyond it was traffic and new sunlight and, most miraculous of all, a line of rickshaws waiting for business. On the ride home, he wondered how it was that a hallucination had left such a genuine memento; for the dead man had been a creation of his mind, but the wetness on his shirt was real. It was full day when he got out of the rickshaw and made a last stop before home. Hello, Dharini, a bottle of Grover red, and two Khajurahos, please, he said, leaning heavily against the counter. It occurred to him that he'd made a similar purchase some twenty-four hours earlier, when all had seemed so hopeful with the world. How things had changed, in how short a span.

'Are you okay, sir? No, no. You're bleeding.'

He was touched, there was no point denying it, he was very much touched by her distress. It was a weakness: he missed the ministrations of women. Dharini came around the counter with his beer and wine, and insisted on carrying it home for him. She helped him up the stairs. She took his key and opened the door. She took charge, finding cotton wool and water, putting antiseptic on his wound. Then she poured a glass of beer for him and helped him get comfortable on the sofa.

He took a long drink and said, thank you, I can't tell you what a day it's been, I.

And he was asleep.

THE ALCOHOLIC AT DAWN

Jeet Thayil

The cup in my hand
rattles like a drum
It tells me my need.

Strange, oh strange to wake
up where the beached whale
skims the sodden sand.

Legs unsteady, undersea
eyes all bleared and brimming,
I twine a blue smoke
from nose to throat

Then the quick stumble to the cupboard.

DANCING WITH MEN

Palash Krishna Mehrotra

Flair Bartender Robin is rinsing beer glasses when I walk in and take my place at the bar. Robin, or FBR as he calls himself, has spiky hair tinged with red dye, and is of stocky build. He suffers from mood swings—cheerful and helpful one minute, brooding the next. I like to think I am responsible for his cheerfulness at least part of the time. He hands me a bottle of Sandpiper across the counter—wants me to check if it is chilled enough. I touch it and say I will speak the truth, and nothing but the truth. FBR grins and opens the bottle. This is our little joke. It has remained so for the last six months, ever since I first made the wisecrack and he responded.

The three men sitting on the other side of the bar have a problem with the cocktails menu. Their uniforms announce that they are from the coffee shop next door; their body language suggests they have just finished a long shift, that they are probably not going to work another one today. It's not so much that they don't like what's on the list or that some drink is missing. They are confused and want FBR to help. FBR, in his turn, patiently explains the concoctions to them: Long Island Ice Tea, Bloody Mary, Tom Collins, Piña Colada, Flaming Ferrari. After much deliberation they decide on orders. FBR pours vodka into three greenish looking glasses, then pulls out a lighter and ignites the drinks one by one. The three sit on their stools, swallowing fire, their backs ramrod straight, their bodies rigid, their eyes bulging with fear.

At three in the afternoon, The Blue Hawaii is full. The regulars are already there: the four politicians in white kurtas, the chubby girl with short hair who walks like a man and is supposed to fuck for money. A stately Tibetan girl sits in front of a background painted with rising blue waves, drinking what looks like a gin and tonic, smoking a cigarette. The elbow of her cigarette hand rests on the table and she tilts her head slightly each time she blows out smoke. I notice the empty aquariums and ask FBR where all the goldfish went. He says there was something wrong with the power supply the other day—all the fish got electrocuted.

A portly middle-aged woman presides over a table of young girls aged thirteen to sixteen. Every once in a while when the DJ puts on a Bollywood remix of their choice the girls break from the table, two at a time, and hit the floor, their long black hair flailing in the multicoloured light. There is an incredible quantity of food on their table, the sight of which makes me hungry.

By five everyone is gone. The match is over, the stadium empty. The few men who remain pull their chairs closer together as if consoling each other.

Somebody walks up to me and extends his left hand.

'Hey man, I think I know you.'

'How do you know me?'

'I have seen you around, everywhere: Meedo's, Polo Bar, Great Value, Quest, here. Where are you headed after this?'

I say I don't have a clue.

He says, 'Hop on then, we're off to Quest.'

'No girls,' I complain; 'No girls…' he replies, 'Yes, no girls…so what?'

I turn to Robin and ask for the bill.

'Sure,' says Robin. 'Quest is getting to be dangerous,' he warns me. 'Too many guys, no?…they are going to have a fight one of these days. No crowd,' he tells me, 'no crowd.'

~

I hop on.

It's a black Honda scooter. I sit in the middle. The man in front, the one in the driver's seat, smells of sweat. The one behind me, the one riding pillion, has got his penis adjusted along the upper crack of my backside. I'm going dancing with men.

The sun plays tricks with the sky. The sky is anything but blue.

The men I'm with are men to whom I would ordinarily have nothing to say. They come from business families. Their fathers own motor spare parts shops and television showrooms, deal in wholesale goods.

It's dark inside Quest. It's full of men in their twenties. Everyone is smoking.

There is a lone girl on the floor. She has long silky, black hair. Another girl soon joins her.

There is a third girl. She's with her reticent boyfriend. When the DJ plays her request, she tugs at his sleeve, tries to drag him to the fluorescent edge of the floor. He refuses. She takes the lead each time but succumbs to his hesitance. She does this again and again until she finally succeeds. The men sitting at the bar turn around and watch the couple dance. The boyfriend dances jerkily He doesn't look happy. His partner sways her hips, thrusts her breasts out, throws her hands up in the air. She seems to be enjoying the attention.

Another couple walks into the bar. They are probably not a day older than fourteen. The boy wears an undersized t-shirt and cargo pants. He seems familiar with the place. They sit at a table close to the DJ's booth. They order vodkas and light up. On the table next to them a man in dark glasses sits nursing a beer. He wears a flowery shirt; his hair is cut short in front, is long at the back. He sits absolutely still. His legs do not shake, his hands do not fidget. The strongest wind will not ruffle his hair. He could be cast in stone.

~

I see Angelo walk into the bar. Angelo is a tall, slim man, with long curly hair and opaque eyes. He is a man of many talents. He works as a shop assistant at a music store, round the corner from Quest. That's where I met him first.

He would always let me step behind the counter so I could have a better look at the tapes. Angelo is also a dog-walker. Often, in the evenings, I see him in Gandhi Park, walking two or three dogs at a time, their leashes wrapped around his wrists. One Valentine's Day, I see Angelo in Paltan Bazaar, a girl on each arm.

Angelo teaches choreography at three local schools. He likes Beyonce and Justin Timberlake. And it is precisely because he is a choreo teacher that Angelo never dances in discos. He thinks it below the dignity of his craft to dance with lumpen drunk men who wiggle their untrained bodies in completely random fashion in small-town discotheques.

Angelo walks over to my table, his slender fingers wrapped around a rum and coke. He knows about my wife but Angelo is the kind of person who expresses empathy by skirting the issue at hand. He is full of news. He has just bought a new Honda scooter. He shows me the keys. Invites me to take it for a ride. I try and feel excited for him, politely refuse his offer. 'I don't drive,' I say, but Angelo refuses to give up. 'Just give me half an hour and I'll teach you how to.'

The place is filling up by now. The awkward couple is long gone. The only two girls in the place have got lost in the crowd. Angelo and I are talking about the weather when something happens. The music stops, people stop talking to each other. In the dim blue light one can make out two girls holding hands, one can hear screaming: 'They don't know who we are. These bastards. They really don't know anything, Sonalika.' Initially, the girls seem to be targeting their fury at specific people. By the time they leave, they are shouting at the world at large, accusing everyone sitting or standing inside Quest of being monsters and rapists. The men stand in groups, mildly stunned, drinking, smoking, sniggering. The girls leave without throwing a backward glance. The party resumes.

Angelo sees some friends come in. He sticks his right arm up in the air trying to catch their attention. Annie, a diminutive but stocky man of about twenty-five, joins us. Annie is the president of the local degree college. 'You must have seen my name plastered on the boundary wall of almost every house in Dehradun,' he says, introducing himself. He has a confident, proprietorial air about him, like this is his chunk of the planet and everyone who enters, enters at his own risk. If you know him and happen to be sitting next to him, like I am tonight, you cannot help but feel safe. We are soon joined at our table by Annie's sidekicks, two Indian Military Academy cadets, and two exchange teachers called Tui and Richard. They all seem to know Angelo who continues to sit facing the entrance, not wanting to miss anybody.

I am not in the mood to talk and am slightly irritated by the crowd Angelo has managed to collect around our table. I came here because I wanted to slink in a corner till the stroke of twelve, the hour when the management turn on the bright fuck-off lights. Except that now, seven garrulous men surround me. They are determined to have a good time, get things off their chest. Every once in a while the strobe light falls on a face in our group. I notice how ugly everyone looks. On the floor, men dance in pairs, their teeth shining like diamonds in the oppressive night.

~

A sailor joins our table. He's got a girl with him. A dark-skinned girl who wears a big pendant and expensive platinum jewellery. The IMA guys are talking about where they are going to be sent next, to an African country on a peace-keeping mission.

Richard and Tui, the exchange teachers, are a trifle shocked at the fact that teachers in their school can beat up kids as and when they want. And, what's more shocking, the kids don't seem to mind it, in fact, they seem to expect it. If you don't whip their asses they think you are a fucking wimp.

The place is smoky. The floor is dirty: the floor is all cigarette packets, crushed cigarette ends and burnt-out matches.

I go and sit at the bar. I light a cigarette. Two Sikh men to the right of me turn around and raise a protest. I am drunk so I say, 'You guys look too white to be Sikh.'

'We are Canadian,' they say, 'but we are Sikh. Smoking is not allowed in our religion. Do not smoke here.'

I want to say: Please stuff your religion up your Royal Canadian ass and yes, might as well give it a good shove while you are at it.

I refuse to budge. There is a situation building.

Fortunately this situation is defused by another situation. There is something going on outside the club door. Everyone seems to be trooping out, then trooping back in. It's some kind of fight. The Sikhs are interested. They leave their drinks on the bar and troop out as well. Everyone is fucking trooping except me.

Everyone is now outside checking out the fight. The sailor and his girlfriend are the only ones who have chosen to stay in. I go and join them. 'Typical,' I say, referring to the fight. 'What's typical?' they respond, with identical quizzical expressions.

Something has fallen into the girl's drink. She complains to the waiter. He gets her a new one. The sailor and his girlfriend decide to tell me how they met. Sailor says, 'This time when I got off the ship I just had one thing on my mind—marriage.' Sailor girl says in a nasal voice, 'Even I was desperate to get married.' Sailor boy says, 'Thank god I met a girl, this girl—I was so desperate to be married I would have married a goat. ' 'Same here,' says the girl.

By now people are coming back into the bar. They resume their conversations. The DJ continues to play Bollywood remixes, Eminem remixes, all kinds of remixes.

The floor is packed. Men arch their backs and throw their hands in the air. The men dance as couples.

I hit the floor and start dancing on my own. I move around trying to penetrate the privacy of these male couples. One of them moves a step back, allowing me to join in. Now there are three of us. The man spreads his legs, throws his head back. I go down on my knees, slide and land under his crotch. My gaping mouth almost kisses the man's bulge. I can smell the smell. I can hear myself singing '*kajra re, kajra re, tere kale, kale naina.*' We reverse roles. The man twirls around like a girl while I thrust my pelvis at him.

The dance floor is absolutely packed. More and more men crowd the floor, clutching cigarettes, drinks, their best mate's hands. A couple enters. They don't look like they are from around here. Everybody turns around and stares. They leave. We get back to dancing. Occasionally, an overenthusiastic dancer loses balance and takes a spill.

Somebody's hand lands on my face dislodging my spectacles. They go flying through the smoky air. I don't even try to find them. I cannot see anything now. 'Where am I?' I ask my dancing partner, a scrawny guy wearing a blue t-shirt that bears some brand name. 'Tum kaha se aa gaye bhai sahib,' he replies. There is affection in his voice. I break away from the guy I am dancing with and begin to work the dance floor. I whirl around in circles, stumble and trip. Someone or the other proffers a hand, picks me up. I go to every dancing couple, I walk over to the DJ's cabin, I can hear myself saying: 'C'mon guys, let's do it. One last time.' I am the foreign coach encouraging his boys to go for the kill. We have to win tonight.

And so the night continues—men dancing in perfect harmony. There is some pushing and some shoving, a bit of aggro but not real, more like role-playing. With no girls around, the men have nothing to fight over. We make the best of whatever we have been given: a floor, a DJ, each other.

I don't know where Angelo is. The sailor and his companion have already left. I feel tired and decide to leave. I pay the bill and walk out into the night. What do I see? An autorickshaw, a smiling mongrel, a desiccated jacaranda tree, sewage water flowing in a straight line, squashed Pepsi bottles, cinema hoardings.

I walk up Rajpur road. After a ten minute walk I see a sign that says The Blue Hawaii. I walk right in. FBR is still there. The chairs are upside down on the tables. They are about to close. FBR is practising juggling. Cocktail shakers fly around his head in rainbow formation. Occasionally, a hyperactive shaker breaks out of the semi-circular arc and smashes to the floor.

FBR fixes me a gin and tonic with lots of lemon. He thinks this is a good idea. I ask him to put on Guns n' Roses. He says, 'Can't you hear it? It's playing, man!' One of the waiters stands on a stool in front of an aquarium. In his arms, he holds a grimy fishbowl. Slowly, carefully, he puts new, wriggling goldfish back into the colourful but empty tank.

Government Country*—Poems

Adil Jussawalla

Paradise

Sufficient unto the day its anaesthetics.
More than sufficient if I take any more.
Who's dead, who's sick?

The walls have multiple bruises,
the floor's out cold.
This place can't take any more hurt.
I'm off.

Ahmed turns up.
He smells of an empty bottle.
I inhale the stars.
They smell of boxing gloves.

Lucky

What made them sick? Why are they doubled up?
Call an ambulance. Take me in too.

It's Friday namaz, you fool, and that's a mosque.

Call an ambulance all the same.
I'll pray like that woman I saw at St Michael's,
shaking all over, bare-headed, crying.

---

*Government country is cheap liquor manufactured by the state and sold in
special bars. The names of six such bars make the poems' titles.

I'll pray I get out alive. The press said
Bottles were sealed at the Tardeo bar
Last night, ten souls too late. A star
burst yesterday. The press has photos.

Picnic

We came to government country
seeking asylum.

Some of us want to leave,
some of us had to.

We got carried away like Subbu,
like Ron, like Jal, like Ahmed.

We got carried away early.

Royal

Kabir, I'm not worthy of your attention.
I spoke too soon.
You worked at your loom till your knuckles broke.
Mine, protruding from foul glasses,
are boils that can't be lanced.

I raised some glasses too many.
I continue.
Their warm liquids silk through me
like urine.

Welcome

Praying hands a steeple,
inverted a cunt.
What am I thinking of
in this filthy bar?

Famous Trinity

Calendar Katy's the guru of Trinity.
Those at the table below her
get covered in talc when she breathes.

Her disciples at other tables
pay her better attention.
Their eyes grow round and wet.
They're sure to get powdered too.

The missal that's Pandu's special,
the papads he thappads,
aren't the magnets that draw us back.

When Calendar Katy does her pranayam,
when Calendar Katy takes a deep breath,
the air is filled with blessing,
the room smells of her talc.

TIPPLE CAKE

Siddharth Chowdhury

I start to worry when Hriday Thakur stops drinking. He is primarily a weekend drinker. Two large pegs of Peter Scot with soda in a tall frosted glass. With three cubes of ice. Every Saturday morning before leaving for work at the Alight Advertising Agency, where he is a senior copywriter, he will check without fail whether the ice-trays are filled and if not will pour water into them from the tap. When I scold him that he should use the purifier and not the tap, which supplies the rusty brown iron-rich South Delhi water, he points out that Peter Scot is as legendary an antiseptic as Dettol and kills all manner of germs, whether physical or mental. I always smile then. He looks forward to his weekend restorative and I take pleasure in his happiness. He used to be a heavy drinker before but is not anymore. He puts the ice-trays inside the freezer, kisses me on the lips and goes off to work. I then go back to sleep. I work in Proscenium Press and Saturdays are usually off for me.

But for the last two weeks it seems that some mental germs have broken the barrier and have taken prisoner of my Hriday again. He has a propensity for depression and as he only drinks when he is feeling at peace with his world, I am feeling a bit anxious. I am positive, he is unhappy. I like it when he drinks, because it makes him so relaxed and mellow and you can almost hear the whisky hit his bloodstream, drop by drop, as the smile grows larger and conversation more tender. As he is so frugal in his speech otherwise, I welcome the weekend whisky-fuelled respite. And later when he mounts me and I wrap my legs around his neck, the whisky on his tongue makes my own rum and Thums-up breath sweeter.

It all started with the phone call I received from Swastika Singh a couple of weeks back. She wanted us to come for lunch on Sunday and admire the new Anunay Chaubey portrait of Zaheer Abdali that Salim had recently brought back from Patna. I realized later that it was only a ruse. An old university friend of theirs and Hriday's too, Charulata Roy, would also join us. She had recently moved back from Jamshedpur to Delhi after her divorce and had joined a travel portal in Connaught Place as a features editor. She had taken a two-bedroom flat on rent in Model Town near the North Campus. Swastika-di and Salim of course stayed nearby in Maurice Nagar in Delhi University where Salim had a cozy little flat allotted to him as a Reader in the history department at the arts faculty.

I think at this point in the story it is prudent to mention that Charulata and Hriday have a bit of a history from their university days. I think Hriday wanted to marry her but somehow it never came to pass. Thankfully she left to marry an engineer at Telco in Jamshedpur. So when I informed Hriday about Swastika-di's invitation, I thought he would be chuffed to meet an old flame again, but on the contrary I saw a swift flicker of dismay pass over his naturally aloof face and he said, 'not this Sunday. Perhaps the next one.' And with that the sabbatical with alcohol and happiness started. Two Sundays have come and gone since then and I quickly became tired of lying to Swastika-di about Hriday trying to complete a long story that he was working on for the new book.

I like visiting Salim and Swastika-di in their flat in the university. It is a place filled with a certain kind of light at all times—a light I associate with the first rays of sun coming out at dawn after a night of rain—which can only come with profound round-the-clock love. Even after eight years of being together, the randy buggers can hardly keep their hands off each other.

Their flat is filled with books on history, on politics, with an entire rosewood table devoted to Marxism, Hindi, Urdu and English works of fiction and poetry and hundreds of LPs brought from Salim Qureshi's ancestral home at Biharsharif. On the walls are oils bought from the Patna and Delhi Colleges of Art and also Swastika-di's small watercolours of the historical monuments of Patna and Delhi. The Gandhi Setu at dawn, the Nizamuddin Dargah in the twilight, Purana Qila by moonlight. Then there is the North Campus series, of St Stephen's College, of Hindu, of Miranda House, of Gwyer and Jubilee Halls and others, for which there is a steady demand through the alumni associations. There is a calmness and 'at peace with the world' quality to her art that exudes instant nostalgia and is very easy on the eye. On our wedding, she had given us two paintings, one of St Xavier's High School in Patna for Hriday and for me one of the St Columba's College in Hazaribagh. Both from photographs taken by Hriday. He had taken those photographs with his FM-10, the St Columba's one when he had come to Hazaribagh for our engagement. We had met for the first time then and I had taken him to see my old college in a rickshaw. Ours was an arranged marriage. It took place just before my M.A. (English) results came out. I remember I was more anxious about Spencer and Chaucer than Hriday's thick moustache on my wedding night. I was twenty-three and Hriday twenty-seven. Later, I got him to shave off his moustache. It was a definite improvement, I feel. Salim and Swastika had met while they were doing their M.Phils from the history department in DU. Swastika-di is the cousin of Pranjal Sinha. Pranjal and Hriday are childhood friends from St Xavier's and were roommates in DU. Swastika-di, elder to them by four years, was their local guardian. Pranjal practices as an ophthalmologist in Patna now.

After his M.Phil, while Salim went to King's College, London, to do his doctorate on the revenue system of Sher Shah Suri, Swastika-di started teaching at Zakir Husain College as an ad hoc lecturer. After Salim came back from London, they moved in together. Swastika-di's mother stopped speaking to her after that but her father visited her every time he was in Delhi to argue a case in the high court. Salim's parents, much more progressive than Swastika's, only wished that someday they would legally marry and have children.

Swastika Singh is one of the best-looking women I know, with dusky glowing skin, thick shoulder-length straight hair, big brown doe eyes with a red bindi in the middle and a long sharp Rajputani nose which makes her look at times like a calendar art Durga. And Salim Qureshi is the tiger that she uses as her mount, and who is no slouch in the looks department either, if you ask me. Not a regulation stunner like Swastika-di, he is broadly built, snub-nosed with short cropped hair to hide the increasing male pattern baldness and is usually dressed in black twill shirts and blue denim. He looks more like a sculptor than an academic. One of the finest Marxist historians of his generation, he also edits, along with the legendary Samar Sinha, *Hand to Mouth*, a peer-reviewed quarterly journal dedicated to history from below. He enjoys the company of women and knows that some women will always find him attractive. Like me for instance and a few more who still wear Cottage Emporium sarees and put big red bindis on their foreheads for target practice. But alas he is totally devoted to Swastika-di. I have had a crush on him ever since my marriage to Hriday six years back when I came to Delhi from Hazaribagh. And he has a terrific sense of humour; last year when he wrote an article about lifting the import ban on *The Satanic Verses* in *Frontline*, the poor Maulanas got agitated and drunk-dialled him to kingdom come. He simply put the Gayatri mantra on his caller tune. Within twenty-four hours, the death threats stopped. 'I always knew the Gayatri mantra would prove to be more effective than the *Internationale*,' he said.

Over the years I have been accepted into the Delhi University circle that Hriday moves in even though I am much younger than them. Over the years I have now grown familiar with the legends and landmarks of North Campus, Delhi University, and do not feel left out anymore. I have worked hard towards this acceptance into their world of books, of art, of politics and activism. Not to mention, of entitlement, of a sense that what they do is of immediate and immense concern to their country. But the good part is that more often than not they are ironical about their entitlement. Their constant refrain when embarrassed about another good cause to espouse or petition to sign or a party headquarter to picket is a belligerent 'For God and Country'. Apparently the old school motto of Salim, Pranjal and Hriday from St Xavier's, Patna. They felt blessed that they were young, liberal and left-wing and hoped fervently they wouldn't suddenly turn right-wing and reactionary when they hit forty like their parents. They hoped to keep God at arm's length all their lives.

I enjoy their easy familiarity with drinking or 'tippling' as they call it. The elaborate ritual of it. The ice, the tall glass, the peg measure which after the second peg is always discarded and then the fascinating discourse on the nationalism of drinking, of Old Monk vs Captain Morgan and Peter Scot vs Glenlivet, till the crows wake up.

To tell you the truth nobody has ever imbibed alcohol in my family, at least for the last two generations, I am sure. So it was quite a shock for me at first as I fell in with Hriday's band of merry friends. 'Matal'was a word used very liberally by my bhadralog father, when he needed to describe someone he disliked. It was usually used with another epithet, 'characterless'. So I found my Hriday to be a 'matal and characterless.' Endearingly so I might add, as soon I myself discovered a buried thirst for Old Monk and Thums-up. And I loved the conversation lasting all night, as the alcohol flowed and made a tributary of our blood.

I can make out the denial of Peter Scot is totally linked to Charulata Roy. It couldn't be anything else. The work on the new book is finally over and he is doing the last edits before sending it off to Tangent, his publisher. This is his second book, a volume of linked stories and we are both hopeful that it will do better than his first, the short novel *Up North* which got a few glowing reviews but hardly sold at all. So the book couldn't be the reason. Can't be work either as a crisis at the ad agency is a routine everyday affair. No one gets unusually stressed about it. Well, there could be one other reason but I do not think Hriday is much bothered by it. At least he has not made it apparent before. For the past five years we have been trying for a baby but no luck so far. We have gone to all the specialists in Delhi and Patna, our mothers to all the gods, but no results so far. There is apparently nothing wrong with us. It is just one of those things. Nothing to be done about it.

'We will keep trying.' Hriday flirts with my petite and grey-haired Malayali gynaecologist in Green Park. 'Is there a particular position we should perhaps try?'

'The democratic one always,' she answers, stone-faced. It is reassuring to know that he can't charm all women. But this craving for a child does get me down sometimes. The rum helps then. I just go easy on the Thums-up. This six-pound heft of a baby, I constantly carry in my arms like an absence. I love children but Hriday is frankly indifferent to them. 'When I was a child, the thing I hated most was when a grown-up would try to befriend me, thinking I was bored or was in need of company. I liked to be on my own. So I leave kids alone. They too have a right to their privacy.' Hriday can prove to be very strange at times. So it can't be our childlessness. Is it possible that he has still not got over Charulata Roy? Is he still in love with her? Hriday's friends are always a bit vague and offhand when there is a mention of Charulata and I am within striking distance. I have noticed that. Also what sets the minute alarm bells ringing in my heart is that nobody ever joshes Hriday about her like they do about other girls he apparently knew in the past. Which means, I realize with a start that it must have been quite serious at one point in time, not really the oh so casual, 'just a girl I was keen on once upon a time' line that Hriday fed me after I discovered a photograph of hers kept between the pages of Zaheer Abdali's *Stormy Petrel*, three months into our marriage. I am positive now that Charulata Roy is the reason he is trying to dodge Swastika-di's invitation. But he can't escape forever.

So this Sunday we finally landed up at Swastika and Salim's home with my signature tipple cake in tow. A full bottle of Sula red had gone into the sponge cake, with raisins soaked in Old Monk encrusted on the reddish brown crust. This cake of mine is justly famous and Hriday in his wisdom has christened it a 'tipple' cake which I think is a vast improvement on the plain old 'tipsy'. A few wedges after dinner with custard, and your night will turn particularly amorous. Swastika-di swears by it. But then with Swastika-di and Salim bhai even tap water would do the trick.

Salim serves Blue Riband and soda, with freshly squeezed lime and bitters. There is Kalyani Black Label but no one wants the lager. Amonkar sings *Basant Bahar*, in a voice you could carve Swiss army knives out of, in the background. Charulata gives Hriday a quick sideways hug and kisses me on my right cheek. Charulata is accompanied by her son Nihal, who is five years old. She is fairer and taller than me. Austere-looking, with thick shoulder-length hair with natural waves. There are streaks of premature grey at the sides and surprisingly it makes her look younger than she is, like sometimes a moustache on a man makes him look younger than he was when clean-shaven. The introductions are made quickly and Charulata passes on a tall coolly sweating glass of gin to Hriday, before I can caution her that Hriday babu is on a sabbatical. But surprise, surprise, Hriday takes the glass and their hands briefly touch. Noticed that. Hriday picks up Nihal and the delight on his face is something to behold. He puts Nihal on his shoulders and they both go on to admire the new Chaubey. Nihal, somewhat startled, looks towards his mother. But Charulata only smiles and thus reassured he settles comfortably on Hriday's shoulders, holding on to his head gently. They both look at the portrait of Zaheer 'Zed' Abdali. It is from the famous author photo on the back cover of *Stormy Petrel*, his autobiographical novel of his days with the Progressive Writers Association. *Stormy Petrel* is one of Hriday's favourite novels. When Salim Qureshi was in the tenth standard at St Xavier's High School, Zaheer Abdali would come down every Saturday afternoon in his sky blue Premier Padmini to teach an hour-long class on writing short stories. It was only for six months but Zaheer Abdali's writing, personality and political views had influenced him very heavily. In Delhi University Salim joined the CPI-ML and became a card-carrying member like Abdali. On the other hand Zaheer Abdali's daughter Sadaf taught Hriday at the arts faculty while he was doing his M.A. (Final) in English.

'He looks like Irwin Shaw here, like in the famous Capa portrait,' Hriday says to Salim and Swastika, who have come to join him and Nihal. I slice some more lemons and look over to Charulata. She in turn is watching me. She smiles and takes a small sip of the gin fizz which the bitters have turned pink and walks over to look at the painting closely.

'He was better-looking than Shaw, I once saw him read at Zakir. The women couldn't keep their eyes off him. Men too. He was over seventy then but still magnetic. Sadaf led him up to the dais. He read "Butcher Out of Gujarat". It was just after the riots,' Sawastika-di said to Hriday.

'A much better writer than Shaw too, if you ask me.' Salim took a sip of his gin fizz.

'True but Shaw wrote some wonderful stories. "The Eighty-Yard Run" is magical,' Hriday pointed out.

'And not to forget "Girls in their Summer Dresses." Hriday once read that story to me long back. Just before the ancient India paper in M.A. Previous to calm me down. I was so nervous. Do you remember, Hriday?' Charulata said softly, pouring some more Blue Riband into her glass.

'Of course, I remember.' Hriday put Nihal down gently on to the sofa and lit a Goldflake.

To calm her down! Really Hriday babu. But then it does seem to be in character. Hriday is a gallant lad, if anything. But I am sure Hriday wouldn't just stop at the reading. He would then have really calmed her down. Even if it took him all night. With friends like these, it is a miracle Charulata could clear her Masters in history.

A cloud seems to have lifted off Hriday and he takes Nihal by the hand and goes over to the small ox-blood Chesterfield by the Grundig. And they keep talking, completely absorbed in each other's company. Nihal is telling him stories of the school he went to in Jamshedpur called 'Lillies of the Field'—more like 'Brood of Vipers', Charulata interjects—and about all his friends. The gin and lime goes down like water in the drowsy February afternoon and before lunch Hriday has already had three large ones. But he is absolutely fine. He is back in character, the despondency had slid off him like a cloak. And it is a relief to see him imbibe and enjoy himself once more. With four large gin and limes, I am not doing badly either. From the corner Suzanne Vega reiterates that 'Blood Makes Noise'.

At the dinner table I sit with Charulata on my left and Swastika-di on the right. On the opposite side, sit the boys, with Nihal between Salim and Hriday eating macaroni and cheese quite adroitly off his fork. While I have cold pepper chicken in white sauce, Hriday has broiled bhetki with Colman's mustard spread liberally on it. According to Salim, Colman's mustard was the one thing that someone called Philby dearly missed in Moscow.

Even though I knew I would have a raging hangover in the evening, it was a wonderful, languid late February lunch and we all felt happy and privileged. As it invariably happens in such gatherings, after a certain point we started talking about caste and privilege and how lucky we are to be born in the kind of families we were born into. Then Charulata narrated an incident that happened while she was coming to Swastika-di's house in an auto-rickshaw. 'At the Kingsway Camp traffic lights, as the auto stopped, a little girl not more than five years old, with a baby in her arms came and touched my arm. She looked as if she hadn't had a meal in days. My heart went out to her. I gave her ten rupees. And it keeps happening at every traffic signal in Delhi. It wasn't so earlier.'

'It was always there. They are all from Bihar, Jharkhand, Orissa and Chattisgarh, caught between the Maoists and the government forces,' Salim said to Charulata.

'Well, the poor will always be with us,' Swastika-di said and filled her glass with the chardonnay that Charulata has brought as hostess present.

'It is a shame. I have been thinking of writing a short story about the child beggars of metropolitan India for a long time,' Hriday said to Salim.

'It is all very well organized. They earn quite a lot. The contractors, that is. You should never give them money. It is taken away from them by the contractors. It is all futile,' I said to Charulata.

Charulata looked at me for a moment and then said, 'Chitrangada, it is hard not to, when you are a mother.' I felt as if she had leaned across and thrown a glass of cold chardonnay into my face. I felt so ashamed and judged. And then angry at Hriday. He should have said something but he didn't. He played the perfect gentleman. He kept quiet and then tried to change the topic by asking Nihal if he would like some more macaroni. I poured myself some more Blue Riband. Salim got up and brought me some ice and refreshed his own drink.

The conversation drifted away. Why did Charulata say something so cruel to me? I had liked her, and whatever there had been once between her and Hriday, I was willing to overlook. I could see that Hriday was still affected by her presence but not so much that it would affect our marriage. But what really struck me like a hammer was the instant bond that Hriday had forged with Nihal. The open pleasure he took in Nihal's company. I realized with a jolt that Hriday probably wanted a child as much as I did. Today his mask had finally slipped.

After my tipple cake and custard are served, we leave. There is ice-cream and gulab jamuns for Nihal. Swastika-di fills a square Tupperware box with slices of the tipple cake for me to take home, as Hriday and I didn't have any at the table.

~

On our way back, at the Kingsway Camp traffic signal, I feel the first stirrings of the slowly creeping hangover and see the light orange matinee sun making everything hazy as some child beggars go from one indifferent car to another with their hands outstretched. Before Hriday can stop me, I am out on the streets carrying the box of cake in my hands, calling out to the kids. Some people in the neighbouring cars roll down their windows and look at me in wonder. The children with their emaciated bodies and malnourished hair bleached blond by the sun, hesitate for a bit and then run over. Just as I open the Tupperware box and start passing the pieces of cake lovingly to them, Hriday comes from behind and snatches the slices back from the hands of the startled children. I hit him from the back, on his shoulders, then, but Hriday pretends not to notice. Still busy playing the gentleman. He takes out of his pocket whatever loose change he has and gives it to the tiny beggars. They run shrieking, throwing their hands in the air. The light turns green and Hriday takes me firmly by the hand and opens the car door. He helps me put the seat belt on, then smiles and has a slice of the tipple cake. He gently wipes the tears from my eyes with his fingers, rubs my chin playfully like a pet dog's and we drive back home.

Mr Majestic! The Tout of Bengaluru

Zac O'Yeah

Chilling Out at the Deluxe Bar

He cursed his laxity, it was unforgivable to keep using the same cybercafé and that too the one he lived next to. Not quite knowing what to do, he headed into the dark hole of Deluxe Bar across the street, an abyss in which many a CD Road champion had drowned.

Its walls were decorated with posters for non-existent packaged water brands that had the same names as existing booze labels. 'Taste the Total High of Knockout: Packs in the Punch! Never attempt to finish the whole bottle of 100 per cent Mineral Water alone!' This early there were just two other customers: one pair of feet sticking out from under an old rosewood table, and the other by the bar, haranguing the barman the way alcoholics do.

'Had your breakfast, Majestic?' the bartender asked in his slurry voice. He was a potbellied fellow who sampled the products he sold.

Hari ignored the breakfast question, it was after all just a way of saying hello, and placed his order. 'Special Mix, boss,' said Hari, who usually only drank coffee until at least 5 p.m. And after work he rarely had more than two or three Knockout pints. Special Mix, the house cocktail, into which went a 180 ml sachet of potent arrack distilled from palm sap, ginger, lemon, rock salt, black pepper, green chili, mint leaves, all topped with a teaspoon of soda water, was ordered once in a blue moon when he suffered a stress overdose.

'Life is that bad or what? Hang on a little,' said the bartender.

Hari rolled his head sideways as he waited for his drink and noticed the other customer reach over the counter and poke the bartender in the belly with a locally made gun. What a day this was! Such unbranded handguns were crafted from parts of old recycled machinery—typically the steering column of a wrecked car was put to fresh use as a gun-barrel—and sometimes they exploded in the shooter's hand.

Hari took a step back.

The situation could turn ugly. The customer maintained that he had been drinking at the bar the night before and had paid for a whole bottle, which had disappeared. The bartender explained that bottles never lasted forever in establishments like this one, and besides, aiming a gun at a CD Road bartender was a big mistake.

He then grabbed hold of the gun's barrel and twisted it hard and fast until the bone in the customer's index finger, stuck in the loop of the trigger guard, crunched and snapped.

The situation was defused. The customer contemplated his busted finger: the pain was going to hit him as soon as the shock wore off. Meanwhile the bartender deposited the gun in a crate he kept behind the bar for daggers and knuckledusters, the more heavy-duty props that customers left behind. Those who returned sober got their weapons back.

At last Hari was served his Special Mix. After a few sips he loosened up.

'Some days are like that only,' said the bartender. 'There's a time for everything and there's another time to die.'

'Yah, nobody's perfect,' he said to the potent liquid in his steel tumbler, lumbering over to a robust cane chair and more or less collapsing into it.

'You can say that again. Just take a look at your uncle,' the bartender said, apropos of nothing.

Hari brooded a nanosecond on this. Everybody thought that Uncle Mamool, full name Ontappa Kallappa Mensinkai, also alias OK (instead of 'hello' he answered the phone with an 'OK' which never failed to impress Hari) had gone deeper downhill than any man in living memory. It was true that he had once tried to start a communal riot at Deluxe Bar by setting fire to the beard of another riffraff customer, after which he had been banned from the premises.

The irony was that the bartender and Mamool had been part of the same gang, way before Hari was born, during the politically tumultuous '70s. OK Mensinkai—an aspiring lawyer—and the bartender used to meet with other social activists to perform street plays on hygiene and democracy to educate the masses.

The drink put Hari in a sentimental mood. If CD Road people started turning against each other, then there was no telling how it would all end. He said, 'It was uncle who taught me everything.'

'A regular guru, is he, your uncle?'

'He isn't perfect, but then what to do?' said Hari. 'My life was good up to seven minutes ago.'

The bartender said sagely, more to himself than for the benefit of any listener, 'The golden age lies in the past, never in the future.'

'I was a fool to think that one can't get busted in cyberspace.'

'Go anywhere, Majestic, and somebody will be there to bust people like you.'

Hari ignored the pearls of wisdom and focused on wallowing in self-pity, trying to scratch his name into the edge of the rosewood table with a fingernail. Then his nail broke. He said, 'Did you know that uncle once sold all of north India to a Pakistani spy?'

'Where'd he meet a spy on CD Road?'

'Not here, in Shivajinagar.'

'So how much did he get?'

'Don't mock him just because your dive doesn't attract a cosmopolitan clientele. Anyway, a quart of rum and some Pakistani state secrets is what he got, which he forgot by the time he woke up next morning.'

'Sounds familiar.'

They stopped their banter when a foreign backpacker walked in—as if to prove that Hari was wrong and that the seedy bar was cosmopolitan after all.

Hari took a closer look. He was grimy; perhaps he had just hopped off the overnight bus from Goa. The expensive digital camera, with its shoulder strap covered in registered trademarks, hung noose-like from his neck. Hari calculated his net worth, divided the amount into a daily budget, and started thinking of which lodge would give the best commission. He hadn't been touting for a while, and some new boarding houses had come up in the deeper back alleys of late. They would be grateful if he brought an overnight guest.

'Hi dude, mind if I sit down?' said the foreigner, but he was already sitting. He seemed a bit nervy.

The fellow may have picked Hari's table because the two of them were about the same age. Or perhaps he just wanted to avoid the aggressive loser, who was talking to his own finger. Analysis time. It wasn't exactly natural to see tourists in Deluxe Bar. As a rule they went for places that kept up the pretence of being hygienic.

Maybe he was one of those travel writers on assignment. Over the years Hari had offered guidance to quite a few who claimed to be working for the *Lonely Planet*.

It was a matter of give and take, but often the writers took more than they gave. Considering that he spelled out everything to them and let them pick his brains clean, he ought to have been given co-writing credit. Being the best tout south of Bombay, he had for years been trying to get listed on page 317 in the guidebook, under the heading 'Information, Tourist Offices'—but to no avail.

The backpacker asked, 'They serve food here?'

As his previous business had just gone bust Hari launched, very professionally, into a spiel: 'No cocktail cherries, but you do get oil-fry Chicken Kebab, boss. If you're a vegetarian I recommend the Gobi Manchurian. Don't touch the beans, they give flatulence.'

That was the essence of professional touting—mix words of caution into your sales pitch, add a disclaimer, and the customer will think you're honest.

The backpacker snapped his fingers at the bartender, 'Hear that? I'll take the vegetarian option, but no beans. And give me a Kingfisher beer.' Then he turned to Hari: 'By the way, the name's Tord.'

'I'm Harry—as in Potter, but better.' Contact established, Hari was about to shake hands, when the tourist joined his palms in a phony namaste.

Then Tord dug out a hi-tech phone that he started fiddling with. So he was one of those who carried the net with them 24x7, one patron less for Doc's cybercafé. More and more tourists had GPS on their mobile handsets, and apps that guided them to recommended eateries and shops, making a serious dent in the tout's traditional customer base.

'Harry?' he said, looking up from his phone. 'That doesn't sound Asian at all.'

'I was adopted, found under the seat in a cinema down the road, so this is as close to home as it gets.' He whipped out a tattered business card, according to which he was a government-approved tourism consultant. 'If there's anything I can help with, just ask me. I work in the tourism sector. I'm going to organize a motorcycle trek to Ladakh; it is like Switzerland but higher.' It was also as far away from CD Road as it was possible to get without leaving the country: first you went 3,000 kilometres north and then you climbed 3,000 metres up.

'Dude, no way am I gonna go to Ladakh, I read in the *Planet* that the Kashmiris rip off foreigners, and fundamentalists there chop off tourists' heads.'

When he got his Gobi Manchurian, Tord gave the food a doubtful look. He chewed on a piece as he checked the messages on his phone, and observed, 'Tastes like chicken.' Then he turned to Hari, a nervous tic under his eye: 'But hey, that reminds me, I saw a lost-looking chick out there in the street. She might want to go to Ladakh.'

'Chick?' The arrack had truncated Hari's depression and the cogwheels were spinning.

It was that easy sometimes: life's ups and downs came and went, and pitch-black nights turned into sunny days. Hari drained his tumbler, he was back in business.

The Highways of Mofussiluru

By the time the battered bus pulled in at the dusty rural bus station, the sun dangled like a used teabag over the boiling horizon.

Hari stepped off and down into a herd of bleating goats being shepherded across the platforms. It was obviously a non-vegetarian town and he was amazingly hungry; very likely a result of having experimented with healthy living for too many days.

He spotted Total Military Mess—nothing to do with the army, just a discreet way of keeping the odd vegetarians out—and crossed the road.

He sat on a wooden bench at a zinc-plated table and ordered some biryani. A radio played a distorted Tamil music channel through its cracked mono-speaker. It was long past lunch and the rice was cool with congealed animal fat, but the rural goats tasted less rubbery than urban goats. It was the absence of discarded plastic garbage in their diet. Unable to resist he asked for another portion; his karma was going to pay for this, but the meat was tender, ah how tender. Mr Total was very pleased when he paid the bill.

After his meal, he started feeling good about Mofussiluru. He returned to the bus station where the newspaper stall reflected the district's borderland location: a heady mix of scripts printed with runny ink—as if they had so much to say that there was no time to let the ink dry—and dog-eared magazines on rent at a fraction of the cost of buying them.

He walked up and down the platform, trying hard to look lost, until the local tout finally spotted him. He had the air of an extinct breed of single-humped camel: a protruding potbelly, a balding head with an oily comb-over, dressed in a Lacoste with too many crocodiles—clearly less wasn't more in this town. One lens of his glasses was cracked and held together with Scotch tape. Judging by the state of its touts, Mofussiluru had seen its civilization peak around 1980.

'Foreign tourist?' the tout said in English, lifting his chin to peek semi-blindly at Hari from behind the crack in his spectacles. 'Russia? Japan? Scandinavistan?'

'Bangalore,' said Hari.

For anyone in Mofussiluru that was foreign enough.

Like all border towns, this too was a nexus of shady dealings. The tout probably reported to the ruling don and kept an eye out for supari killers and investigators arriving by bus. So Hari handed him his Sandalwood Starring Multi-Agency business card. It'd go blank in a blink in the hands of the sweaty tout, and cover Hari's tracks. 'I'm scouting for locations. The next installment of Mission Impossible will be shot in Bangalore. On CD Road to be precise.'

'Oh, you're a movie man…Had your lunch?' asked the tout.

'Yes boss,' Hari said. He did the one-thumb-in-the-mouth-fist-suck, globally understood to mean it was time for a certain beverage. 'Now I need something else. The lead actor has a bit of a hooch habit. He can't perform impossible missions without his ration of rocket fuel. Any good bars around here?'

'Plenty of top class restaurants.' The tout rattled off the list—from half-star to minus star to black hole. 'You might prefer AA Paradise Garden, where film people sometimes go to drink.'

'Deadly!' Hari immediately recognized the name of the dhaba from the card in the bhai's wallet; it was very likely to be the place where Madhuri had been taken.

The tout was full of gossip, proud of his hometown. According to him mostly minor Kollywood stars drove up from Tamil Nadu for drinking binges. This side of the border, liquor permits were easier to get, so there was more competition. Rum cost twenty rupees and a Smirnoff Rs 45 per peg, and the lodges along National Highway 4 were sufficiently anonymous for weekend romances. Of course no megastars drank here; they and the hyperstars were rich enough to down their sunset cocktails in Bali.

'Boss, want to go for a drink?' Hari suggested. A decent tout was the best guide to local areas of ill repute and he didn't want to go to the highway bar alone: it would immediately single him out as an outsider.

'Puttu,' said the tout and they shook hands, English-manner.

It didn't quite sound like a proper name, more like an alias. Naturally. What a lovely town. It was like a bucolic version of CD Road, he thought, and somehow he trusted this fellow would be a good guide to it.

Although Puttu looked like a long-dead camel, the camel was a noble animal belonging to a better era. Puttu had his own unmetered rickshaw and drove Hari out to the national highway. A private rickshaw was a perfect getaway vehicle if things got rough. Puttu smartened himself up by tying a bandana around his head: its colourful grease pattern suggested he sometimes slept face down in his plate of Chilly Chicken Boneless, local fashion.

The sun had set, the sticky-wet darkness poured out of the jungle and Hari stared at the lit-up highway dhabas, each brighter and more alluring than the other with their offers of multi-cuisine and a good time to be had till you blacked out.

Each was adjacent to a liquor shop, so even if the dhaba wasn't licensed the waiters procured drinks against corkage. A cluster of two-, three- and four-wheelers stood parked in the unpaved parking lot in front of AA Paradise Garden Family Restaurant and Riverview Bar. The board in front advertised Royal Stag whisky and 'Big Drinks with a River-View.'

Somebody had used spray-paint and altered the 'Drinks' into 'Drunks'; there was a lot of comedy in life as long as you knew where to look.

The river view at AA Paradise was purely hypothetical. A murky smell suggested that it had been built next to a drain. The dhaba was the sort Hari was familiar with since childhood. Something of a men's club, a refuge of the alphas and omegas, the last bastion where gents still had the upper hand. Out in front stood a crumbling concrete fountain adorned by milkmaids in various stages of undress. The basin was dry and in use for chucking scrunched cigarette packs in. The beverages were served, very sensibly, in stainless steel tumblers because sweeping broken glass off a dirt floor was time-consuming. A bony youngster in a deep neon-lilac nylon shirt greeted them by tilting his head and staring at them; this was the cool barman's way of asking: 'What do you want?' Hari asked for the Private Deluxe Compartment, like his uncle used to, and Puttu followed his lead self-importantly. The idea of being in a place frequented by stars—minor, major or middle-sized—was thrilling.

Deep Lilac Nylon guided them to the back with its two facing rows of 'rooms'. Mostly customers who brought in ladies used these and screens of split bamboo strips guaranteed confidentiality. As a kid, he had been to similar places, strung all along the roads leading out of town, whenever his uncle was seeing someone other than his official mistress. Little Hurree was given a bottle of local cola and told to play with the stray dogs. Mamool went into the 'room' for a consultation. (Perhaps the aunty needed a complicated legal document, an endorsement stamp for foreign travel on her passport, or some other bureaucratic issue solved quickly.)

Hari and Puttu were given a room next to one occupied by a group of youngsters who had driven their bikes into the compound. These boys had spilled out of their space and some of them sat on their Royal Enfields, passing around bottles of extra super-strong beer while the rest smoked joints inside. Another customer lay supine in the position known as 'had enough' under the prominently displayed warning: 'Liquor Ruins Country, Family and Life'.

Deep Lilac Nylon was their waiter and he rattled off the specials, including an Ayurvedic anti-hangover Party-Smart pill that came free with each order of foreign liquor. Except for the imported booze everything was cheap and hangover-inducing. Hari asked if the proprietor might be coming in that night. Deep Lilac said that A.A. Sura usually dropped by after finishing his other work to have a little something.

Puttu wanted coconut hooch and a side order of Goat Brain Fry, which, taken along with the drink, lined the tummy with grease and protected it from going acidic. Hari asked for his favourite vegetarian bar snack, Gobi Manchurian, but Puttu talked him into sampling the local Chinese inspired specialty, Manchurian 65, which turned out to be a chicken dish which tasted exactly like the vegetarian version.

The underworld gossip got going without much prompting because smaller fry naturally want to impress bigger fry. 'You wouldn't believe it, but…,' Puttu started bragging about how much he knew about the owner of AA Paradise. Apparently, the highway with its heavy cargo traffic had a tendency to develop into a flesh market at points such as this, where the truckers had their long-established rest stops. So that was one part of A.A. Sura's business. The borderland was also the major conduit for stolen motorcycles: two-wheelers from the state were sold in Tamil Nadu, and Tamil motorcycles were shipped to Bangalore in a never-ending exchange. It wasn't unheard of that the same motorcycles were restolen, and then resold again here. If Hari needed an almost brand-new bike, Puttu said, he could broker a deal with the smugglers, who it turned out, were the same young men smoking pot in the next room, relaxing after having driven in the day's cache of two-wheelers from Tamil Nadu. A.A. Sura's fingers were in so many pies that he reminded Hari of Uncle Mamool in his heyday—from illicit arrack to land racketeering to owning a fraudulent business school that issued certificates against cash. Then there was that detail about the wedding filming service. This had to be the man.

Hari hadn't had alcohol for a week and so felt out of practice. After a few rounds he went to the bathroom in a separate concrete building at the back. It was a remarkable toilet for such a seedy bar. Apart from the porcelain cowry with neat footrests sunk into the floor, it was equipped with a bathtub into which Hari projectile-vomited in order to not get too drunk. When he saw what came out he was amazed. It was as if half a national park had been poached, oil-fried and stuffed down his throat. He hadn't eaten so much meat in a long time. No wonder he felt dizzy. Somewhat green-faced, he came back to the room to see that a newcomer had joined the party. It was a large man with a scarred face and lots of crooked teeth that gave him the appearance of a shark after a trainee taxidermist had done a shoddy job.

'That's him,' Puttu slurred, low-key now, an indication that the local don was in attendance. Hari sat down, a bit nervously, uncertain about how to make his pitch. There was something conspicuously dishonest about Sura. Perhaps it was the flowing shirt, block-printed Hawaii-style with coconut palms, combined with sunglasses that had LED-disco lights built into the frames. The pulsating lights made it impossible to guess what Sura was thinking.

'Don't shut up on my account,' Sura said.

That didn't do anything to boost the conversation. Hari handed over his card and received Sura's in return—the ceremony was stiff. Studying the card, Hari pretended to be impressed by the don's business empire.

Sura called in Deep Lilac and ordered platters of grilled meat and bottles of Knockout, the extra-strong beer popular with highway motorists (you didn't have to stop to pee as often); a beer brand that Hari favoured too for the practical and quick intoxication it gave. Hari was glad that he had done some preemptive upchucking in between rounds, or he'd have hit the dirt floor in less than seven minutes.

After the awkwardness of the initial round of drinks, everyone was soon cheering everyone else and Hari was so deep undercover that he drank anything that appeared on the table. Puttu's ears were red and sweaty from the excess and he fainted, face down in his food.

'So tell me,' said Sura when he heard Puttu snore. 'What you want? I hear you've been asking questions about me.' He spat out a large animal bone he had been chewing on. A stray dog caught it mid-air.

Best to be cautious.

Hari plucked at the beer label, the social courtesies were over. Luckily he was one of those who turned slippery when wet, and so his autopilot went on. 'Same that everybody wants: business.'

'As in?'

'I'm in the filmy trade, about to break new turf, boss. I need to rent a studio.'

'Then go back to your Sandalwood. That is where the big-banner production houses are.'

'I don't require a large studio.'

'Is that so?'

'A small facility for budget filmmaking; the work has to be done with a low profile and hence it can't be done in Sandalwood—where too many idle gossip reporters drift around.'

'I don't follow. Why would I be interested in your films?'

'You're the owner of a wedding video company as well as of this wonderful garden resort. One has to use resources creatively for optimal result. We want a place where we can bring—nubile—' Hari emphasized the idea with a suggestive English expression thrown in for good measure.

'—wannabe actresses to the casting-couch, is that what you're saying?' Sura filled in. 'And make dirty films?'

'Somebody has to do the dirty jobs, no? So how's that wrong if we save someone else the trouble?'

After pausing to deliberate the karmic consequences, a greasy smile appeared on Sura's lips and his tone turned menacing: 'How many Xs—single, double or triple?'

'I aim at a lot of Xs, ten to twenty X minimum, the most X-rated film ever made,' said Hari, although the mere thought of what that might look like gave him a foul taste in the mouth.

'That's a film I'd love to watch.'

'Yes, boss, you'd be the first. That is why the studio has to be here at Paradise Garden, far away from town. Do you follow now?'

'Correctly you have come to me,' said Sura as he too switched to English to pronounce the key idea of the evening. 'It isn't as if nobody has suggested this to me before. Time for more whisky. Boy! Show him the studio.'

Deep Lilac had stayed in earshot ever since Sura had come to the room. He put a bottle of Royal Stag on the table and then, after a quick toast, the boy whisked Hari off to the back of the compound.

It turned out that he had already visited the 'studio' facility when he'd gone to use the bathroom attached to the Presidential Honeymoon Suite. That explained the incongruous bathtub in a restaurant lavatory—the backdoor of the suite's bathroom was falling off its hinges and so it was a convenient place for customers to answer various calls of nature.

The front entrance to the suite was more attractive. The porch was painted to resemble the Taj Mahal and its pillars had replications of attractive Khajuraho sculptures. A dried-up pool overlooked the drainage ditch. While he struggled with the key in the padlock, Deep Lilac explained, 'Infinity pool with river view.'

It must have been planned as a luxurious hideaway for amorous couples...and this was what was left of love, Hari thought as the door swung open. Madhuri's love for cinema had brought her to this tomblike hotel room and here her dreams had ended.

The room had a heart-shaped bed; its sheets were red, discoloured by mould. The remaining half of a shattered ceiling mirror hung precariously over it. The grill of the air-cooler was broken and empty beer bottles were stashed inside it. But he didn't spot any extreme bloodstains. The sordidness of it all made him sober up fast.

(***Editor's Note:*** 'Chilling Out at the Deluxe Bar' *captures the ambience of a seedy bar in the Majestic area of Bangalore. 'The Highways of Mofussiluru' is set in one of the booze dhabas that line the highways out of Bangalore as far as the Tamil Nadu border.)*

CONTROL

Indrajit Hazra

Imagine there is no limit to your threshold. You drink.

The alcohol slowly mixes with the blood. Your head feels expansive.

You drink more and the expansion that your head feels is now shared with the space behind your eyes.

As you drink even more, your body starts betraying you just the way you had always wanted it to since you witnessed the intoxicated as a child, wondering without actually wondering how it was possible to be under the influence of anything and be free from any control at the same time.

But in this imagined sequence, there is no limit to your threshold. You drink more. The alcohol—slowly for some people, quickly for others—drives the blood into the corners.

There cannot be any poisoning because your body has stopped distinguishing between poison and blood. Even blood can't tell the two apart. You drink on.

You are floating. A balloon in the sky. Then a star whose place in the skies had been tenuous to start with. You drink more.

The blood is driven away by alcohol like surges in a crowd.

But in your case, in this special case, no one gets trampled or done under.

You do not get sick because in this imagined condition everything stays and accumulates. There is space for all. There is no violent expulsion. In fact, there is no violence at all.

Causes keep gathering and effects keep piling up. You can't collapse, pass out, or enter into a coma.

You drink and you drink with the alcohol sloshing around the insides of you, even under your lids and under your nails. That is until, without any fanfare, it starts seeping out of your body, primarily out of your pores. There is no old blood left inside you. Yet you manage to continue to drink.

Then, the alcohol starts to capture the space that lies outside and around your body, claiming it the way a particularly ambitious race or nation or even Hernán Cortés himself claims new territories. In this disposition, this new civilization, your body will be anointed not emperor, but vazir, a position that usually demands one and only one thing: sobriety. But no longer.

~

He wa walking aimless on footpath straightish. Evening outside night falling. Had no marks of usuphoria as he spoke in voice: 'Go away! Or I shall call the police,' as if us were goonda.

Abey sala not knowing that we were the police hee ha. White cleank shirt jean tucked he couldant be more tan forty-fiffish. He looked losht but insisting was walked just to take evening stroll. We see evening stroll people but this man was diffirent. Had no sweat on face, nothing.

'Look, here is my PAN card. My name is Satish Kanwal. I live in 23/C College Road. Why are you harassing me like drunken idiots! I have been here in Nashik for the last one month and work for *Hindustan Times*!' Which after he showing us press card hee ha.

But he said 'drunkw idioms' and tha was infuriation. So we took Satish Kanwa in our car left his polybag of tomato Motha Diary carton back behind.

It was straynge. Satish Kanwa had white eyes seemed suffer brain blank like not before we had shown. Not dull red normal. I was offered him a dring of paper cup inside Tata Suma police car but he ignored. Was then we downed him down as a anti-socialist peace disruptor.

'I want my cellphone back! I want to call my office. This is ridiculous!'

Satish Kanwa murburred inside shortcut to polish thana. Majid my man was watching into Satish Kanwa's mobile. IPL was score tight. Mumbai Indias Majid checked line batting at Mike Huzey 28 off 6 balls and Pragin Oza in just on nothing with 66 for six. Kakeyr was a good team and we support all watching Mumbai Indias.

The van outed Satish Kanwa. He stepped out angry but strange soft. He looked as if sleep steps as we walkered either his side now knowing Satish Kanwa has may something wrong.

'If Huzzey stays another last three overs 150 may possible,' constable fellow Arvind says me when we enter polish thana and me take my hot cap out.

'It is may be. But Kakeyr has batting—Gautam Gambli, Jacus Kalli, Rovin Uthpah. So it not easy na,' I said after fill upping my paper cup with round of whiska from thana drink machine.

Satish Kanwa was bringed and sat. Inspector Ranade was showed IPL on TV but with sound slow when he showed the man we suspicious brought to polish thana.

'There has been a mistake. I was walking back home from the market—I live in 23/C College Road—when your people took me into custody. All of them have been drinking and I really think this is shameful!'

Ranade turning seat showed to Satish Kanwa as I brought Ranade Satish Kanwa's PAN card press card mobile with last score card 90 for 6.

'I am new to Nashik, not been here a month yet. I work as a senior journalist at *Hindustan Times*. Why doesn't someone just check. I know Damani-saab. Ashok Damani, MLA. You can check with him. My wife and I were in Delhi for eleven years and now I work here in Nashik.' Satish Kanwa said now. Adding again together like point, '23/C College Road.'

Ranade has high taste to tongue. White Mischiev he keeps for alone unless big event like Raksha Bandha Dusra or Diwli. Paper cup filling Ranade shows once at PAN card then shows once at Satish Kanwa. Satish Kanwa is less abnormal face now. Is sweaty and shows around room looking one time even at me.

'Satish Kanwa?'

'Kanwal.'

'You are okay?'

Satish Kanwa hands are curling on Ranade's table and forward leaned says, 'Yes. I don't know why I am here, inspector. There has been a mistake.'

But Satish Kanwa is not calm as calm. He seed Ranade take White Mischiev in paper cup and then ask Ramdulal for Limca. Or 7 Up. Or Sprite. Ramdulal slow turning from dring brings glass bottle supply of Limca and opens with cap opener and goes back to corner. Ranade is self help and pours own Limca bubbles doing on surface of paper cup.

Satish Kanwa shows Ranade paper cup and shakens head.

'Are you okay, Kanwa-ji?'

'Kanwal! My name is Satish Kanwal!'

Then just as full-toss Umesh Yadav hitted by Huzzey goes into plop hands of Morne Morkel in mid-off running place with score at 124 for seven with two overs kept, Ranade mops his black hair head with hand towel and picks up landline.

'Hello? Dr Mukhjee there? I will hold,' Ranade spoke as showing to Satish Kanwa.

At this point Satish Kanwa stands upward to moving gesture still straightforward. On eyes on eyes from Ranade me and Majid walk to him paper cup in our hands still and push Satish Kanwa down to chair.

'Shut up!' Ranade shout making Satish Kanwa plop more inside chair. 'No Dr Mukhjee. Sorry. But we have some man here needing look. Can you please come? He missing person may be or disorientating.' Click out landline Ranade asking Satish Kanwa.

'What are you drugs?'

'What? No! Please call my office. Satish Bose is the editor. His number is on my phone.'

Ranade raises hand calling for paper cup sign. One was nearest inside one other so I put double paper cup on his table.

'Kanwa-ji. Vod? Or like more whiska?'

Eyes roundy and mouth apart, Satish Kanwa put eyebrows frown and murble, 'I do not drink, Inspector-saab. And certainly not inside a police station. What kind of place is this?'

The Mumbai Indias innings fulled at 138 and Kakeyr players happy looking on television. On cans and plaster bottle were being taken by ground staff off field with players walking crooked tired way back to dressing room. Camera showed crowd happy and loud and some drooping in sitting. They have may be unhappy by score. But not too much unhappy. The TV then showed studio. Harsha Bogles was having dring and talking to Sidu who like always like shouting when dring down. Which is when Dr Mukhjee holding bag and wall walk in.

'Ah, Dr Mukhjee. Sit, sit. This is person Satish Kanwa my men found walk with suspect in street.' Then Ranade addit grave, 'He does not take dring. But examine him? I think drug actish.'

'What nonsense is this?' Satish Kanwa rupted. 'This is harassment!'

Majid and me came and put our hand on side shoulders of Satish Kanwa. I needed more soda for paper cup. But I contained.

Dr Mukhjee unrolled pressure pump after told Satish Kanwa to open his mouth. Hr notice also Satish Kanwa's eyes white with no normalcy red. Dysfunctional agreed too by doctor as he put stethoscope to ear and pumped out air around Satish Kanwa's arm.

'Inspect he needs to come to hospital at right now. Can I have this?' Dr Mukhjee spoke taking paper cup White Mischiev left half on Ranade's desk.

I was assigned to company Satish Kanwa to hospital and though mind was frowned that I would not see Kakeyr innings, duty is duty is fact. So filling my plastic bottle with DS and soda and water I took Dr Mukhjee and by now angry as dog Satish Kanwa in Tata Suma. I looked once at board message next to dring machine:

In Case You Are Caught In a Riotous Situation

1. Do not panic.

2. Quickly go away from the riotous mob.

3. Take shelter in built up areas or behind solid objects (wall/big stones etc).

4. If possible take photograph (from safe distance) on your mobile's camera.

5. Move away to safety at the earliest possible opportunity.

6. Pass on the information with you to the POLICE at the earliest opportunity & be available for answering queries.

I don't know why thinking went like this but as I taking Satish Kanwa head covering with my hand to enter him into the car, I thought of riotous situation possibility and I did not like the look of the night ahead. Pandey was in front holding wheel to drive and when we moved to hospital way with Dr Mukhjee followed I had niggle.

I big gulped from my plastic blue bottle that with yellow inside showed green. Satish Kanwa was looking mad and shaking his head very much like there was big insect that had inside through his ears. I thought I can give him one dring gulp but with his hands handscuffed and previous times Satish Kanwa refusal I did my dring alone.

Nashik in night time looked darling. From my side of window pane I looked the dring shops lined up with families on happy plastic chair tables as the Godvari comes goes comes goes behind the house line. It was in the Kumbh of 2003 where I decide to be polish. I had gone with my mother to dip down in the Godvari with all. I bought two books from the Ramkrishin Mishin stall and I saw uniform polish. The control was there. And the control was everything.

Control went missing on the day Wednesday when my board exam watch gift said 1.24 afternun. Mother looking finding back our chappals when we turned to heard loud people sound. Control broke in the lane next to Kalaram Temple and bamboo barricades were untied from ropes. But I had not seen dead persons. That I saw on television but with bad sound later. It was after that bad day that control was brought again with big seriousness since it was first brought in in 1925.

Much after alcol the first wine yard was decided to be made in Ozar near Nashik town 1925 two years after stamped deaths of 110 people happened in Panchvati. Not like the one where mother went that time the crush dying took place on the Godvari river side on the ghat next side of Kalaram Temple.

This stamped impede was not on Kumbh but still. The same Kalaram Mandir had Balasaab Ambkard outside with thousands harjans in 1930 wanting to get entered in the temple. It was only after this satagrah that the haramis let everyone inside Kalaram.

But it was the wine yard growing in Ozar and then in Narayangaon and then in everywhere else in Nashik that made people here change

for the happiness. Wine after other alcol was first dring that brought
a dring policy by law and custom and habit. Doing dring made equal
whether man woman or harami caste and low like everyone else. Even
childrens dringed water wine with meal.

Dring bring control for everyone. Apart people with liver sickness
and other sickness of parts who would not have dring as of death
reasons and need doctor certificates everyone dringed drings. But
when I joined the force of polish two years after the Kumbh crush
in 2003 there still had people in Nashik who secretly did not dring
drings. Some dringed only sometimes but they were less hard to be
unlawful and melt with the happy regularity.

But many still did not dring drings *at all*. Especial women who
had problems thinking dringing is sinking in badness. Men of their
homes were bad after dring but control was not right because only
these women were out of chaos.

But but but now Nashik is dring persons full. No problem comes
becomes control. In training we were learned how to identificy non-
alcolis and then how dealing with them. A non-alcoli is straight
walking, one foot then other as if in machine steps zombie pagal. They
speak like words in writing and not like diffecurrent.

On asking non-alcolis speak with short sentence. So you ask from
taxi window, 'Cuse me Yashwantrao Chavan Maharashtra Open
University?' He will say back in speak like writing: 'Okay, from Dwarka
Circle take the second turn. Then there will be a gol chakkar. Take
second road to Tilak Road. You will pass Indira Medical Stores on your
right. Take first road turning left to Shivaji Road and you will pass
Savatabhai Desai Children's Hospital. Then turn right to Old Agra
Road…' Some non-alcolis try thicken their tongues with pretence to
sound alcolis but give way. You can not hide non-alcolis sign.

By this time, normal persons have made you lost in your head never
mind in real place. Non-alcolis are like this. They may perhaps not
be bad meaning but with senses all ticked they make as much use as
birds inside water or fish inside the sky. It is this that brings problems.
This mismatch of people with heads cleaned dry with no thing inside
bodies except the body was many more problems before. And funny

that the non-alcolis or people who dring drings but only sometime thinking that it was they with control. Pagal sad.

'I don't want to lose control,' I have listened some of them tell me in my career. Hee ha. What way can you lose control? It is not like slip of paper with a girlsh number of phone you worry about letting lost. Hee ha. Control is somfing you have to get and gather. Like fuyel in a tanka for it to happen work properly.

With no dring people are ghosts. Like when we sleep and the first minutes of waking. With no dring hum sound we are vulnerous unsafe. With no dring hum we can be unsafe to others. With no dring inside like in Satish Kanwa there is no control. There is no tune to play. Hollow pagal these non-alcolis.

As Pandey turned the car inside Matoshree Nagar to be wayside of the hospital in Trimbak Road he turned his head and told me, 'Mahesh, pass that plashtic bottle that's back.' Just as I body turned to get the bottle from backwards the car moving slow speed stopped.

'Hey hey! Get down!'

Three men wearing cloth on faces were in the face of headlights. I was leaned to get rifle but Satish Kanwa harami one number jumped on my face and I felt his body push heavy while I fell outside my bucket seat. Minute passing the door on both sides opened up by two men both speaking in non-alcolic way of straightforward. 'Get out chutiya! Ajit get into the car. You two, stay still or I'll blow your police heads away!'

Ajit who I thought up now was Satish Kanwa stampled out of car almost as if he did have some drings. But on the outside standing he showed me that his face was still like straight and stopped sweaty. He was even hands handscuffed made a sick smile at me. It was the chaos smile of someone who gets a rush of blood when no dring has stopped any natural all sider rush from happens. Dr Mukhjee standing next from his tall thin starey driver had the same smile face but with a wet glint of dring inside him. He was them people!

Pandey me was handscuffed and our mouths taped with tight tape to stop any shout tapes. The three figures with face covered walked straight arrow with no in-built falter or slowness that normalcy people do. Dr Mukhjee and his driver engine started away and left before. The white Maruti Steem with Ajit also Satish Kanwa turned in the road front of us and left and left until we saw it driven into a blink point in the orange road ending in black. On Trimbak Road five minute distance away in civil hospital we were stuck tied with radio making cackly sounds.

How long before any person would seed us inside car handscuffed I worried. Mouth shutted and stuck Pandey and me sat sitting in the shut darkshade window of the now keyless Tata Suma. My blue bottle turned green with yellow was going out of reach for hours.

More than to be afraid of non-alcolics out there and out of control in Nashik town, more than again to be chaosed, more than our men women children with dring inside them as always protection now target of sick mindaddicted to straight inhibitionery I was to be afraid of something much much more to be afraid of: depleting and reach shameful sober.

Police Uncle

Anup Kutty

Vasu Mama hands me a bottle of cheap cologne, turns around and asks me to spray some on his shirt.

'It will help you. You won't have to smell the sweat,' he says. I do as he says.

He wears his helmet and kickstarts his motorbike to life. I grab his thick shoulder and climb on. It's been a few years since I've been back here in Ponnani. Each time, I feel like a weary world traveller returning home to catch my breath. Except this is not really home. This was where I spent my summer vacations. But vacation playgrounds turn into empty buildings before you know it. Buildings crumble. Fences disappear. Boundaries appear. And your arrival becomes so unexciting that no one even looks out of their windows anymore.

'Let's check out this new Karma road. They're building it along the Nila river from Chamravatoom bridge right up to the old Ponnani port,' Mama says. Early monsoon clouds have been gathering above us, threatening to explode. But we know they won't. These are empty threats and we are not carrying a raincoat, or even an umbrella.

The Hero Honda Splendour makes it way through the laterite stone corridors wide enough for an Ambassador car but too narrow for a man and a woman to cross each other without turning sideways. It delivers us to the state highway.

A right takes us through the old town once haunted by lepers and men with legs the size of tree trunks. Down this way lie the warehouses built by the British, the 500-year-old mosque that looks like a temple because of its legacy of forcible conversions, the town court with its colonial arches, the jail with its formidable stone walls along the river delta, the lighthouse that locals wanted to close down because one could peep into their open bathrooms from it, the beach where fishermen meet sand and the filthy Arabian Sea that lashes furiously over shit-stained rocks.

We turn left.

'How's it living with a woman?' he asks me.

'Ha…you tell me.'

'I mean a live-in relationship. What's that about?'

'It's the same as being married I suppose. The pain is the same,' I laugh.

'But there's no loyalty, right? I mean, you can just walk out anytime and carry on with someone else. Right?'

Beautiful women in hijabs smile back at me through hoardings faded by the sun. Sabina Fashions. Zulfi Fashions. A mother and daughter, both in burkhas, walk purposefully into one of the stores. I see more women in burkhas walk by. They are waiting for buses, buying groceries, waving down autorickshaws…I don't remember so many burkhas in this town.

'I wish it was that easy.'

We take a left at the junction onto a road that runs parallel to the Nila river and immediately turn into an alley between two rundown buildings. There's a long queue of men sticking out of a dark doorway that says 'IN'. A door beside it says 'OUT'. A window next to it says 'BEVERAGE' in big bold letters. Two men sit and pass bottles from behind the window in exchange for little paper slips, swiftly and silently, like pharmacists handing out medicines for fake prescriptions.

We get off the bike.

An old man in a checkered lungi hobbles across to mama. 'Ten crores to win. Guaranteed win in every ticket book. It's my last one. Get it off me so I can go home and stretch my limbs,' he flaunts a stump and an ugly toothless smile.

Mama remains cool, gazing at the window. He gets a palm comb from his pocket and runs it through his thin hair and then combs down his heavy moustache. I notice his receding hairline for the first time.

'You are wasting your time,' he tells the lottery-seller in a tone that only cops can deliver.

'Are we going straight to the counter?' I ask Mama.

I've been here before. I know he's got connections in there.

'Yes, but give it a couple of minutes. We don't want these poor souls to protest. Let's blend in first,' he points with his head to the long line of men.

Like thirsty animals they crowd at the only watering hole within miles. We wait and watch like old cats. Sunlight breaks through the black sky and a shadow falls upon us. Vasu Mama takes it as a sign and moves in for the kill, walking in long hasty strides towards the window.

He waves to one of the men lifting cartons inside and speaks gently through the window, 'What's special? In brandy.'

'Morpheus and British Empire,' the man walks up to take a better look at me.

'My nephew. He's come from Delhi.'

We exchange nods.

Mama turns to look at the beasts waiting impatiently for their turn at the hole, their scrawny brown legs glistening with sweat in the humid May sun.

'British Empire and two strong KF beers,' he says.

I offer to pay but he won't let me. The bottles come gift-wrapped in newspaper. Mama packs them neatly into his leather carrier and gets back on the bike.

We leave the beasts to their fate.

'Does she drink?'

'Who?'

'This woman you're living with.'

'Yeah, sometimes she passes out and I have to carry her home.' He is delighted.

When I was a kid, we discussed Bruce Lee and Sylvester Stallone each time I came visiting from Delhi. He'd take me on buses and ferries to find a lone theatre in a faraway town playing *Fist of Fury*. As I grew older, our conversations were about women and alcohol. He'd take me to local bars and toddy shops and tell me tales of his drunken behaviour in return for mine. He'd tell me of the time he caught twenty bottles of pure ethanol off a hooch gang but only reported eighteen. He drank the rest at home, bit by bit, mixing it with water, feeling the glass grow warm in his big firm hands, getting a kick that no IMFL could ever match. I'd tell him stories of all the women I met in Delhi, falling in and out of love with them and everything in between.

We're the best of friends when we meet. But the time we're apart, we won't stay in touch. Not even a phone call.

'Should we do a quick stop at the Kallu shop?' he asks me. I was hoping he'd ask. After all, it's become a ritual. We drive by confectionaries, mobile phone stores and shops selling toilet seats. Brand new houses in fluorescent hues of green, yellow and pink whiz past and finally make way for lush paddy fields and gentle canals. We race over the new highway from Kuttipuram to Guruvayur, between corner shops selling sherbet and plantains, and finally stop at a betelnut tree with a familiar black and white signboard.

This time there's outdoor seating. Benches are laid out under a tin roof supported by crooked bamboo poles. Some are already occupied. There's an awkward silence as we shuffle courteously onto a bench under drunk scrutinizing eyes.

'One pot to drink and one to parcel,' Mama tells the waiter and looks around.

'You see how everyone falls silent when someone new walks in? We'll do the same when the next guy walks in. Watch out,' he says.

A lazy brown cow tethered to a bamboo pole moos in affirmation. I am surprised I never noticed it till now.

The waiter comes with a pot full of fresh toddy and two glasses. Mama asks for a third glass. The waiter checks us both out and then looks away. Stranger requests have been made. He gets another glass.

Mama fills all three glasses to the brim. He dips his index finger into one, takes it out and flicks three drops. Then he clinks his glass with mine and finishes it in one swift gulp. I sip on mine like its expensive wine.

He pours again. We both turn to look at the third glass waiting for its owner to claim it. But he's been long dead. Mama's father, the man who taught him the art of drinking, my grandfather, my Ammachan.

'I've never asked you but what's the flicking business all about?' I begin taking big gulps to match his pace.

'One for our elders, one for Mutthappan—the liquor god—and one for…I don't know, luck maybe,' he says.

Someone from the adjoining bench smacks his lips. A fish curry has found its spot.

'Does brandy mix well with toddy?' I ask him. He loves mixing brandy with everything—beer, whisky…even pure ethanol. Once we got so hammered on a concoction of beer and brandy that I was talking to imaginary people by the pond.

'You know how I found out? Anthony had banned arrack many years ago, and liquor became expensive. Achhan was short of stash. He had less than a quarter brandy in his cupboard, a gift from a friend. He offered it to me so at least one of us could be happy. That's the kind of man he was. You know what I did? I mixed it with some of this cheap stuff so we could both get high. And what a great idea that was,' he takes a quick swig from his glass and points at mine. He hates people nursing their drinks. I knock back the brew and slam the glass on the table.

'It's a good kick,' his eyes turn as red as the soil under our feet. I ask him what he plans to do after he retires from his job in six months.

'This is the plan,' he laughs pointing at his glass. I laugh with him and we order another round to celebrate our silly drunkard joke.

'When did you and Ammachan begin?' I ask him.

'I used to steal from his bottle of Hercules rum in the cupboard. I'd measure it with a pen and fill it up with water. Then one day, Amma said, "Achan says you are welcome to drink from his bottle but please don't mix water",' he grins.

After that, they drank together every evening out in the courtyard. I have watched them drink under a dark sky that shimmered every few seconds with the light from the distant lighthouse. They spoke about cricket and politics. I remember my father being part of it on occasion.

My father was like a principal at a school farewell. There were limits to how much fun you could have. A third drink meant crossing the line. But I always played along…seeking his approval each time I poured myself a small one, secretly laughing about the number of times I'd blacked out and woken up in strange places with strange people.

A lonely egret tiptoes through the garbage floating along the paddy field dripping with fresh sunshine. It reminds me of my girlfriend walking around my messy room. I wish there were some women around here, drinking and discussing their dull lives. They'd be wearing hijabs and talking about men and their strange perversions.

'What about Vishu Mama? He never drank with you guys when he came visiting?' I ask him about his elder brother.

'He was always awkward about it. When he came over from Delhi once, he got us some imported whisky. Achan sat in his room and sipped on the whisky and watched TV while Vishu and I sat in my room. Every once in a while, I'd excuse myself and go over to Acchan to give him some company. Then I realized the pointlessness of the whole thing and I took Vishu with me,' he says, finishing his drink.

A couple of men walk into the bar and we all look up. We wear the suspicious eyes that met us when we entered this hideout.

'Toddy makes your sweat stink. Should we leave?' he looks at his phone for the first time since we left home.

I finish my drink and insist on getting the bill for this one. It's only 200 rupees. The man behind the counter says, 'Let it breathe,' and hands me a bottle of toddy.

'So how does it work when you are travelling? When you check into hotels what do you tell them? A girl and a guy…' Mama asks me as soon as we hit the road.

'Nothing, no one's asked us anything. In any case, it's not illegal.'

'Yeah, but the police could still harass you,' he says.

Is that a threat?

'Then I just call my friends in the police to help me out,' I tell him.

His shoulders shake. He's probably laughing. I want to smoke the weed I have in my wallet but maybe it's not a good idea.

~

We slip into a dirt road, down a steep decline, through chickens scurrying to get out of the way. I see green tree cover lose to blue sky. We are near the river. Large iron gates appear, the entrance to a crematorium.

'Do you want to see where they buried Achan?' Mama drives through the open gates up to a cabin.

A man with bloodshot eyes looks up to greet us. He's burly, dark and looks familiar.

'How's business?' Mama asks him.

'Got one coming right now,' he points over our shoulders. I turn to see a head bob above the mossy stone walls of the crematorium. And then another, and some more.

'Bury or burn?' Mama asks.

'Got a pit all ready for him,' he smiles at me. I remember that smile. It belonged to a man who came to fetch me and my parents from the railway station in his Ambassador every year.

'We came to check on Achan,' Mama pulls the bike on its stand and leads me through unkempt wild grass. I feel a drop of rain on my cheek.

'Wasn't that Radhakrishnan, the driver?' I am stuttering.

'You remember him? He sold his Ambassador. Everyone's got their own cars these days.'

Two men, sitting on the stone wall that separates the crematorium from the Karma road are drinking straight out of a small bottle of whisky, looking out at the river. Mama stops nexts to a young tamarind tree growing out of the fence and sighs.

'He's somewhere around here. This tree is the mark,' he sways and lights his first cigarette of the day.

I can't see any graves. Only shrubs.

'You mean you don't know for sure?'

'He always wanted to be in an unmarked grave,' he says, looking around, trying hard to remember where they buried his father all those years ago. I fumble in my pockets for my phone to take a photograph.

'I brought Vishu here once. He got a bottle of imported rum and emptied it here. Can you believe it? Halfway through, I begged him to stop. Quality booze wasted like piss! "Don't worry, Vasu. I have two of them for you," Vishu told me.'

The drunkards on the fence laugh at their own private joke. Their laughter precedes thunder. We turn back towards the cabin where the funeral has arrived. A dead man is wrapped in a shroud with his sons standing around him wondering what to do next.

Don't worry brothers, you've got Radhakrishnan in charge.

We drive out onto the dirt path up to the river. I can see where it meets the sea, under those nasty black clouds, with the fishermen that look like little ants scrambling for shore.

'Did you drink with him the night he died?' I ask him.

He slams his brakes. I look over his shoulder to see the road broken into two with a stream in between. It runs with a newfound ferocity to join the river. We are on the edge.

'No. I was in a hurry. I had just returned from work and they called me back. I remember him in front of the TV with his drink. They were announcing the World Cup Team. He said "They dropped Ajay Jadeja. It's a bad idea." I said "Yes" and left. That was our last conversation. But I was anxious all night, like something had gone terribly wrong. I couldn't quite put my finger on it.

'When I got back home in the morning, Amma told me that Achan wasn't waking up. I went to check on him and found his body cold as stone. I ran to get the doctor but I knew he was dead.'

The rain comes down like curtains after a show.

'At least he died painlessly. In his sleep,' I tell him.

A boy runs past us, waving his cricket bat at the sky, begging for it to stop.

'But I had so much more to say to him,' he whispers to himself.

I bury my heavy head in his back drenched with rain and sweat. It smells familiar.

Mohan Bhaiji

Mayank Tewari

For the record, alcohol is banned in Haridwar. Consuming it in any form is a punishable offence. In my family—we're Kumaoni Brahmins: first class, number one—to even talk about alcohol is a sin. Yet Haridwar is full of illegal drunks, mostly Brahmins, like my Mama's son, Mohan Bhaiji. People say Bhaiji is half the man he used to be, that alcohol ruined him. I think not. Haridwar ruined him and was ruined in return.

Bhaiji hates Haridwar. Dvesh Bhakti, the devotion with hate, he calls it. Alcohol is just a prop in his great Brahmanical civil disobedience. Even then Mohan Bhaiji is the most cheerful drunk I know. He brims with the boisterous belligerence that can only come with serious daytime drinking. As a child it scared me; only in late adolescence, when I had begun to drink heavily myself, did I realize how much love could be transmitted via foul language. Mohan Bhaiji is my favourite cousin. Our family would like to believe that alcohol binds us more than blood, but if you ask me, it's the other way round. Alcohol unbinds, unhinges us; it unlocks the love.

If he starts early, Bhaiji can polish off a bottle of whisky by lunch. A bottle and a half by breakfast on busy days. A bottle of whisky is only a standard of measure here: Bhaiji hates IMFL. His poison is country liquor. Packed in small transparent pouches, it looks like Gangajal till it hits the gut and a few seconds later, the head. According to the family legend, Mohan Bhaiji began drinking under the influence of Carbon Baba. I don't buy this theory for two reasons: a) my family proposed it, and b) no one in Haridwar will believe it.

Carbon Baba did not work the buses like Mohan Bhaiji. He was in the extortion department. His real name was Bengali. A wicked shot, Bengali was conscientious about his drinking: only on Tuesdays or on the days he killed someone. Bhaiji and Baba met on the job. There had been a dispute with the police over weekly payments and Carbon Baba had been sent to settle it. As is the nature of such business, the negotiations broke down suddenly and Carbon Baba had to pull out his gun. A police inspector died, and disappeared. That night on a ghat somewhere, Bhaiji and Carbon Baba became drinking partners. And my family thinks that was the day Bhaiji began drinking—at the age of twenty-three. I don't know who they are deluding.

It helps the family that Carbon Baba isn't alive to tell his side of the story. He died in a police encounter a few years later. The general reaction in the family leaned towards karmic retribution, a fitting punishment for corrupting a bright Brahmin boy. Losers. When my family can't find a fact about Mohan Bhaiji it invents one. A bunch of ambitious but powerless Brahmins, my family cannot accept the fact that Bhaiji, self-contained and self-satisfied, is a self-taught drunk corrupted by the Haridwar he was born in. Who knows why people drink, what alcohol does to their heads, their hearts? I am not sure what alcohol does for Mohan Bhaiji but I know it doesn't corrode his soul.

Seldom bullied by guilt, Bhaiji comes across as honest when he loves. Most people don't care but to his wife and daughter, these things matter. Always getting his act together on the street, Bhaiji never comes home drunk. He wakes up at 5 a.m., goes down the ghat to Gangaji for a bath, says his prayers in the temple, has a heavy breakfast and, unless it's a busy day, goes back to bed. Bhaiji's second sunrise happens sometime around ten, he gets to work by half past, and is hammered by eleven. Only God knows how he works in such a state but he manages a decent living. Bhaiji drinks through lunch and stops around half past four. An hour later Bhaiji heads for the Vishnu Ghat nearby where he takes a dip and says his evening prayers. By the time Bhaiji's done and gets home, he's either feeling fine or needs to vomit in order to feel fine. What adds a touch of spiritual banality to the whole exercise is that his wife knows everything.

Hanging out with Bhaiji's Brahmin booze brigade, the situation can appear tragic and comic at once. But only to an outsider, let me warn you, to someone from New Delhi, like me, or to someone from Mars. It's very different for Bhaiji and gang. Imagine water resistant timebombs floating tick tock tick tock in Gangaji, pilgrims floating around them, some with a hint of annoyance, others calmly, safe in the knowledge that none of them is ever going to explode—that's Bhaiji and gang. As a result the Haridwar they know is schizophrenic, abusive. The air is parasitic, the streets stink. Gangaji, a no-frills low cost Goddess, is fucking dirty—on a good day, buoyed by belief and blinded by prayer, shit floats, hopelessly, with half naked pilgrims. Yet like Bhaiji's pouch of potent country liquor, Gangaji delivers what it promises: a taste of afterlife in this life. Generous pilgrims are always on the prowl and the pimp—the hungry, uneducated, Sanskrit-babbling Brahmanical baboon—pockets everything.

A 4000-year-old city, Haridwar drips with history and as a result tends to see its own past when it looks to the future. Drinking helps people like Bhaiji deal with the present. Of the future they have given up all hope. Bhaiji's daughter will finish her schooling in a boarding after which she will be sent to either Delhi or Mumbai to study. There is no hope for anyone in Haridwar except for the sinner, the tourist, and the tout. Mohan Bhaiji's Haridwar isn't Varanasi. There are no riverboats, no music, no predatory prostitutes, no bombs of bhang, no vagabond bulls, no white tourists with backpacks and hash pipes, no poetry, no literature, no art, no theatre, nothing but Mohan Bhaiji and his Brahmin buddies, drunk all day, foolishly floating in the void between sin and salvation. Most of them are employed, some are self-employed in the transport business like Bhaiji, some are drivers, some experts in Vedic rituals, yet once they get drunk, sometimes as early as eight in the morning, they ceaselessly complain about there being nothing to do. Haridwar attends to pilgrims all year long but for its prosperity it is heavily dependent on the March-August tourist season. Mostly cash-based, the economy of Haridwar is what we talk about when we talk about the unorganized sector. Unless one really wants to, it is extremely difficult to be unemployed in Haridwar.

One could do anything as long as one did not question the work or
the payment. Allegedly a precocious child, Mohan Bhaiji didn't just
land a job by the time he was eighteen, he took off with the most
fashionably fastidious, the most demanding, the best paymaster of
them all: the mafia.

~

In hindsight, my family unambiguously blames the flying squad
of the education department. Its fault: punishing the innocent.
Mohan Bhaiji was appearing for his Class 12 board examinations. In
the examination hall, according to the official flying squad version
released later, everyone was openly cheating from thick textbooks.
(Mohan Bhaiji contested this claim alleging that everyone except
him was openly copying.) Too scared to act, the invigilators watched
helplessly. (The official version glosses over this fact: what scared the
invigilators so?) Unfortunately or fortunately or as fate would have
it, the flying squad raided the examination hall. Something strange
happened next: the students in the hall, seventy-five in all, buzzing
like a broken beehive, threw the textbooks they were copying from
at the flying squad. The attack lasted a few minutes. Three members
of the flying squad were hospitalized with serious head injuries. The
examination hall was sealed. Mohan Bhaiji didn't get a hearing and,
along with the other seventy-four, failed the board exams that year.
The reaction in the family was along expected lines: on the face of it
everyone was shocked and shared Bhaiji's pain, but secretly everyone
agreed Mohan Bhaiji had it coming. If Mohan Bhaiji was a genius,
as all first-born children are expected to be in a Brahmin household,
then perhaps the education system had failed to nourish him. Bhaiji's
talents were never under any doubt. The problem was his precocious
drinking, his head, his thinking and his soulful but sentimental denial
of his bigoted Brahmin heritage. But working buses for the mafia?
What sort of talent went into a job like that? A talent for conmanship,
it turned out.

To work the buses for the mafia entailed robbing pilgrims. Bhaiji
made millions. And drank maybe half of it. In two years, by 1992,

he was heading the mafia's bus operations in Haridwar—the single largest revenue generator after real estate—and was beginning to hit a bottle a day. I was only twelve and didn't understand much of what was going on but I did get the gist: suddenly and strangely, everyone was scared of Bhaiji.

When it was clear that Bhaiji would not be going back to school, the family had no choice but to accept his new line of work. The money was fantastic too. Not that anyone had ever openly protested. There had been murmurs which Bhaiji's meteoric rise had all but silenced. Plus my cousins and I volubly hero-worshipped him.

Bhaiji's boss was a retired brigadier of the Indian army who believed that as long as people will commit sins and come to Haridwar, the mafia's invisible hand would be mistaken for God. Seeing that the Brahmin boy had talent, the brigadier took Bhaiji under his wing and taught him how to hold his drink all day without getting drunk. An infantryman, the brigadier drank like Winston Churchill and talked twice as much. He was the only God Bhaiji believed in. Anyone who wanted to do business in Haridwar first had to do business with God. To the transporter the brigadier offered blanket protection from authorities of all kinds, for crimes of all kinds. In return the transporter sold him all the seats on buses leaving Haridwar at 30 per cent of the price. Bhaiji and his gang would then sell these seats at whatever price they liked.

There were ugly scenes daily. People went crazy when they discovered that the person on the next seat had bought his ticket for half the price. Sometimes the entire bus would clamour for a refund. At this point, which happened a few minutes prior to departure, which itself was delayed by two to three hours, one of Bhaiji's boys would pick on the strongest-looking passenger and thrash the daylights out of him. No one who ever sat in Bhaiji's bus ever set foot in it again, but Bhaiji never cared for customer service. There were always new people to con in Haridwar, which to Bhaiji was the biggest con of them all. According to Bhaiji, people who come to Haridwar deserve to be cheated because they deeply crave the experience. Getting conned in Haridwar rounds off their spiritual experience; gives them an opportunity to balance their spiritual soliloquy with some semi-serious crime reportage. As a child I would often play hide-and-seek with my cousins in the parking lot where Bhaiji carried out his business. Every now and then, hiding in one of the half-filled buses, I would hear pilgrims praying for the death of whoever had caused their misery. I found the sentiment ironic, since most victims were convinced that in some way or the other Haridwar was to blame.

What alcohol couldn't conquer in a decade, the brigadier's violent murder, sometime in June 2000, plundered in a moment; overnight, Brahmins with bigger guns and better political backing forced Bhaiji out of the mafia business. His body shrunk, his skin grew darker and his eyes acquired the suspicious stare of the fearful, an expression that hasn't changed till date. Suddenly, at thirty, Bhaiji started sounding like a retired rockstar. A lot had happened by then: Bhaiji had married, fathered a daughter, and lost his father. Bhaiji rolled with the punches, laid low, and even as most of his comrades were shot dead in the fields of Saharanpur, Bhaiji remained as silent as a meditating sage before the cops. At one point, Mohan Bhaiji was so sad that he stopped drinking for almost a month. He could have joined the other side, indeed there were many offers, but Bhaiji was only a Brahmin by birth not by habit. He did what came naturally: drink.

~

When it comes to alcoholics, fate doesn't like happy endings. People in the family say Bhaiji is drinking himself to death. Bhaiji peddles philosophy when elders try and pigeonhole him—now they can, now that he's no longer what he used to be. To any opposition to drinking, Bhaiji has stock meditative responses: Aren't we all doing something that's killing us faster than usual? What is the usual speed of approaching death? If we are all dying why not live honestly and do what we really like? What is there to love about life? Etc, etc. There is no shortage of money. At forty-five, Bhaiji runs his own buses, sells his seats at 30 per cent, and still makes enough to not care about trifles like a fatty liver or a malfunctioning pancreas. In the last decade and a half, ever since the brigadier died, fate has conspired unceasingly against Bhaiji. When it couldn't kill with disease, fate handpicked accidents. When that didn't work, it seduced him with gambling not knowing how impatient Bhaiji was with card games (he wanted to bet on boozy brawls instead). Each day Bhaiji takes on fate, face to face. There is a view in the family that Bhaiji is plain lucky. I would have to agree with them here, even though good luck doesn't even come close to describing his wife, Gauri Bhabhi.

Gauri Bhabhi is what happens when Gangaji decides to bless a man. One reason why my family thinks Bhaiji is plain lucky is because they cannot imagine a half-breed poverty-stricken (till she hooked Bhaiji) Nepali girl doing anything right in a Brahmin household. They cannot tolerate her tolerating Bhaiji. With her the family is fighting a moral battle. For them, the fact of her happily tolerating her alcoholic husband somehow makes her impure which, paradoxically they all agree, she already is by birth. For years I have heard rumours that Bhaiji beats Bhabhi though I have never found the slightest evidence. It's not that Bhaiji isn't the beating type, who knows which Indian man is or isn't, it's Bhabhiji who has had her share of beatings and won't take anymore. Theirs is a Shiva-Parvati union, a daily play of ifs and buts, unspoken assurances and eloquent silences, acknowledgements and indifference, hate and humour, a game Bhaiji participates in with every bit of his drunken soul, grateful, to the point of going on and on about it, for not just playing but losing to his wife every single time. No one in the extended family has the courage to say a foul word around Bhabhiji, but behind her back the women say the worst. Bhabhi doesn't care. Married for fifteen years into a Brahmin household, she has taken her time figuring out that no matter how hard one may try one cannot Brahminize one's soul.

Bhabhi's mother died while delivering her. When she was twelve her father remarried. He sold flowers; they lived in a slum. Bhabhi's stepmother used to beat her and did not like her going to school. For the first two years Bhabhiji managed housework with school but once her stepbrother was born, even her father suggested she drop school and stay at home. That year Bhabhiji had topped her school in the Class 10 board examinations. When the school principal learnt that

Gauri Bhabhi wouldn't be coming to the school any longer he did not think it wise to speak to her father, even though her academic talents lay revealed. Instead he let the local newspaper know, and it pounced on the story like a hungry cat and demanded a photograph of the girl from the school records. When her stepmother saw the newspaper the next day she broke Bhabhiji's right arm.

At the hospital, Gauri Bhabhi bumped into Bhaiji who had brought a friend with stab wounds. Bhaiji too had seen her picture in the paper that day. Unsure about how to react upon meeting the girl of his dreams and feeling strangely sincere on top of that, Bhaiji asked for her hand in marriage. Bhabhi's laughter can be heard even today in their bedroom. When they first met, Bhabhi was fourteen, Bhaiji eighteen. One day Bhabhi noticed Bhaiji looked like Ajay Devgan. Left without a choice, Haridwar nodded in agreement. Since then, every time Bhaiji looks into the mirror, Ajay Devgan looks back. One by one he fulfilled all the promises Ajay Devgan made to Gauri Bhabhi. The day Bhaiji joined the brigadier he went to Bhabhi's house and warned her mother against hitting Bhabhiji again. Intense as a screen idol, Bhaiji threatened to kill her only son. Doubtless, to Bhabhij, Bhaiji offered escape but more than that he was strangely entertaining. Bhabhi had known such characters existed but she never imagined herself in love with one of them. More vulnerable than dangerous, Bhaiji connected with her at levels she did not know existed. To her Bhaiji opened his heart. He tried to open the bottle too, but she steadfastly refused, year after year. Bhabhiji took the longest time to say yes. For years she wanted him to quit the mafia. But when he got so powerful that assassination was an actual possibility, Gauri Bhabhi discovered that she was happier being a gangster's moll than a dead gangster's widow. Of their sex life I know next to nothing. Bhabhiji and I are not frank with each other and Bhaiji behaves more and more like the reticent Godfather he never was. Yet, I am quite sure things are excellent on that front. I am not sure how Bhaiji makes his moves, but I have a feeling he's a missionary position or a woman-on-top man who likes to look at his wife when he ejaculates.

The story of Mohan Bhaiji's rise and fall in the mafia has had a life of its own in Haridwar. Soon after the brigadier was murdered, there were murmurs that Bhaiji was a snitch, that in order to save his life he sacrificed his God. Rumour had it that Bhaiji too would be killed. But Bhaiji did not die. He stayed at home and drank for a couple of years, refusing every offer he got from the brigadier's killers. Then one day Gauri Bhabhi decided enough was enough and drove him out of the house to go look for his soul, which roamed vacantly in the ever-populous parking lots of Haridwar. Bhaiji began where had left off and within a year his business was bustling like before. The mafia, not used to Brahmins with balls, stayed away—happy with the 30 per cent Bhaiji gave them every month. No one expected Bhaiji to live and here he was, running his show under the mafia's nose. Naturally, the narrative in Haridwar twisted itself to suit the new developments. Bhaiji was now regarded as a fighter, an incarnation of Ajay Devgan, born to fight the mafias of the world. Bhaiji's own version, that the brigadier was alone when he was murdered, was improvised many times over with one story claiming that Bhaiji killed at least two assailants before the murderers could even touch the brigadier. Bhabhiji, knowing fully well how harsh historians can be with alcoholics, especially oral historians, keeps her own record. It is rumoured she writes in a little black book every day before going to bed but no one has ever seen that book. A satisfied housewife who needs no reassuring, (except by her husband), Bhabhiji is a woman who loses an argument only when she wants to, a fact my family has learnt the hard way. Gauri Bhabhi expects less, suspects more and is usually rewarded as a result. Every time I think of Gauri Bhabhi I stop worrying about Mohan Bhaiji.

DRINKER TAILOR SOLDIER SPY

Aditya Sinha

'To your motherland,' RAW chief Singh proposed, his vodka hovering in the air.

'To *your* motherland,' chief of the former KGB Vyacheslav Trubnikov said, knocking his shot back before you could utter Stolichnaya.

The two spymasters looked at the bottle and then at each other. 'Another one?' Trubnikov asked and without waiting for an opinion poured another shot.

Singh was disoriented. It was ten-thirty on a cold November morning, a little over three hours after his Aeroflot flight landed in Moscow, and he was already downing his second vodka. Or was it his third-plus-fourth—the shot-glasses here were 50 ml, as opposed to the standard 30 ml back home. Should he be drinking like this? He was, after all, the head of India's external intelligence agency, the cabinet secretariat's Research and Analysis Wing (RAW, though insiders as well as pretenders insisted on the ampersand after the 'R'); he did not want to sully India's image by getting drunk and then drooling on the flag.

Singh was in Moscow on a working visit; part of his job as RAW chief was to liaise with foreign spy agencies. He was hosted by the Russian Intelligence Service—whose acronym was SVR but whom Singh still referred to as 'the guys who used to be KGB'—and it had lodged him in a safe-house deep inside Moscow. He de-planed, checked in, hot-showered, and as soon as his eyes were flushed of jet-lag, Trubnikov heroically burst through the front door clutching a frosted bottle.

'But chief, it's just…' Singh gestured at his wrist.

'I know, I know. I would have come earlier but Yeltsin telephoned,' Trubnikov shrugged, setting the bottle on the coffee table and his compact build into the sofa.

Singh was at a loss. It had been ages since he had had a drink this early in the day, even though he himself was a Punjabi and thus the embodiment of endless joi de vivre. But he could not deny his host, especially in view of the close historical ties that tightly bound their republics. What if Trubnikov felt offended and complained to President Yeltsin—which man could afford to be the one who destroyed India's closest foreign relationship? On the other hand, if he showed up plastered at the official engagements, the Russians might cluck their disapproval. Worse, excessive drink, beyond what even he could hold, could compromise the secrets he held: basically the secrets of identities, operations and information. After all, he was the boss of India's spies in countries near and far, friendly and hostile. Plus, he had a weak bladder and suspected that the more you frequented the toilet, the less of a man you became in the eyes of others.

'To India-Russian friendship,' Singh said, bracing himself as his vodka levitated above him.

'To Yeltsin and Vajpayee,' Trubnikov declared.

And he proceeded to pour the third shot.

Oh well, Singh mused. Best to surrender.

Being RAW chief was not easy. You ran the agency; you monitored the various desks and the outstations; you ran agents; and then the prime minister needed strategic intelligence to figure out his foreign policy. There was also the onerous burden of travelling the world and liaising with other spy outfits. RAW talked to every spy agency in the world—everyone except its arch-enemy Pakistan's Inter-Services Intelligence, known by its sinister acronym ISI: three letters that struck icy fear into the heart of every Indian newspaper editor (though readers seemed a bit more phlegmatic). It was a shame, really, considering that even at the height of the Cold War, the USA's CIA and the USSR's KGB (whose first directorate turned into the SVR after the Soviet Union disintegrated) never stopped talking to one another; there was no reason why RAW and ISI did not talk and in fact there was every reason they ought to talk. So much did they fear and loathe one another.

As part of his liaison work, Singh had done a bit of drinking with counterparts from around the globe, including the Chinese and the Israelis; he had even had a few with George Tenet. The CIA director had landed in New Delhi from Islamabad with his own take on the General next door, who had seized power not too long back. Tenet came to Singh's official Tughlaq Lane residence for dinner and slugged back four double-scotch-and-sodas in double-quick time, leaving Singh shocked and awed (the other twenty guests—espiocrats and station-chiefs, and their spouses—were left stirred, not shaken).

When Singh poured him his fifth drink, Tenet suggested the two of them leave the rest and spend alone-time in another room. There was no top secret discussion of the planet's biggest secrets or the sex gossip of lesser world leaders; there was just chit-chat about the weather and the wife. Aides from both sides peeked in but Tenet waved them off; he and his best buddy were too busy bonding to be interrupted by something as prosaic as a toast.

~

'To the RAW,' Trubnikov said, raising his third shot.
　'To the KGB,' Singh responded, and then bit his tongue.
　'To them as well,' Trubnikov said. 'Did pretty well. Rest in Peace.'
　'And to the SVR,' Singh said.
　Trubnikov tipped the bottle for the fourth shot.
　'No, chief, no,' Singh said, grinning. 'I can't.'
　Trubnikov looked heartbroken.
　'Chief, chief,' Singh said, in consolation.
　'You want to go meet Putin?' Trubnikov suggested.
　'Sure,' Singh shrugged.
　'Okay, come on,' Trubnikov said. 'But we will need a shot. To see the prime minister more clearly.'
　'Sure,' Singh sighed.
　Their shot glasses floated together, their sides touching, from side to side.

'Does Putin drink?' Singh asked.

'Not with me.'

'Wasn't he in the KGB too?'

'Da,' Trubnikov said. 'He was junior to me. He joined when I was posted in India.'

'I've heard,' Singh said. 'You were a journalist.'

'With *Izvestia*,' Trubnikov said. 'How did you know? You were briefed?'

'No briefing, chief,' Singh laughed. 'I just know.'

Trubnikov looked at him. 'I know that you know,' he said.

Singh smiled. Trubnikov might not have known that back in the 1970s, Singh was in counter-intelligence. He knew a bit of the blast the Russians—or the Soviets, rather, back then—were having in New Delhi, one of their favourite postings. He also knew of how the middle-level Soviet diplomats were sleeping with each other's wives.

But he could not say any of that, no matter how much vodka they drank.

'I know that you know that I know,' he said.

Trubnikov roared with laughter. Singh felt the vodka's fumes lick his lips.

As they departed the Kremlin an hour and a half later, Singh wondered whether they should have just stayed at the safe-house and drunk themselves blind. In any case, the ordeal called Prime Minister Vladimir Putin was now over and done with. Putin had promptly invited them in, seating them at the large, round table in his anteroom. It was the first time Singh had seen a round table inside the office of a senior political leader. Putin was unsmiling. He seemed to have detected the whiff of vodka when the two spymasters entered; he rhetorically asked Trubnikov if they had come directly from Yeltsin's office. The rest of the conversation was cutting-edge in its banality.

After wearing out the afternoon with additional mind-numbing diplomacy, Trubnikov took Mr and Mrs Singh to dinner. The restaurant was a converted old church with the distinctive architecture of the Moscow Patriarchate. A narrow set of wooden stairs led up from the ground level to the restaurant which, to Mr and Mrs Singh's surprise, was completely empty, though each and every table was fully set and lamp-lit.

Had the Russian spooks cleared out a whole restaurant for them, Singh wondered. Maybe this was a KGB restaurant. Perhaps the RAW should also set up its own restaurant. He would mention this to the principal secretary when he got back home.

Two tables had been set up alongside each other. On one, the SVR chief sat facing the RAW chief; on the other, the wives sat, Natalia and Mrs Singh, cheerfully occupying a separate universe altogether. A bottle of vodka magically materialized.

Trubnikov poured out two shots. Natalia and Mrs Singh looked sternly at the vodka, so Trubnikov offered them the shots. They refused and turned back to their conversation.

'To Gary Kasparov,' Trubnikov said.

'Three No-Trump,' Singh said.

They downed the shots. 'I used to have a son,' Trubnikov said. 'He died over ten years ago. In a road accident. Natalia has never been the same since.'

Singh momentarily pondered the world of difference between hearing about an event and reading about it in a file.

'He was a good boy. He liked music, and played football. Girls used to fawn over him,' Trubnikov said. 'I was so busy with work that I didn't spend as much time as I should have. But I loved him so.'

Singh wondered whether he himself had been a good father. He studied Trubnikov silently. The Russian was three-four years younger, but looked more worn out. He wasn't boxer-like, as Singh had decided earlier, but life had beaten him up.

'I was so busy with work that Gorbachev gave me a second Order of the Red Star. I got the first one for my posting in New Delhi in the '70s,' Trubnikov said.

'All of us had a great time in Delhi,' Natalia said. 'We can never forget.'

'Have some caviar,' Trubnikov said, passing Singh a tablespoon.

A few shots later, Trubnikov leaned towards Singh. 'I'm going to propose that we set up a Russia-India-China forum,' he said. 'What do you think?'

'It's a great idea,' Singh said. 'But it'll never happen. The Chinese.'

'You leave it to me.'

Several shots of vodka later, and after a dinner whose details escaped Singh though its tastiness did not, it was time to stop.

'To Laika,' Trubnikov said.

'Who?' Singh asked.

'First dog in space,' Trubnikov said. 'My son was a big fan of this most famous Russian puppy.'

Singh raised his glass and downed his drink.

They stood up slowly, leaning heavily on the tables, the restaurant staff smiling nervously, aides waiting at a respectful distance to spring to the rescue. Trubnikov praised the chef, the chef praised Natalia, and Natalia praised Singh. They staggered out.

The cold stung Singh's face and suddenly the stairs down to the street looked like a giant slide. Ignoring his vodka-induced vertigo, Singh grabbed a banister.

Trubnikov stepped tentatively and swayed dangerously. Halfway down he stumbled and Singh caught him, just in time. The security detail stepped forward but Trubnikov was okay.

'*Mera joota hai Japani*,' he declared.

~

The next morning Singh drove out to the Aquarium, at the Khodinka airfield. This was the office of the GRU, the Main Intelligence Directorate, which handled military intelligence and signals intelligence. Singh and his team would have a look at the Russians' SIGINT capabilities. Trubnikov was not sure if he would make it, providing a glimmer of respite to Singh's hungover liver.

'But what if they serve wine anyway?' Srinivasan asked. He was a technical man, from RAW's Radio Research Centre, posted in Moscow. In total there were four RAW officers accompanying the chief, the other two being the Moscow station chief and, from headquarters, the fellow heading the Moscow desk.

'Do the Russians even drink wine?' Singh wondered.

'Sir, beer, vodka, all the same wine,' Srinivasan said. 'I'm a teetotaller.'

'Also, sir, Srinivasan is a vegetarian, he is Tamil Brahmin,' the station chief volunteered.

'Just concentrate on the briefing,' Singh said and everyone shut up.

At the Aquarium, things went swimmingly. The GRU chief, Vladlen Mikhailov, showed Singh some of his toys. It was an impressive display and it seemed to match anything that the Americans had.

'Even we have that,' Singh said at one point.

'Yes,' Mikhailov said. 'You bought it from us.'

Electronic eavesdropping was a mixed bag. During the 1999 Kargil war, the government told Singh to release an intercept of a telephone conversation between General Pervez Musharraf, who was visiting Beijing, and his second-in-command, General Aziz Khan back in Rawalpindi. They discussed the tactics of the Indian Air Force and Army, and whether their prime minister, Mian Saheb, had begun to panic. While the intercepts scored a propaganda point and got India the world's sympathies, it also dried up a source of reliable information from inside the Pakistani army.

Now the government wanted a separate technical intelligence agency, carving it out of the RAW's Aviation Research Centre, much in the way the RAW had been carved out of the Intelligence Bureau back in September 1968. This suggestion, ironically, came in the government's post-mortem of Kargil. Now his guys were squabbling over who would leave ARC for the new outfit. Sigh. Even espionage suffered from the tedium of bureaucracy.

Mikhailov and his men had finished; it was time for lunch. Singh and his team went to a spacious hall where a semi-circular table was set up. He and Mikhailov sat at the centre of the table, with both delegations sitting on either side of the two chiefs. Stewards stepped forward with plates of cold cuts, black bread and heaps of caviar. They also set down several bottles of vodka.

Singh sighed as Mikhailov poured them a shot. The stewards poured shots for everyone at the table, including Srinivasan the Tam-Bram teetotaller. Singh raised his glass and saw Srinivasan do the same. Mikhailov proposed a toast to Semyon Aralov, the first director; Singh responded with a toast to R.N. Kao, the first RAW chief. Srinivasan quickly emptied his shot glass.

Singh was spellbound by Mikhailov shovelling caviar onto pieces of toast which he then shoved into his mouth. Yet he still kept an eye on Srinivasan. He counted as the Tam-Bram knocked back three vodkas, and prayed Srinivasan wouldn't be sick; otherwise there would be no end to the 'vomint' jokes.

Mikhailov clapped his hands and a colourful group of pretty girls appeared. Singh wondered if the girls were GRU. Musicians also appeared; GRU had arranged entertainment.

The music began to play and the girls began to dance. It was a Russian folk-dance, with the girls holding hands and dancing and then kicking in the air. It was lively and had nothing to do with espionage. Maybe it was a honey trap.

'Khorovod,' Mikhailov shouted out in excitement.

'I want to see the Bear Dance,' Srinivasan shouted back.

Singh shot Srinivasan a dirty look.

Mikhailov turned to Singh. 'Why don't you dance with the girls?' he asked the RAW chief.

Singh was taken aback. Where was Trubnikov when he needed him?

'I'll dance if you dance,' he said to Mikhailov.

To his surprise, Mikhailov agreed. He stood up and Singh reluctantly followed. They walked around the semi-circular table to where the girls and musicians waited. And then the two old spies folded their arms and kicked their legs, the girls cheering them along.

Singh was enjoying himself. But then he noticed Srinivasan sitting in a tight coil, as if he were ready spring out of his seat and onto the dance floor. So he shot him a preemptive forbidding look. Srinivasan deflated.

After a couple of dances the two spymasters took their seats and vodkas were poured.

'Listen,' Mikhailov said. 'Why don't you stay for dinner? We can keep dancing with these girls all night.'

Singh had to admit that the girls were good dancers.

'I can't, chief,' he said with genuine regret. 'I have tickets to the ballet tonight. I'm taking my wife. It's at seven so I have to be back at five.'

'But this is better than the ballet,' Mikhailov protested.

'Yes, but I have tickets,' Singh said, wistfully. 'And it's my wife.'

'I'll send her an escort,' Mikhailov said. 'But don't worry, not Spetsnaz.'

'Chief, thanks, really,' Singh said. 'But I have to go.'

Mikhailov looked crestfallen. Yet he knew when to beat a tactical retreat.

On the way back, Singh looked at Srinivasan. 'I thought you said you never drank alcohol in your life,' he said.

'It's true,' Srinivasan said. 'But what to do, Sir, they kept giving me. It burnt my throat.'

'Yes,' Singh said. 'But what if it had made you ill?'

'I felt ill,' Srinivasan confessed. 'But I had to be okay in front of my boss, the RAW chief, didn't I?'

~

Three months later, Trubnikov came visiting New Delhi. Singh lodged him at a five-star hotel in south Delhi, and directed the protocol officer to stock Trubnikov's room with an endless supply of vodka. The protocol officer coughed.

'Sir,' he said. 'Our Moscow people say that Trubnikov prefers Scotch.'

Singh was taken aback: 'Are you sure?'

'Sir, they say he probably has no choice but to drink vodka on home soil, but when he travels he only drinks Scotch. In fact, sir, in the '70s he consumed more Scotch than the entire Japanese embassy.'

So they stocked Trubnikov's room with Black Dog Scotch Whisky.

Trubnikov telephoned Singh. 'How did you know I love Black Dog?' he asked. 'Reminds me of Laika.'

Singh was still trying to recall who Laika was, when Trubnikov said: 'Listen, must I come to your office? Why don't you come here and we'll have a drink.'

'Chief, you have to come to the office,' Singh said. 'We've set up lots of fun briefings for you.'

Trubnikov groaned. 'Okay,' he said. 'But you have lunch with me tomorrow.'

The next day, Singh asked the minders stationed at the hotel to let him know when Trubnikov was ready for lunch. He had work to wrap up and he figured if he got a call at one-thirty then he would arrive promptly for lunch.

But there was no call at one-thirty. The minders said Trubnikov was still locked in his room.

Singh waited. One-forty-five. Two o'clock. Singh's tummy growled.

Then at two-fifteen, the call came. Trubnikov was ready.

On arriving, Singh asked Trubnikov: 'Chief, I hope everything's all right?'

'Sorry about the delay,' Trubnikov said. 'You see, today is Yeltsin's birthday.'

'Okay,' Singh said. Yeltsin had resigned but Trubnikov obviously still felt loyalty to him.

'I wanted to wish him but had to wait for him to surface,' Trubnikov said. 'As soon as I did I was ready for lunch.'

After a couple of Black Dogs, Trubnikov said: 'I want to see Vajpayee.'

Singh nearly choked on his whisky.

'Chief, I hate to break this to you, but Vajpayee doesn't meet intelligence heads,' he said. 'It is out of the question.'

'What do you mean, out of the question,' Trubnikov thundered. 'I took you to see Putin, didn't I?'

Singh had no choice but to request the prime minister to make an exception and to his credit, Vajpayee did. Trubnikov was thrilled. The rest of the visit went by in a blur.

~

Shortly after that visit, Singh went to Beijing, where the Chinese secret service and Minister of State, Security, Xu Yongyue plied him with a vile-smelling and worse-tasting concoction that was either a rice-brew or an industrial-strength paint-stripper. Singh being a pious devotee of Scotch whisky nearly spat it out. 'Are you trying to poison me?' he asked, jokingly.

The Chinese fell silent. Finally, Xu replied: 'No.'

Singh downed that drink and then raised Trubnikov's suggestion for cooperation between Russia, China and India. Xu said nothing. Two drinks later, Singh raised it again. Xu examined his own tie and said: 'A very interesting idea. We must examine it.'

It was not the first time Singh had encountered this conversational cul-de-sac in China.

He wanted to complain to Trubnikov, but soon found that Putin had removed Trubnikov as the head of the SVR, kicking him upstairs as first deputy minister in the Ministry for Foreign Affairs. And a couple of months after Vajpayee left office, Trubnikov was made Russian ambassador to India, where he was more popular than David Mulford, the American ambassador.

Singh retired, and while that marked the end of his drinking days with serving spy chiefs, it kicked off his drinking days with retired spy chiefs. This included not just Trubnikov and assorted others like him, but also, on a visit to Islamabad as part of a diplomatic initiative, something no one would ever have contemplated: the ex-RAW chief having a few stiff whiskies with an ex-ISI chief. Yes. But that's another story, to be told only if the telling of this one survives the Official Secrets Act and lodgings at Tihar Jail.

Hanging on Like Death

Anjum Hasan

> The whisky on your breath
> Could make a small boy dizzy;
> But I hung on like death:
> Such waltzing was not easy.

—Theodore Roethke,
My Papa's Waltz

It rains in Neel's dreams and when he wakes up it's still raining. Like all optimists, Neel takes the long view. He is able to look beyond all signs of disaster to that fixed point in the distance upon which turns the axis of the perfect world. Good, he thinks. Let it rain now, then it won't rain later. Who knows, the sun might come out even, and by evening the puddles will dry. He puts on his glasses with his standard morning air—one that suggests there is nothing remotely frivolous about life—and packs his schoolbag, slipping in books neatly, two by two.

His costume is waiting to be ironed. When he saw it for the first time yesterday he couldn't believe its loveliness—a shimmering cream satin cape with silver piping and matching tights. He gently opens the tiny umbrella that has been painted dark brown with white freckles to represent a mushroom. This, with the aid of the elastic band that hangs from it, Neel must wear on his head. He puts it on for practice and brushes his teeth, looking up at himself in the mirror flecked with his father's toothpaste spit, silently repeating his line—*If a mushroom could talk what would it say?…If a mushroom could talk what would it say?*

He realizes, in the momentary silence in his head after he has ensured that the precious line is still with him, that the sounds coming from the kitchen are not mother but father sounds. He knows the difference. His mother is clear and continuous—the filling of kettles, the stirring of sugar into tea, the measured chop-chop of knife against board, the hiss of onions hitting hot oil.

No, this is his father—he always makes low, rustling sounds like he's secretly searching for something in a stranger's house and then all at once, as if to prove that the quietness was just a joke, will come the shattering of many glasses, or the crash of a chair, or the noisy collapse of the man himself as he stumbles on apparently nothing and embraces the floor. Neel goes on brushing even when he is done, a man's way of suppressing the thought of something like tears. If his father is in the kitchen it means his mother is gone. If his mother is gone, his father has a mightier reason than the rain not to come and see Neel play a magic mushroom in 'The Hood and the Hoodlums'.

Why today? Why today? Why today? Neel asks himself to the rhythm of his superfluous brushing. But soon enough the optimist reasserts itself and he thinks of all the things his father will be pleased about because his mother has gone—he can play his music so loud, people walking on the street will glance nervously at the house; he can read the stories he used to write, and drink straight from a bottle of whisky at 8 a.m., having failed to extract a clean glass and ice cubes from the mess in the kitchen. Perhaps something of this happiness will eventually rouse him and remind him of the importance of this evening in his son's life.

~

Because it was chance, not glamour, that led to Neel's being singled out as a mushroom, he has treated his role with grim seriousness.

During the first two weeks of rehearsals, he was—like most of his seven- and eight-year-old peers—part of the chorus. The boys stood in the galleries afternoon by afternoon, looking out for the cue to break into song. The wait between songs was so long and they knew the lines so well that when the time came they roared out into the empty hall with the full force of their bottled-up enthusiasm. Brother James's thin shoulder blades ground under his white cassock as he kept the piano in pace with them. Then they must be quiet again while the chosen ones up on the stage—Robin Hood, some spastic children, a falsely corpulent politician in a Gandhi cap, Gandhi himself, Hitler, a talking mushroom in an enchanted forest, Batman and a pair of rickshaw pullers—screamed out their lines and were ridiculed by the long, lean, unsmiling Brother.

On the golden afternoon of Neel's promotion, Brother James was angry rather than just sarcastic. A scuffle had broken out between Robin Hood and Gandhi which they half-heartedly tried to conceal, poking elbows into each other as Brother called them upstage to thunder at them. Neither seemed to mind; they were both glorious actors in Neel's view, boys who seemed to have never known shyness. Meanwhile the spastic children, who were genuine and accompanied by two ever-watchful chaperones, grew fretful at the shouting and a contagion spread causing them all to lie on the floor and bawl. All of Classes 2 and 3 watched in disgust as the girls soothed and hushed in voices meant for infants. Brother James paid no attention; he returned to creating cascades on his piano and the chorus took up the notes. Then he stopped abruptly and addressed his keys.

'Which idiot is singing out of tune?'

The singers froze as if the slightest movement would betray them.

'Who?' he shouted, turning around on his stool and surveying them with murderous intensity. Miss Dhillon, the assistant director of the musical, walked up and down before the galleries, smiling as if to assure the boys that there was nothing pretended about Brother's anger.

'What's your name?' asked Brother. 'Yes, that's right, you.'

It was eventually established that the boy in question was Neel.

'When did you last cut your hair?'

Neel could not remember, nor did he think Brother had the patience to wait for an answer. For long stretches of time his parents forgot about ordinary things like haircuts.

'Just look at him,' said Brother and the whole hall looked, including,

it seemed to Neel, the now quiet spastics, while he desperately sought
out Miss Dhillon. He was wedged between two tall boys, his hair
sticking out in clumps from his head like a battery of antennae and
his over-sized glasses catching the almost-three-o'clock sunlight that
slid out in dusty planes from the ventilators. He looked like an ant
with goggles.

'He looks like a mushroom,' Miss Dhillon said, rewarding him
with a slowly expanding smile. 'Do we need another mushroom?'

So Brother James, perhaps only because Neel was spoiling the
symmetry of the middle row with his bad hair and opaque look, had
him pulled out.

'But no glasses. Better a blind mushroom than those ridiculous
glasses,' he said, falling upon his piano again.

Neel, burning with love for Miss Dhillon, was led up to the stage
and given his line: 'If a mushroom could talk what would it say?' The
question was answered with this profundity from his companion
mushroom: 'The oak tree has eyes, the pond will betray; what remains
tomorrow could have gone yesterday.'

Neel was soon hearing the roars of his fellow actors in his dreams.
Robin Hood rushes into the forest in pursuit of a fat politician. *Which
way did he go*, he asks himself, unaware of the listening mushrooms.
Their timeless lines provide him with the vital clue. He looks in the
pond, sees in it a reflection of his shiny-eyed quarry hiding high up in
the branches of the oak tree, brings him down with a flurry of arrows
and compels him to explain why he's oppressing the rickshawallahs.
Hitler arrives, pounding in his boots, shouting at them to move
out of the way because it's World War II. The mushrooms run off
screaming and Robin Hood sings: 'Wait a minute Mister Hitler, you
have gone all out of gear; you are desperate to make history, but it's
time I interfered.' There is a crash of cymbals and the chorus joins
in. Lots more follows—Gandhi and Hitler do a war dance, Batman
organizes the spastic children into an uprising against the politician
who proposes to tear down their school and build a parking lot in its
place, Robin Hood time travels in search of Gandhi, both join forces
with Batman, surmount Hitler, send the children back to school and

bring succour to the rickshawallahs. In the end, as the mushroom had prophesied, war is narrowly averted and history rewritten.

~

Neel takes off the mushroom umbrella and creeps into the hall, clutching his costume. He can feel the music in his heart, stone striking stone.

'You write to exceptionally moving effect, yet steer clear…Neel…' his father calls and Neel can smell drink across the waterfall of music. 'Listen to this…You write to exceptionally moving effect, yet steer clear of any sentimentality associated with…'

'I'm going to iron my clothes,' Neel calls back. He's dangling the cape and tights from his arm in a way that his father might notice the creaminess of the cream, the excitement of the polished silver edges. He's too shy to actually hold it up and say, 'Look,' the way his father can proudly read out from the letter he got from an American magazine before Neel was born, praising his stories and offering to publish them. *You write to exceptionally moving effect.* Neel recognizes the words as a source of everlasting happiness.

He stands on his toes and flicks on a switch. *If a mushroom could talk what would it say?…If a mushroom could talk what would it say?*

'Let her go, Neel,' says his father consolingly. 'If she wants to go, she can. I'm not here to oppress anyone.'

A couple of times a month, Neel wakes up to find his mother gone. There's no way of predicting these disappearances. Sometimes she's been angry the previous evening. She yells and his father smiles. He tries to make her see that there's nothing to shout about, he shushes her like she's a child with a tantrum, he jokes, he brings out the famous letter, he reminds her of her beauty, but the more charming he is, the crazier she gets. She stops listening to him, discovering in her own yelling newer reasons to yell more. At other times, nothing—a perfectly ordinary evening, his father drinking till he cannot move, his mother indifferent—and yet the next morning she's gone.

Neel drapes his ironed cape on a chair and goes to the kitchen where ants are running excitedly between the previous night's unwashed dinner plates. He carefully pours cold milk into a bowl of cornflakes.

Sometimes his mother is hiding in the neighbour's house—an old lady with six cats whom Neel must dodge to get to her. Sometimes she moves in with her cousin. Once she checked into a hotel and they couldn't find her till she came back on her own the next day. The times following her homecoming are always the best. She hugs her son and makes kheer or jelly and custard. When Neel returns from school, he keeps going to the fridge to check if the jelly has set. This repeated opening and shutting of the fridge door is another thing that contains in it the potential for lifelong joy.

But this evening Neel and his father cannot go out looking for her because this is the evening of the *musical*. She has forgotten. If she were here, both his parents would make it somehow—despite misplacing the house keys along the way, arriving late and squeezing past everyone with their wet umbrellas, despite forgetting to wear their best clothes. Yet the fact that there are still ten hours to go is a source of hope. That Neel has not yet been disappointed is a source of hope.

'Cause I couldn't stand the pain. He becomes properly aware of his father's songs only when they shift register. This line moves the music to a different, sadder place. Neel leaves his empty bowl to the ants. His father is unfolding the letter yet again, looking like he has managed to convince himself that he doesn't know what it contains and that soon his world will be awash with the news. Seizing the moment, Neel rushes up. His father peers as if through a fog and asks, 'You're awake?'

'You're coming for the musical, no? I'll be on the stage for ten minutes very near the start, so don't come late; if you come late you'll miss it.'

Alone with his father he is cautious, though. There is a balance in him that should not be upset, and demands of any kind invariably upset it; his smile becomes the smile of a man who wants to hurt himself. Neel is aware that his father's world should stay simple but he also wants his father in the dark hall watching him say his mushroom line. His mother would do, but his father is the one who matters. He understands the importance of that letter, for instance. Even though he's unable to get past it.

It's raining like heartbreak. Once, walking down the lane from their house on a day when the world was water, Neel's father had slipped and broken his arm. He told everyone it was nothing but ever since he considers the rain a traitor and doesn't go near it. Even so, Neel is hopeful. *If a mushroom could talk, what would it say?* Let it rain now, then it won't rain later.

'You want me to make you breakfast—toast-omelette?' his father slurs, his eyes widening slowly as if toast-omelette would be an act of incredible virtuosity. Because both father and son know that no such thing is possible.

'You're coming for the musical, no?' answers Neel, retreating, for his father is immersed again in his letter.

~

They are fussed over, given orange juice and samosas, powdered, rouged, told a dozen times not to move or breathe a single word backstage once the play starts, and then taken in a majestic line past the classrooms—where the others are getting dressed in mere pyjama suits—and down to the hall. Neel sees himself in the glances of the chorus. Through their eyes he notices the brighter make-up that he and his co-actors are wearing, how nervously Brother James scolds them, and the two teachers importantly leading the way. The grandness makes him feverish. He can no longer descend to everyday worries such as whether it's raining. He is reckless now. If his parents don't come, he will never again pick out the lines in his father's music or care about the jelly in the fridge. The atmosphere of the school building at night—shadows and voices where in the daytime there are none—cuts off Neel from everything ordinary.

When they are seated backstage like a row of competing princes, Hitler wails, 'Miss, my lipstick's gone.'

'Don't eat it then,' says Miss Dhillon, laughing as she applies more.

'Miss, Gandhi is sitting on my cape.'

'Miss, my grandmother-grandfather are coming also.'

'Miss, Neel looks like a monkey.'

Neel has been separated from his glasses and everything is an electrifying blur. He tries to follow Miss Dhillon as she moves between the boys—as long as he can make out her blue sari-clad form he is safe. His love for her lacks expectation. He is happy just to be near her and hear her laugh. She lifts Neel's chin and pulls his umbrella low over his forehead.

'He doesn't look like a monkey...' she says, 'he looks like a mushroom.'

Then Brother James silences everyone, including the largely unaware spastics, with the first resounding note, and Neel's stomach hurts. Miss Dhillon knows he cannot see and takes him by his damp hand to deposit him in the still dark enchanted forest, while upstage the rickshawpullers groan under the weight of the fat politician. Then the lights blaze, a second layer of curtains is pulled back, the audience gasps with wonder at the lifelike trees and the unreal sun, a song proclaims the wonders of the forest, and Robin Hood dashes in.

'To left or to right did that scoundrel escape, in which direction should my arrows make haste?'

Neel brings the whole force of his being into the answer.

'If a mushroom could talk what would it say?' he screeches.

'The oak tree...the oak tree...'

There is a pause of a few seconds in which the other mushroom seems to be dying.

'The oak tree has eyes, the pond will betray; what remains tomorrow could have gone yesterday,' fills in Neel proudly. The two mushrooms are statues then while Robin Hood berates his foe. By the time they scatter under Hitler's boots, the second mushroom has recovered his wits and yells convincingly but it is too late.

Backstage, Neel is a minor hero. Robin Hood dashes in and knocks him hard on the head in affection, swigs distractedly from a bottle of water like a grand slam tennis player, and dashes out at his next cue. The boys yet to make an entry and still sitting stiffly in their places smile gingerly at him and Miss Dhillon hands him back his glasses, laughing soundlessly.

There is nothing to do after that but wait and glow till the larger heroes have defeated the forces of evil and can dust their hands. Finally, they all emerge on to the stage and, standing in a line made untidy by the uncontrollable spastics, sing the school anthem along with the chorus and the audience, which has risen to its feet.

Neel cannot bear the thought that he isn't out there watching him, his father.

~

When he comes out into the night from the backstage door with his make-up off and, in his bag, the cape—his to keep—he can see how in the distance the rain is flashing off cars that are revving up to leave. A few parents remain—waiting to receive their heroic, main cast sons with the reversed looks of children watching out for adults. He knows just from the outline of the shapes they make against the glittering dark that his parents are not among them.

He starts to walk across the courtyard slowly; because he has never thrown tantrums—he must work at one now—a grand tantrum that will outdo his mother's. But what good would that do, asks the now only superficially positive voice inside him. For deeper within him is forming a more disastrous idea of how to express disappointment. He wants it to stretch for days and weeks and months—the delicious pain of this.

He sees Miss Dhillon running towards him but she goes past without noticing and on to the waiting parents he has left behind. Neel walks on; he is almost by the cars that exude their warmth into the wet air like happy beasts, making his misery more clear-cut. Miss Dhillon rushes back with a torch under her arm, punching a number on her phone; she overtakes him and goes clattering down the steps that lead to the path below. At the far end is the small gate through which walkers like him leave the campus.

Neel cannot understand why she doesn't see him. She knows he saved the mushroom scene. She knows he is parentless in the rain. The knot in his heart pulls tighter. He goes to the low railing and watches her make her way to a bend in the path where a man lies sprawled as if fast asleep after a tiring day. A small huddle of people try to make up their minds about him by flashing the lights of their phones, their hands unsteady. Above them, leaning over the railing of the courtyard, the parents he passed earlier shout out: 'Did anyone notice him fall? Should we call for an ambulance? Is he a parent?'

Below, still talking on her phone, Miss Dhillon pushes aside the crowd and shines her torch on the frozen man. In that powerful glare, Neel sees that it is his father, that his eyes are wide open, and that sticking out from the pocket of his raincoat is the yellow handbill for the play.

And all at once he is flying over the steps, his heart pinned on a single realization: his beautiful mushroom line has echoed in his father's ear. He is beside Miss Dhillon in seconds. Looking up at her with an eight-year-old's solemn pride, he says, 'My father.'

Poems

Manohar Shetty

Ten Feet Tall

In my drinking days, I never slept,
Only passed out and woke up
My eyes red as Mars, my head
A rattling alarm clock, amnesiac
To the past twenty hours when
My tongue ran away with itself.
I know how it felt to be ten feet tall,
Lurching about like a leaning,
Beaming Tower of Pisa. Now sober,
I remain mostly quiet,
Content with a lime and soda,
A humble penitent not given
To garrulous argument or loss
Of temper or making bosom chums
With my local fisherman and barber
Or tipping the waiter half
My wages. In fact, I've become
Somewhat timid, diffident,
A little remote, even reclusive, certainly
Not the high spirit of the party
Inviting the cop on duty for a nip
Or two into the speakeasy with
A gangster swagger. But unlike
The Phantom with his wolf,

I haven't switched to a glass
Of milk at the bar counter.
In times of extreme tension
I keep my patience and don't
Attack the bottle with that
Resultant loss of dignified
Balance or, fully dressed, drop
Half-dead under a running
Shower in my bathtub, the doorbell
Ringing at milkman dawn like
Church or temple bells
In a storm. No, I don't cringe
From that same old taunt:
'Yeh sala Manu ban gaya bewda'.
I know how it felt to be ten feet tall
And to wake up crunched into a doll,
My head unscrewed from my neck,
My fingers digging and clawing myself
Out from a ditch ten feet tall.

Wastrel Song

After your life's work's been done
You still want a few things undone

Like that feud with a friend,
Its spark and fuse long forgotten,

Or your last visit to a gambling den
From where you fled with a debt

Still shadowing your head
Or those designs on your best friend's

Mum when you were quite young
Or that sure bet on a jinxed gelding

Which trotted off with all your savings
Or that pickled night when you showered
The rows of plants in a public garden
One by one and woke up at one
In a garbage bin, the sun blinking
Down as through a magnifying lens,
Your hair rough as coconut husk,
Your shirt unbuttoned, and strangers
Shying past in disgust or amusement
Or plain embarrassment if they

Knew you as the neighbour's
Son or that furtive tryst in a brothel
Which smelled of minced mutton
And flavoured betelnut and you were far

Too gone to get it done and left
That bottle half-drunk.
Now that you've passed sixty you think
It's all part of your momentous history.

You've scaled that peak where neat Scotch
Or rum, country or fine brandy are all one.

You who've never loved or been loved,
Lying drunk as any bum seven hours

Past the rising sun, your fingers trembling
Like false guitar strings, your head

An empty drum, and not song but all that
Phlegm and gall flooding your tongue.

Taverna

After twenty years of yoga
And mastery of its
Acrobatic asanas—forehead
On the floor, feet round
The neck, total breath control—
He tripped over the doormat
And died of cardiac arrest—
All of 44. Clean living,
As he put it once,
Is the path to nirvana.
At the Goodluck Taverna
Eddie, 74, pours three
Quarters of cashew feni
Topped by a shot
Of *dotor's* brandy
Down the hatch below
A picture of Mother Mary
Between sunset till
The bar shuts at twelve.
He goes home on his
Moped without
Troubling the potholes
Or the pigs and sleeps
The sleep of the just.
This his ritual the past
Forty years though every
Christmas doc warns him
It's his last.
I asked him once
Over a peg, boiled eggs
And a saucer of peanuts
The secret of his long life
And sound health.

He blinked behind his soda
Water bottle lenses and said,
Drink. Siesta.
And God bless;
What for you is poison
Is for me tonic
And medicine.

Unknown

(For Ashq, songwriter)

You can be sure if
The Scotch swigging czars
Don't know who you are

Or if you don't belong
To the right family tree
You won't set the screen

Ablaze with your songs
Or be part of the orchestra
Or play even a bit role.

You can be sure you'll
End up as that unknown
Citizen found on a
Cracked pavement,
Your number stamped in
Sequence in a police outpost

After you're buried
In an unmarked grave
Or sent up in casual flames

Or fed to the birds
With due respect
To your lost faith.

The Morning After

After all that smoke and hot
Shot air, and one more,
And one more for the road,
You wake to a false dawn,
Your throat sandpaper,
Your tongue curled up
Like a dormouse,
Your head
The empty drum
It always was.

Denial

He's on the wagon,
Quite reformed but gives in
On aggrieved or those
Imminent moonshine

Moments to his secret
Stash, to that giddy loss
Of inhibition, that ersatz
Whiff of freedom. He

Slips from one sip
To a drop more, to
That hearty spirit.
He pretends those puffy

Red eyes are from
Sleepless nights and that
Minty mouthwash,
Chewing gum, cool

Colognes and fragrant
Aftershaves are
     Newly acquired
Tastes and he never

     Sways.

Poems

Vijay Nambisan

First Infinities: Need

Desperate with knowledge, opened wide by drink,
How I've thrown my need about the houses
I've partied in; how tainting the responses.
How crudely eager to be loved, and how
Vile next day, with J flinging in my face

My sottishness, not allowing me to think,
His poisoned tongue flickering, my vulgar vows
To be good again. I took my chances
And paraded them; and now,
Put out to grass in an accustomed place
I count them one by one. To find a city
Where I have not been foolish: Difficult lies
And truths despicable in their fragility,
Both lack the charm of inadequacy.

First Infinities: Hospital

The doctor's hand was asking what my liver
Meant to do. I thought behind the curtains of
This purpose of my birth, to lie and act
Like one soon to be a corpse. Wayside station
Blues, city living blues, writer's cramp blues.

I had of countless bottles made a river
And discovered its source. Yet one more dropped its love
Into my slow veins. The tiled walls did not in fact
Confine; they wrung from me definition
And made me what I am. Tell me now what use

The pills, the fruit, nurse's disgusted eye
Or glucose, or molasses. No life is short
That at its centre has this clarity.

First Infinities: Drying Out

For I asked my spirit, What is worth this pain?
And my spirit said: Do not think of Hell
Or hope of Hereafter. Breathing this filth
In a stale room, aching for the fire
To flow in you again—only believe this.

Only ashes clog and clot my veins.
It is in another life that I was well
And time moves like the sea. I spew and spit
The yellow bile. My bones are torn entire.
They look at me and laugh. I am what is.

And what is this I am, in a rude day
Bright with the flame of fever? Spirit replied,
I am the Truth, and the Life, and the Way.

Part Two

Essays

Rehab Diary

Vijay Nambisan

On my fourth morning, after my first night of wholesome natural sleep, I wake at 6.30. I wasn't called at 5.30 for prayers and tea; why? Everyone downstairs is clotted in groups, talking in hushed whispers. I'm told two of the youngsters downstairs had tried to escape in the night. They gagged the guard and were fumbling with his keys when they made a noise and were caught, at 1.30 in the morning. What happened to them? They were stripped, doused with cold water (in early January in Bangalore) and thrashed black and blue—by the other inmates, who welcomed an outlet for their frustration. Their screams had roused everyone, except me. I'm glad I missed it. Later that day I see their heads shaved by the barber who comes from across the street once weekly. They are also 'sanctioned'—no tobacco, no cots or beds to sleep on, toilet-cleaning-with-a-toothbrush duty, and no talking or being talked to.

One of the two youngsters is a rich roughneck, used to having his own way, who seems not much affected by this treatment. In several sessions of coming clean over the next month—akin to old-style Communist Party confessions following 're-education'—he says what he thinks his interlocutors want to hear, professing repentance. The other youngster is just a spoiled kid with little moral fibre, which is what I guess is the defect of most of us. Several times over that month I have to drag my eyes away from the look in his: a cowering, desperate look, anxious to please, like that of a whipped dog which is sure it will be whipped again.

Neither of these youngsters is an alcoholic; but given the

encouragement this centre gives, they might well find an escape in heavy drinking.

~

The building is tall and narrow, with two floors and a terrace enclosed in tall chain-link fencing. We go up there for a little exercise every morning, under supervision, and once a week to wash our clothes and hang them out to dry. We have to be guarded: Most of the clients have been brought in against their will, on false pretexts, their freedom signed away by over-zealous (or, sometimes, designing) relatives. Akash, the rich roughneck who planned the breakout, doesn't seem to be an alcoholic, as I said. Apparently his family didn't like his behaviour, his late nights, the company he kept, the reckless way he spent money.

The technique for abducting clients is simple. A crew from the centre drives up to the victim's house in a van. (The crew often includes a trusty inmate or two.) They tell the victim they have come to take him to a marriage or some such function some distance away, and with the active connivance of his family get him into the van. On the way they make sure they stop and persuade him to have a drink or three. Then he can be brought into the centre with alcohol on his breath, and the papers (saying he is an alcoholic and needs treatment) are duly signed by the family and some willing medical man.

This racket is big, and has more nuances to it than you might suppose. I heard of a very wealthy Chennai man who signed over all his rights to his wife, including I suppose a power of attorney. He just wanted to be left to drink in peace. She promptly had him dumped in a rehab centre, and he's been in one or the other for five or six years. Every eleven months he's shifted to a new one, with the papers signed by her. Meanwhile she's one of Chennai-Bangalore's social butterflies, 'she goes to Singapore to have her hair done,' I was told.

~

The name of this centre is a synonym for mercy. There is another, better-known institution of the same name, run by Jesuit priests with centres in Mumbai, Pune and Goa among others. At least one of the inmates in this Bangalore centre where I found myself had been misled by the name into coming here. This young man—he is not yet thirty—is a building contractor from Chhattisgarh, a sweet chap, who had tried to solve his drinking problem by taking Alprazolam, a tranquilizer. He no longer drank but had been on up to thirty 10 mg tablets of Alprax a day. That's practically a killer dose; just one occasional 5 mg tablet knocks me out for the night.

The name might signify mercy, but there's precious little caring, even between clients. Strangely, few of my twenty-five or so fellow-prisoners seem to expect it. One of them has been in rehab twenty-eight times. He's almost sixty, and his wife and he seem to have given up. This is a fact of their lives. He says rehabilitation has become a racket in Bangalore. 'Anyone who's been sober for two years opens a new place. And then,' adds the cynic, 'as often as not he relapses and is admitted in a friend's.' I never suspected there's a social network of alcoholics and addicts, but there is, and it's got plenty of the creamy layer. There's also a lot of money in it: I paid 22,000 rupees for a month at one place, and that was three years ago.

This centre is not too bad, though. That's what the regulars tell me, anyway. There are places in Bangalore, and other cities, where the first thing which happens to a new admission is that he is stripped and made to spend twenty-four hours in a bare isolation cell without windows, food, bedding or sanitation. This is to break his ego. The task is carried on by a systematic humiliation in which fellow-inmates take eager part, culminating in a session in front of his family. I am told the State Human Rights Commission raided some of these centres the previous year and forced them to stop such practices. They've probably started again.

It's not caring or treatment these centres are after. 'Fear is the only way,' intones one of the two counsellors who take classes, one Mr Simon who quit drinking three decades ago and has since been helping Church and State by instilling fear into his charges. He's an okay guy when I relate to him in private sessions, but has the obnoxious habit of picking on one inmate every day and doing his best to reduce him to a stammering, defensive wreck before the end of the hour. Worse, he reads out tidbits from the confidential file for other inmates' edification and to the victim's impotent rage. When, later in the month, he takes off with his wife on a holiday to Singapore, everybody's happy.

~

Alcoholics Anonymous is a noble organization, and should have won the Nobel Peace Prize long since, but who would step on stage to claim it? They're very strict about anonymity. So it's galling to find Simon doing this sort of thing. 'Have you stopped beating your wife?' is never an easy question to answer.

The second or third day Simon picks on me, but I've resolved not to be bullied and give back as good as I get. The chap who sat next to me in that 'class', Raghu, for whom I translate, tells me later in Tamil, 'Ore sirippuvandidu'—I felt like laughing when I heard you both. The next day he is not laughing, for Simon makes him the butt of his jibes and revelations and sarcasms, and he is helpless. I'd like to help him but am sitting next to him again and have to translate.

Raghu is rather a sad case. He is a Reddy from the rich lands north of Chennai, where Andhra farmers have been settled for generations. He's become the butt not only of Simon but of his own fellows, because of his endless tales of having been defrauded by his maternal uncle who is also (following old usage) his elder brother-in-law. His idea of a good time is to spend all day in a mango tope, with a bottle or two by his side and the film songs written by Kannadasan in his headphones. No one believes his assertion that he once drank fourteen quarters in one session in these conditions.

Raghu was abducted using the classic ploy: The van sent by the centre purported to be taking him to a wedding. (That's not unusual: The web reaches as far afield as Tiruchi.) He says he drinks because of what his brother-in-law did, and solemnly avers in class that when he gets out he'll kill his sister's husband. He'll do it as much because he was robbed of his estates as because it was the brother-in-law who arranged for his abduction. All of this is perfectly probable. Those who run the centre are, however, listening not to Raghu but to his brother-in-law, who's paying for Raghu's treatment. If he is.

~

The classes are ill-organized. No one seems to care much; I'm the only one who takes notes, more out of journalistic habit than anything else. Strangely, in a centre which locks in people, discipline is lax. It's made worse by the presence of a bunch of Maldivians, who are pampered because they pay double, in US dollars. They are drug users and dealers, who escape jail terms of from twelve to seventy-five years at home by opting for three months' rehab abroad, in India, Sri Lanka or Malaysia. They have a house to themselves, get meat daily and can go out with minimal escort. We are told they go to 'malls'. We all think they take advantage of this: They are not serious about giving up drugs. (One of them tells me that former President Nasheed smokes ganja, which is why he is lenient with the drug users.) It's always a mistake to mix drinkers with druggies, and particularly these druggies. They come from an area of Malé where casual violence is a fact of life.

The Malé men provoke a stupid incident which ends with their threatening to kill me. I cannot remember any provocation from my side: I asked one of them not to sit in the chair next to me because the Chhattisgarh chap was due there (I used to translate for him too, he didn't know English). The Maldivian said 'fuck you', at which I rose and waved my finger under his nose and said, 'Don't talk to me like that.' The Maldivians rose in a body and came at me; one hurled a water-jug which shattered on the floor; but my compatriots wrestled them away, 'effing and blinding' as they used to say in England.

We natives finally lose patience and go to the top brass (himself an ex-druggie with 'a very violent past'), who hints that next time they step out of line we can 'deal with them'. That means physical business. Much rolling up of sleeves. The Maldivians apologize and even touch my feet. They have years and years to lose if they don't get their certificates, and the management is adept at using the inmates against each other.

~

There's supposed to be a 'Group Leader', who ensures discipline within the group. While I'm there it's a Bengali named Deep, who is everybody's darling. Simon even calls him 'Deepu', and defers to him, and of course he takes advantage. He and a crony are permitted to surf the net on the computer upstairs, which is supposed to be strictly out of bounds. This crony, a tall, very dark Bangalore Telugu, broke open his grandfather's safe in order to get money to drink. Now he is the life and soul of the place, but he is also Deep's chela.

One earlier Leader—they change each month—Joseph, from Shimoga side, takes his leave of us. There is a ceremony to rid us of him: Various criteria are chalked on the board, and we are all supposed to say what we think of the guy in those terms. Of course, it's a tamasha. I ask Joseph, on the side, to give a message to my wife. He's a straight guy, and I think I can trust him. He doesn't call. Later, I hear Joseph has gone back to his native Shimoga and started a rehabilitation centre.

~

Deep doesn't like me, I know. That's strange, because I like him: He's a natural leader. I've known many of them, and they're generally fearful of someone else usurping their authority. They have to keep on hectoring, though 'hector' is a slur on the Trojan hero. There's an in-house AA meeting every evening, which means we all sit in a circle, with one chap presiding, and speak our minds. Deep has gone out; I'm next in line. But Deep has told someone else to take the chair. I sit mumchance, silent. What idiots we are, to resent being passed over at an AA meeting! But there it is, such we are.

Three weeks, and I get to go out to an AA meeting. This is a regular one, outside, and only trusted inmates are taken. We go in the famous van, those of us who can be trusted—more or less. Roshan is with us, I haven't told you about Roshan.

Roshan is only about 5 ft 10 inches, but enormous on every side. He has a beatific smile; he looks like a sweet guy and he is, until he flexes his arms. He's the resident tough, the only one of the management who sleeps on the premises. He started the beating of the two escaping youngsters earlier this month, and boy, I wouldn't want to be beaten by Roshan. Towards the end of my stay at this centre I have a few words with him, and discover he used to be a bouncer in a nightclub in south Mumbai. He got into drink, went the rounds of the rehab centres and ended up here. He looks on non-drinking as a religious mission.

At the AA meeting outside, in a church, as usual I'm impressed by the feeling of brotherhood. 'Normal' people think of addicts as weak-willed degenerates (but think of how gays were regarded just twenty years ago); Simon thunders, 'Fear is the only way'; but it's the brotherhood which works. It's striking how the blue-collar men are candid and selfless, while the executive types begin, 'I started drinking when I was working for an MNC in Bombay...'

This is my lasting impression of AA: It is a wonderful thing, and the Twelve Steps are a programme which even teetotallers would do well to follow. I see how 'recovering alcoholics'—they never call themselves 'recovered', indeed when they speak at AA meetings they always introduce themselves as so-and-so, 'a recovering alcoholic, who by the grace of God and thanks to this wonderful Fellowship has not had a drink today'—recovering alcoholics are such *nicer* guys than the average. Some say, indeed, that they were lucky, because they had to dig deep within themselves. The Fourth Step says: 'We made a searching and fearless moral inventory of ourselves.' How many are granted that chance, or take it?

~

Deep is the 'leader' of the group. That doesn't mean much, except that he's in with the management. In fact, he's well in with the Maldivians— they sit together and talk for hours in the dormitory downstairs—and has to be persuaded that his authority will crumble before he throws it behind the anti-Maldivian throng when they threaten me. Before him as leader there was a Bangalore Tamil named Muthu, a big dark guy whose job before he came here was as enforcer in the K.R. Market area, twisting the arms of small merchants who hadn't paid for protection.

Muthu is an asshole, that's clear. But he's also a dada, and he keeps dropping in—ostensibly keeping this centre as a base while he finds a job—until one day he goes out for a job interview and comes back drunk. That's the problem with rehab centres, there's no guarantee. That wouldn't matter if only the family would believe there's no guarantee.

After a month, I've had enough. There's no space here, no place to walk. The food is not sustenance. It's undermining me morally as well as physically: no milk, curds or butter, no fresh veg, eggs once a week, chicken on arbitrary special occasions. Sometimes it's rice thrice a day. I find myself chewing and relishing the kadi-patta and other seasoning, just for some roughage. The centre is short of funds, it owes all the local shopkeepers. The owner, making an infrequent appearance, tells me he hasn't 'seen a paisa of profit'. Hah.

The owner is an ex-alcoholic who's been off for seven years. When he comes, late in the month, he brings with him a big guy, Philip, who bowled in the Ranji Trophy. Philip's twin brother, Martin, a sober guy as so often happens, runs a rehabilitation centre, but understandably Philip doesn't want to go there. Philip and I play a game of table-tennis; I haven't played for twenty years, but the smashes come out all right, as do Philip's.

The owner of the centre phones soon after, and talks to me because Philip is in the bathroom. He tells me Philip's teenage daughter, who has leukaemia, is dying now in hospital. He tells me to tell Philip, and that he will be coming soon to take him away.

~

Everything that has to do with the abuse of alcohol is a shaming thing, except, mostly, the actual use. When you drink, you forget the shame. When the drink goes down the gullet, however the drink is obtained, all shame is forgotten. These lines will never go away:

> I often wonder what the vintners buy
> One half so precious as the goods they sell.

There are so many specious reasons for drinking. I can always, no matter what the circumstances, convince myself of the need, and so have so many before me. This is from the eighteenth century:

If all be true that I do think,
There are five reasons one should drink:
Good wine; a friend; or feeling dry;
Or lest I should be by-and-by;
Or any other reason why.

One way to cure alcoholics is to make them feel good about themselves. This centre is taking the easy way. Fear is not the key. You, the teetotaller or social drinker, may think of alcoholics as moral degenerates who take a shortcut out. But it's not easy, not at all. The point is, we'd rather not partake of this society or its fruits. Yes, that makes us degenerates, weirdos, misfits—or simply weaklings.

It's a good thing I came here of my own will, and can get word to my family that I want out. Families tend to think rehab involves meditation, yoga, intensive counselling. They also think of it as a magic bullet. Several inmates would like to see their families shut up here. The worst of it is, we're not allowed outside contact without supervision; and we know our families are being lied to.

I go out feeling I've rendered unto Caesar what is his. Now, does the coin go to the gods or to the neighbourhood liquor shop?

Confidence Trickster

Pavankumar Jain

Navin got his high from whoring and gambling. He was a close friend of my youth. I, on the other hand, was more interested in learning the ABC of boozing.

I believed that women were kidnapped and forced into whoring. I felt that having sex with such a woman amounted to raping her, and so I'd never do that. I also had a mortal fear of contracting venereal disease.

Gambling didn't hold any attraction for me either. Navin placed bets on cards. You could get Rs 9 against one rupee for a single card; or Rs 81 for a pair, i.e. 'jodi'; or Rs 130 against a rupee for a sequence of three cards, i.e. 'paana'.

My logic for this was simple. I didn't want to risk losing my one rupee. I drank cheap and indigenously-made country liquor, and it unfailingly gave me a 'kick'. I often coaxed Navin to accompany me. He was free not to drink. On one such occasion, when we were sitting in a cheap bar, a couple walked in. Normally women didn't enter such bars. We were quite curious. I told Navin that the woman too will drink. But, to our surprise, only the woman drank, and not her companion. After the couple left, I asked the bar-boy, Lalmani, how it was that only the woman drank? He said that they were husband and wife. Every day, at the appointed hour, the husband brought his wife to the bar. After she'd had a few, the husband would take her home, feed her, put her to bed, then leave for work. This little arrangement had been worked out in order to prevent her from drinking excessively in his absence.

Years passed. Navin finished his education. He moved out of his parents' house. He got a job. Got married. He quit whoring and gambling. We lost touch. When we'd bump into each other accidentally, we had little to talk about.

I too finished my college. I joined NID—the National Institute of Design—in Ahmedabad, acquired a degree in design. I didn't like the idea of being employed, whether in the private sector or public, a large set-up or small. I couldn't do any lucrative activity of my own. I wrote short stories and poetry. I didn't marry. I remained a pauper. I'd decided that I'd live my life by the modified maxim of 'plain living and plain (not "high") thinking.'

In the meanwhile, I had learnt my alphabet of drinking so well that I could repeat it forward and backward umpteen times, without halting once to breathe in between.

Then I came across Ramnikbhai. He sold the coasters which I designed from acrylic sheets. I'd put paint in the centre, before pressing the sheets together. The colours would spread out into abstract shapes. Ramnikbhai drank at any time of the day. But he shunned the government approved country liquor that I was fond of. He preferred to drink hooch, the illicit, slyly-made, often spurious country liquor. He had five daughters and was past the age of producing children, yet he firmly believed that since the government-approved country liquor destroyed a man's virility, he'd better stay away from it.

Ramnikbhai was not the first or only person to offer me this gem of truth—of course, free of cost. It was a widespread, deeply-entrenched, and firmly-held belief. It had plenty of takers. Who could have spread this rumour? Naturally, it was the USP of distillers, carriers and sellers of hooch.

I drank hooch (or 'bewda' as it was called) to keep Ramnikbhai company, but rarely on my own. The papers often carried reports of people going blind, and even dying after drinking poisonous hooch. I thought to myself: this really couldn't be the best way to die, at least not for me.

For many years though I drank hooch on certain fixed days of the year:

January 26—India's Republic Day
August 15—India's Independence Day
October 3—Gandhiji's birth anniversary
The various voting days when municipal, state and parliamentary
elections were held.

On these designated dry days, I had an uncontrollable urge to drink.
The illicit liquor addas were the only places I could wet my parched
throat.

The tradition of distilling illicit liquor in the suburbs of Bombay is
quite old and widespread. For several years (1950-1973), the distilling,
transporting, selling, buying and drinking of alcohol was prohibited,
in Bombay as well as the rest of Maharashtra. Those who were thirsty
could choose a speakeasy of their liking; there were plenty around.

~

In my parents' house, where I grew up with my six siblings, there
was no tradition of drinking. No one from my caste group, or the
Gujarati-Hindu neighbourhood we lived in, drank openly. Drinking
liquor was considered a vice, a sign of bad character. I too shared
this general impression: that only members of the theatre and film
fraternity, only the very rich and the very poor, were not bothered by
the stigma attached to drinking. The compound of our rented house
shared a wall with a shanty. The men in that shanty drank cheap
liquor every day and beat up their wives and children. You could hear
the foulest abuses being hurled around at the most unearthly hours.

So, you see, there was no reason for me to be attracted to alcohol
in the first place, or even have an irrepressible curiosity about alcohol.
And yet, there was no denying that it was there, this curiosity.

~

When I entered the hallowed premises of a reputable college at the
age of sixteen, I was skinny, weighing around forty-four pounds. My
height was four feet something, and I still wore shorts. I worried day
and night about how to improve my English, as I had studied at a
suburban Gujarati-medium school.

The college had a tiny library in a secluded corner, which was meant for the use of research scholars. The librarian seemed bored in the set-up as hardly anyone ever went there. Two years went by. Sometimes I met this man and conversed with him. On one occasion I noticed him sipping something. He said that it was cashew feni. I asked him what it tasted like. Was it bitter? Did one get drunk and fall down after drinking it? He said, no, not if you consume it in small quantities. He asked me if I'd ever had a drink. No. Never. Would I like to try? My heart was in the grip of fear. But my curiosity won. Give me a little, please. No, no. Less. Even lesser. Are you sure that I won't get drunk?

I gulped down a teaspoonful of it. It had an unbearably strong and unfamiliar smell. Very bitter. A somewhat burning sensation in the throat, causing short spasms of dry cough. What? Nothing happened. Why does the librarian sip this useless stuff? Anyway, that was my initiation ritual, deeksha if you may, to enter the adult world.

At this moment, someone whispers in my left ear (or is it the right?) that the journey of a thousand miles begins with a single, however shaky, step.

In the quiet deserted library, I had some more sips of feni in small quantities. Possibly, I was looking for greater adventure. So one day I called my classmate Lewellyn (or Lulu as we called him), a big tall fellow, aside. I requested him to take me for a drink. I repeatedly assured him that I'd pay for his drink too. In those days of Prohibition, he took me to a nearby illicit country liquor bar. It was a dingy dark room, part of someone's house. The room had a few tables and chairs and was crowded. An old woman, the owner of the house, served the drinks. Lulu ordered drinks for the two of us. I took a very small sip (I was scared of getting drunk), and passed the rest of it to Lulu. He gladly gulped it down. On a stool was a plate with some salt crystals and boiled eggs. It made the taste of hooch more bearable. This was my first experience of hooch and a hooch joint.

The entrance of this hooch joint was covered with a dirty cloth curtain. Outside the joint, hawkers sold hard boiled eggs, pieces of fried fish and boiled chana. Over the years, these two markers—the dirty cloth curtain on the door and the hawkers selling fish or chana nearby, always helped me locate a hooch joint, even in areas totally unfamiliar to me.

~

In my 35-year drinking career, there were times when I'd stop drinking completely. One evening, after I had given up drinking, my friend Pradeep and I went to the house of a common friend, Ashok. Ashok had a small bar with a good stock of excellent liquors. I was confident and comfortable in the company of drinkers. Ashok and Pradeep would drink alcohol, while I stuck to plain water.

At one point in the conversation I told them that there had been times, two or three at most, when I couldn't recall how I reached home. I must have crossed roads with heavy traffic, boarded a local train, got down at my suburb, climbed the railway overbridge, and reached home. Pradeep recalled that he on some occasions had reached home riding his motorcycle, without any knowledge or memory of how he had done so. I was scared to hear that. Ashok too sometimes drove home in his car, and didn't recall how. I was gasping for fresh air. I don't approve of the idea of luck but that evening I thanked our lucky stars that we were alive to share our mind-boggling experiences.

As a writer, I have been sharing my views and experiences with my readers for more than forty-seven years. But I learnt the great value of honest sharing during my visits to the meetings of Alcoholics Anonymous, in my attempt to give up alcohol for good.

I was struck by the brilliant narrations of some sharers, who otherwise seemed ill-equipped to comprehend philosophical or literary complexities. Coming mostly from humble economic backgrounds, they didn't mean to spin gossamer-fine webs out of nothing. Their experiential truth was expressed in a forthright manner, without the pretence of linguistic skills. How charged was their narrative sharing! They seemed more powerful to me than the characters we 'create' in our writings.

When I was somewhat set in the business of drinking, a fear started lurking in my heart. Suppose someday I discover that I am pulled into the vortex of liquor, what will I do? I had a secret hope that I would seek the help of Alcoholics Anonymous, though in those years I had not the slightest idea if AA existed in India or only in America. I didn't worry much though. My getting addicted seemed only a distant possibility In those initial years of drinking I frequently abstained from drinking for a month or longer, and assured myself that I possessed a lot of willpower, that I'd never become a 'gone' case.

Like all the others around me, I had the impression that I was a timid person, with middle-class values, who was born to follow social norms and would never feel the urge nor have the courage to cast aside any taboo. All through my childhood and teenage years, my self-image of being a 'decent person' remained intact. My introduction to liquor, and the deeper affair with it that followed, shattered that image.

Urdu poetry, which I read in the Hindi script, romanticized drink, drinking and the drinker so much that it seemed like an authentic prescription to cure you of all the miseries of the world. It must have been an indescribably powerful influence in my formative years. In my early childhood and youth, I was one person; thereafter, a completely different one.

Even during my years of heavy drinking, I noticed that before drinking I was quiet, withdrawn and reticent. But after about three drinks my voice became loud, I talked a lot, laughed much, and got the courage to fight against the whole world. In short, drink altered my personality radically. After giving up alcohol, whenever I was in the company of friends, I'd observe them keenly. Whether they drank a lot or in moderation, they remained themselves, unlike me who was transformed into a different person.

At times, I tried to apply and use this theory of liquor-changing-my-personality. I put it to work in the real world. Once I went to record a short story of mine at All India Radio. I'd only read a few sentences when a hammering sound was heard in the otherwise soundproof recording room. The recording was stopped. I was shifted to another room. I started reading the story from the beginning but the hammering sound was heard in that room too. The recording was stopped again. I was given yet another room. I began to read. After a while, the recordist stopped the recording. He came to me and said that I was reading too slowly. I promised to read fast. The recordist paused the recording again. He said I was now reading too fast, that it shouldn't sound like I was reading something, that it should sound natural, as if I was narrating something. I asked for a break of ten minutes. I went out of the radio station and asked a cigarette seller where I could get something to drink. He pointed out a place close by.

I got suspicious. Was the fellow taking me for a ride? The place had three buildings in the same compound. But I was desperate and in a hurry. I entered the compound. My eyes gleamed at the sight of a row of glasses laid on a table near the window of a house. I asked the hooch seller for three drinks, gulped them down in quick succession and rushed back to the recordist. I was composed, my voice was well-modulated, the pace was natural, and the recording successful.

There was another time, another place, and another recording. It was a television quiz show on matters related to art. It was called *Mashoor Mahal*. There were several prizes to be won. A friend had prodded me to participate in it. The thought of facing lights, about three cameras and a dummy/studio audience to enliven proceedings made me very nervous. So I had a few drinks. Just when I felt comfortable and mentally ready to shoot, the fear returned with double the force. I sat down and drank some more. This kept happening. Then I asked myself: if I get drunk, how will I perform? The answer I gave myself was this: in that case I would go to the organizers and tell them that I was unwell and unable to participate. Surely, they must have a backup. They'd get another contestant to replace me.

I soon reached the venue. I decided that I'd have my say once the cameras were rolling. I'd say that winning or losing the prize was inconsequential, what mattered more was to play the quiz game with utmost interest and concentration. I imagined viewers watching the programme being telecast. I am a performer. I must perform so well that the viewer should feel I was the best contestant, even if I didn't win the prize.

The shooting went off smoothly. It was faultless. After the show was telecast on Doordarshan, people came up to me in local trains, at bus stops, while walking on the road, a cyclist once, a group of girls in a park…they'd come up and congratulate me, express their sympathy that I'd erred at the penultimate question and lost the handsome prize.

There was yet another instance where alcohol was a help. A friend's young daughter had died after an unsuccessful cardiac surgery in the US. On his return home, I got the news. I didn't know how to go to his house. I didn't have the courage. I didn't know what conversation to have with him. Should I drink and then go? It was a sad occasion for the family. It might be offensive to go there smelling of liquor. Talking over the phone, and not meeting him personally, would appear rude. I drank. I went. I was myself. I expressed my grief and sympathy. My friend seemed consoled and comforted.

Drink worked fantastically on some occasions. But, on occasions when there was absolutely no possibility of drinking, what would I do? My innate timidity and reticence depressed me. It took the first AA meeting for me to realize that one could be confident without alcohol. It marked a new beginning.

CONDUCT UNBECOMING

Manohar Shetty

'Ankur' means seedling in Hindi and true to its name, it was the
first restaurant established by my late maternal uncle, back in 1941.
Since then he set up or ran several more, both in the Fort area of
Bombay and in the suburbs. Before it was rechristened as Ankur
with a bar or 'permit room', as such places were then known, it was
a popular Udipi-style outlet known as New Welcome which catered
to the hundreds of office-goers in the area, especially during lunch
time. It was so popular that it issued monthly lunch coupons to its
regular customers. Oldtimers in Tamarind Lane—rechristened now
as M.P. Shetty Marg, after my uncle—and the surrounding areas still
remember the place with more than a hint of nostalgia for its excellent
and modestly priced food. Many of them were perhaps not too happy
when it changed to its new avatar as a swanky, air-conditioned bar in
the early eighties—a bar which curiously only served vegetarian food.
My uncle by then had turned to his sons to carry the business forward.
The younger generation saw little sense in continuing to dish out the
same old fare with small profit margins in a highly competitive and
labour-intensive business. A permit room was the way forward and
the vegetarian menu, which many were skeptical of, actually made
sound business sense. There was no other similar outlet in the area and
more pertinently, the Bombay Stock Exchange was close by, teeming
with Gujarati stockbrokers and speculators who were predominantly
vegetarian. After all that hoarse shouting in that tension-packed bear
and bull ring, they needed to unwind with a drink or two and some
wholesome vegetarian food. As a veteran stockbroker once put it

to me: 'Both ways you win: if we make a windfall we come here to celebrate; if we lose a fortune we come here to drown our sorrows.' There were also a few other regulars who quaffed a bewildering variety of 'Doctor's brandies' on medical advice.

Like those share bazaar brokers, I embarked on my brief two-year career at Ankur with purely mercenary motives—to become a partner in the business, make a killing, and marry my ladylove who just happened to be from another community. But my gamble didn't quite come off. My extended family rightly didn't see me as an astute businessman nor someone who would for purely pragmatic reasons marry a girl from my own community. With my long hair and somewhat unconventional attire, I was at best a bit player in their grand designs. I hung in there for two years, but no miracle happened. Indeed what happened was quite the contrary. I began to drink. Not that I was a stranger to Peter Scot or Hercules, but it was at Ankur with the bar literally within reach, that I became a serious drinker.

The long hours only compounded the habit. The peak crowd would usually thin out by around ten at night as most of the clientele lived in the distant suburbs. Incidentally, the paanwala outside did brisk business as almost every customer picked up a fragrant Banarasi to disguise the unmistakable aroma of hard liquor. No one, it seemed, had enlightened them on the impossibility of camouflaging the smell. If some crafty distiller were to invent odourless booze, I'm sure the sales graph would resemble vertical lightning.

I had, as someone who managed the show, to stay on at least till midnight when the restaurant closed, to check the accounts. As often happens in such bars, customers would troop in just before closing time. The 'last order' before the bar counter closed would invariably be a clutch of three or more large pegs, lingered over garrulously till well past midnight when the swaying customers would be politely ushered out.

During these hours of utter boredom, I usually planted myself behind the dumbwaiter, quietly sipping on my fourth or fifth whisky. This became my daily routine before I took my regular taxi back to my home in the suburbs. If the customers lingered on longer, my own intake rose to a sixth drink or more, usually progressing from 'small' (30 ml) to 'large' (60 ml). I was never a sporadic binge drinker, never the life of the party, but always nursing my drink in a quiet, unobtrusive corner. The government-ordained 'dry days' were often a nuisance but such days only served to intensify the regulars' thirst for alcohol and liquor was served to select customers under the guise of 'soft drinks'. Indeed, on such days excise officials themselves whose duty it was to enforce abstinence were regular freeloaders, quite happy to drink whisky mixed with colas.

Looking back, I doubt it was the easily accessible free drinks—part of the perks—that contributed to my burgeoning addiction. It was akin to a second nature within me to drink, and in any case I often bought my own liquor on Sundays which was supplemented by new and free sample brands given to me for promotion at Ankur.

People find it somewhat novel that an aspiring poet should run a bar, and in the biographical notes in anthologies that feature my work, this fact is often highlighted. But it was actually nothing more than a purely mercenary sidelight—with noble intentions of course. And indeed several poets have led far more interesting parallel lives. Ted Hughes, for instance, was once a night watchman. And in the *The Oxford Companion to Twentieth Century Poetry* which covers about 1,500 poets, the editor Ian Hamilton remarks that among the 'zany professions' some were involved in were that of 'lumberjack, tax inspector, furniture remover, carpet salesman, and policeman'. One poet was even an international hockey player and nineteen of them had served time in prison. Rather surprisingly, only fifteen of them 'were diagnosed as alcoholic'. Out of 1,500 poets, this to me is not a credible figure, and the operative word is 'diagnosed'. There would surely have been dozens more, who like most seasoned tipplers, would hardly allow themselves to be officially 'diagnosed' as alcoholics. Self-delusion and denial are the hallmarks of a habitual drinker's psyche.

My plans thwarted, in 1984 I left Bombay for a job in Bangalore, but not before a fellow dipso presented me with a book inscribed with the following ditty: *'I drink to your health when we're together / I drink to your health when I'm alone / I drink to your health so damn often / I've almost ruined my own.'* My health was the last thing on my mind when I worked for two years for a Sunday evening tabloid in Bangalore. As a chief sub, my duties involved late-night editing and ensuring that both the 'dak' mofussil edition on Thursday distributed to the small, surrounding towns and the main city edition on Sundays met their deadlines. The press was at some distance from the city and its main priority was printing an Urdu newspaper. The printing of my paper could only be taken up long after midnight. The proof-reading was a little tricky as I had to check the main headlines right to left as the printer found it too cumbersome to change the process from the Urdu formatting. I remember a particular edition well, the day when Indira Gandhi was assassinated. The urgent edition very nearly went to press with the 60-point typeset headline 'PM SHOT DEAD' reading DAED TOHS MP, almost getting past my bleary eyes which were no doubt shot red too with the Hercules rum which was my constant companion. After the editions went to print, I would sit on the crumbling steps of the press alone, nursing that companion till the first rickshaw sputtered into view usually just before dawn. There was not much of a market for a Sunday evening paper in Bangalore and soon after it closed down, I moved lock, stock and barrel (no pun intended) to Goa.

As all tourists know there is no, or a minimal excise, tax in Goa and liquor is sold at roughly a little more than half the price prevalent in the rest of the country. But I was not led there by the availability of cheap booze. My motives were far more wholesome—to have a home of my own and start a family. I did of course continue to drink, quite steadily, every night after work. What made my drinking habit imperceptible and almost anonymous to others was that I never drank during the day, only at night after eight or so till around midnight. Three-quarters of a bottle or three nips a day—and a drop more— was for me quite regular. I envy people who refuse a drink after their quota of two 'small'. For me that would only be the kick-off point, the appetizer leading to the main course. After the fifth large, when inhibitions are down and garrulity takes over, the intake is usually more rapid, one 'repeat' following the next and if you have run out of your particular brand, so be it. After half-a-dozen large drinks, the brand takes a toss and there's little difference between the desi Diplomat and Chivas Regal though, curiously in Bombay, even before I joined Ankur, I never developed a taste for the country liquor 'aunty' joints in the Dhobi Talao area and, in fact, even in the floor above Ankur from where at night customers tumbled down the stairs. In Goa I did, though aficionados here will jump at your throat if you lower cashew or coconut feni to that crude country level.

Put off by its naturally sickly and fruity odour, it took me two years before I was drowned by the lure of cashew feni. And for the next twenty-odd years, I drank nothing else. I stopped fooling myself buying two or usually three full bottles of IMFL (Indian Made Foreign Liquor) every week with their delusional, macho labels like Officer's Choice or Black Knight or the occasional Johnnie Walker. It was cashew feni distilled from fermented cashew fruit with all its sweetish reek and nothing else. And bought wholesale from a regular supplier from Colvale who, on his motorcycle, home-delivered twenty litres at a time in a plastic jerry can. Initially for storage I used a garafão, a traditional, large, curved and bulbous bottle wrapped in a crisscross coir design. But one night the garafão slipped from my hands and broke. (The horror! The horror!) My distiller and supplier, Mahableshwar, a short, stocky man with a white moustache, would then fill twenty bottles in the kitchen sink from the jerry can. I dreaded the days when he came to refill my stock as the entire house reeked of feni. Indeed after bouts of heavy drinking, even after several hours, its smell poured forth from the very pores of your skin. But at less than Rs 30 a bottle, it was worth the olfactory intrusion into domesticity and the dark, glowering looks all around. During work, not many people actually knew of my abundant intake. In terms of tippling, I was a day scholar: studious and industrious by day, and something of a brooding villain after sunset, though I never got into brawls, brandishing a menacing knife, swaying, with bloodshot eyes.

But intoxication was part of my intrinsic mental make-up though I've never understood the romantic notion of alcohol as a palliative to a broken heart, as exemplified in some old Hindi movies. I was also not unfamiliar with the hash-addas of Churchgate and Colaba. After a few drinks I often made my way to these joints, trying to attain some outlandish acme of nirvana. (The difference between booze and grass: booze aggravates, grass accentuates). Alcohol may be a time-tested icebreaker, but it's also the quickest way to a fool's paradise, even if the next morning, the tongue turned dry as tanned leather, serves as a reminder of the previous night's folly. An endangered liver may be the last thing on a seasoned drinker's mind, but I feel a little concerned when I see people quaffing liquor neat or on the rocks. Some drinkers even surreptitiously put down a whole pint within minutes to escape detection. I never drank in that perilous manner, but always with the peg topped with water to the brim in a tall glass. And always accompanied by a meal or snacks. But the problem with booze is that the higher you are, the higher you want to go. Once you have conquered the lowly Alps, you want to conquer Mt Everest.

I'm often asked if liquor is conducive to the writing of poetry. My straight answer is no. Drinking offers no profound insights into the mysteries of the universe or the soul. Booze is not some mind-expanding drug, leading to super-consciousness. It makes you less inhibited, but is of no help in exploring the dark (or radiant) recesses of the mind. I've often written what I perceived to be brilliant, original lines under the heavy and heady influence of liquor, only to find the most banal scribblings the next morning with, if I'm lucky, not more than a line salvageable. For me at least booze was a false god. Its physical intoxication was a path to bravado and little else. This is of course not a golden rule for all poets. Perhaps poets like Dylan Thomas and many others found inspiration in drink. But what is a magic potion for one may be poison to another, as it eventually proved to be with Thomas. I cannot deny that liquor helped me socially in opening out from my normal morose, withdrawn self and that there is much to be said for sociability and good fellowship. But it provided no revelatory spark to set off a sheaf of poems. Indeed quite the contrary happened. After I gave up serious drinking, my output burgeoned manifold. From 1994 to 2010, I produced no book of poems, only a few scattered ones still confined to my notebooks. Since 2010, after

I gave up heavy drinking, to the present time, I have published three full-length books, with another in the hands of a reputed publisher, each one quite substantial at least in terms of the number of poems in them. I cannot obviously vouch for their quality. That I leave to readers and critics. But the fact is I was soberly alive to grab those moments of lucidity with alacrity which otherwise would have been lost to the fumes of alcohol.

The battle with booze is, however, never over. It is an ongoing conflict. Alcoholics need their 'quota' just as intensely as a junkie needs his fix. Perhaps excessive boozing has coarsened my taste, but I've never fathomed how people can get high on beer or wine—whatever the vintage or 'bouquet'. To me, they are poor substitutes for hard liquor. Occasionally, especially at weddings or parties, I still find myself slipping up. When I do, I feel deeply ashamed of myself, of my lack of will and of my infinite capacity for self-indulgence. I remind myself that I have vanquished the habit once and can do so again, despite the passing years. I know for certain that I will not again become the daily three-quarter-bottle (and the occasional full bottle) man again. There are those who say to break this habit, you need the support of people around you, your family and friends, of organizations like Alcoholics Anonymous which no doubt does good work. But I've never had the humility to go to an AA meeting. My mind has never functioned in that fashion, of seeking a remedy outside for my own misdeeds. Indeed the more a boozer is harangued and chastised, the more he will drink. My best defense is that I know all too well that the worst form of deception is self-deception. Booze is possibly an ally for our soldiers in the extreme cold of our borders in the mountains. But here, in the pleasant environs of Goa, it is neither an ally nor your enemy. It is just another intoxicant that in the end leaves you high but dry, and ultimately, out in the cold.

A Glass Too Many

Adil Jussawalla

I had gone to meet Anil Dharker at the *Mid-Day* office. The office was in a building that looked as though it had been made of a number of tatty filing cabinets stacked one on top of the other. It was the sort of building that looked as if a finger pushed at it would bring it tumbling down. I pushed a finger—at the lift button, but the building didn't come tumbling down. I soared into the *Mid-Day* office.

The office was like a bloated midriff, its intestines lined with glass. I followed one loop of the intestine and found Dharker sitting behind glass. He beckoned to me. I pushed at what looked like a door. He beckoned again. I pushed again. The door didn't yield an inch.

Perhaps it was meant to be pulled. I looked for a handle and found none. A little frantic now, I began pressing the glass panel all over with my palms, hoping I'd find the one miraculous electronically sensitized patch that would unlock it. I saw Dharker rise and come towards me. I heard his voice.

I discovered he was standing behind me, unable to hide his smile. In my mind's eye, I saw several *Mid-Day* employees unable to hide their smiles. What I'd been trying to get to was Dharker's reflection. His cabin was directly behind me, the whole caboodle being reflected in obstinately unyielding glass.

That wasn't the first time that I stumbled upon the open treachery of glass, its transparent insolence. Nor the first time I questioned the motives, not to mention the depravity of architects who use the material freely. I've got into trouble with glass more often than I can remember. I've slammed into it when I thought I was walking through space and baulked at space, usually at airports, railway stations and congested public buildings where there was no glass, leading to human traffic snarls and bodily collusions behind me.

I've been deeply traumatized by glass, though not so severely, perhaps as a highly-strung colleague of mine who, eager to leave a dentist's chair after having had two broken teeth fixed, smacked his head into glass and broke his nose.

When did our contemporary obsession with glass begin? You see it everywhere in Bombay. Old buildings are no longer pulled down. Instead they are draped in acres of cloth behind which ragged construction workers flit. They are the city's newest and worst-paid plastic surgeons, giving its structures a facelift. Three to six months later the buildings emerge from their chrysalises, shimmering butterflies, most of them glass-fronted.

There's a liberal use of granite too, both on the buildings' surfaces and inside them, so liberal that even as you admire your reflection in some glassy sheen you can feel your feet slipping, you're about to fall, help! And there's nothing to hold onto for miles.

Come the monsoon, smooth polished granite will become slippery polished granite. Come the monsoon, bosses and stenos, peons and executives will slip on smooth polished granite. Come to think of it, nothing is so great a leveller, not death, not sex, not travelling on a cart behind diarrhoea-hit bullocks—it happened to me once—as smooth, polished granite.

Why do our architects and designers not think of it? What country do they think we're living in? As a student of architecture in London, I learnt about curtain-walling. That meant some buildings had outer walls which were not structural but were like curtains, mostly of glass. New office blocks had them, new department stores had them. They were among the worst buildings in Britain.

That was in 1957. Haven't chrome, glass, steel and granite, used as liberally as we do in our new and renovated buildings, really had their day long ago? We know slippery surfaces make for a fall and as for glass, apart from its treacherous quality, with so much pent-up fury in us, well, glass is just a stone's throw away.

I'll tell you one more story about glass. It happened yesterday and the glass was in the shape of a bottle. Some bars serve liquor in quarter bottles and as I was halfway through mine before having to leave for an appointment, I asked the waiter to fill the bottle up with soda. He did. He was about to put the bottle into a brown paper bag when I thought, hang the bag, I have one made of cloth, it'll do, and then again I thought, let him put the bottle in the brown paper bag.

I dumped the wrapped bottle into the cloth bag and caught a taxi. Halfway to the five-star hotel where I had my appointment, the bottle exploded. Whisky and soda bled through the cloth bag, my lap was soaked with its injuries. It didn't make for a respectable entry into the hotel.

But the point of the story is this: the brown bag contained the explosion, no glass pierced it. I had taken the bottle along with the idea of having a swig in the taxi. It would have been out of its brown paper bag then. I can see the headlines still: Bottle Explodes in Columnist's Face…Piece of Glass Pierces Taxi Driver's Neck…Taxi Goes off Road, Pavement Dwellers Crushed to Death.

And the two morals of the story are: One: never take anything fizzy along with you during a heat wave, with the temperature well above 35 degrees Celsius. Two: you can never see through glass, you only think you can. Though openly treacherous, its motives are well hidden. In this cruel world, there's always one glass too many.

THE THEKA

Abhinav Kumar

For young Indian men of modest means who came of age in the last decade of the twentieth century, their first visit to a theka was a rite of passage. Almost as significant as your first kiss, sometimes more because often that came later. The first time a young man had the confidence to hitch a ride with a friend to a theka (the first time was seldom alone), and have the courage to walk up to the counter and pull out a crumpled note from his trouser pocket and ask for a beer, and actually get it, was the day you properly entered the hallowed and harrowing gates of manhood. Never mind that the transaction was performed with more than a generous amount of nervousness and furtive side glances, after all you didn't want any prying neighbours to catch you in the act, and the bottle was instantly tucked away inside a bag or on your person.

Once you had done it, you had become more of a man in your own eyes. Not only did you have the means to go to a theka, you also had the courage to order your drink, and in the battle of being handed over your first bottle, finally you had silently announced your arrival as another adult Indian male. Never mind that the alcohol burnt your throat and, more often than not, it made you retch, and you lived in mortal fear of being caught out by nosey relatives for a few weeks. You had conquered the theka.

While Harivansha Rai Bachchan may have immortalized the tavern in *Madhushala*, the humble theka still awaits its bard. The tavern was always celebrated as the house of refined pleasures, both of the palate and other areas beneath it; the theka has always been its humble country cousin. Neither celebrated in verse or prose, nor in song or celluloid, the theka was the cultural equivalent of the toilet. It existed in a state of non-being, under a constitution that was implicitly committed to Prohibition, though just not yet, and a culture which was obsessed with notions of purity and piety which simply refused to acknowledge it. For the middle class, the theka existed to be used discreetly, with an appropriate sense of coyness and embarrassment. For the lumpen, it was their refuge and playground rolled into one. An entire ecosystem would develop around the theka to cater to its more reliable and involved customers. A shop selling snacks, masala peanuts mostly, a paan shop, with a side alley or a backyard to enable the excessively inebriated to relieve themselves in a manner of their choosing.

A well-informed young man was expected to know not only the location of the two or three closest thekas but also their timings. In fact timing was everything. Summer closing time was 10 p.m. and winter was 9 p.m. Dry days had to be planned for well in advance too. This was the pre satellite, pre malls, pre iPod, pre mobile, generation we are talking about. If you didn't stock up for declared dry days, your social life was essentially over. For most of my holidays that I spent shuttling between Delhi, Bareilly, Aligarh and Lucknow as a college student, the quarter was the preferred currency of street cred amongst young males. Unlike a girlfriend, which for most young men consisted of an undeclared crush on a woman mostly unaware of their existence, a quarter, or sometimes a half, was for real. Possessing one was like owning a cricket bat and ball as a school kid, you didn't need to be invited to play, you were the game in town.

As a college student in England, where eighteen was the permissible age for drinking, the culture of drinking that I was initiated into there could not have been more different from the one that I had to reckon with back home. Compared to the turmoil around the theka, with its jostling, badly lit stalls, prices that often fluctuated depending on the size of the crowd of tipplers thronging the sales counter, frequent arguments and occasional fights, the British off licence of my college days increasingly seemed like an oasis of calm. And all this when the legal drinking age in India was a respectable and mature twenty-five. And of course there were no women to be seen within miles of any theka. The sale and purchase of drink remained a male preserve in the early '90s. And despite the growing number of young female drinkers, especially in our metros, I suspect that this gender barrier around the theka is yet to be breached. For now, the theka remains a testosterone temple, a segregated celebration of aggression, bravado and brashness, that passes for early manhood in India.

When the twists and turns of fate required me to wear the uniform of a police officer, my perspective on the theka was to undergo a radical transformation. From being a grimy source of guilty pleasures, it became a crucible of crime and depravity. From a police viewpoint, a theka was the epicentre of the forces of crime and disorder. It had to be monitored with a hawk's eye and dealt with a firm hand. The excise laws and the penal code conferred ample authority on the police to be the primary arbiters of the drinking habits of our society, and it was a role most policemen performed with added gusto. Often at the cost of other more important and demanding duties. Policing the theka, swaggering around it with a lathi, admonishing the staff and customers for infractions real and imaginary was the dream assignment for any self respecting beat constable. But not for reasons of professional pride and social vanity. I realized soon enough that the theka was an important source of illegal gratification that greased the gears of the entire police and criminal justice machinery. A police station that did not have a theka or a bar in its jurisdiction, was literally and metaphorically regarded as a 'dry' police station and did not have many willing takers to do a stint there.

The theka and the police have a symbiotic relationship. Each needs the other for different reasons. The proprietor of a theka keeps the police in good humour so that the countless daily violations of our cumbersome excise laws go unnoticed and are not acted upon. The police need the theka to serve as a lightning rod for young drinkers, who in their opinion are the demographic most likely to cause trouble, as compared to law-abiding teetotallers. And of course they also need the theka to serve as a source of 'perks', in cash and in kind.

It seems to me that the politics of policing vice is pretty much the same around the world. With pretty similar consequences. A vocal puritanical minority gets together and invokes some religious or cultural norms to demand a ban or strict regulation of a particular vice. The large majority is either indifferent or too embarrassed to resist. The result is a ban or tight regulation that places enormous trust and authority in the hands of law enforcement agencies. With great power comes greater irresponsibility. And gradually the police become the staunchest supporters of public morality. Amplifying public anxieties, the police encourage the impression, often without empirical evidence, that without giving them the authority to carry out the regulation and prohibition of vices such as drinking, gambling, prostitution and drugs, the more real challenges of crime and public order cannot be tackled effectively. As a policeman it is perhaps in my class interest to welcome any and every expansion of police authority. As a citizen I am not so sure. Especially when the police in India simply do not have the resources to carry out their primary responsibility to protect the life and property of our citizens.

Over my two decades and more as an active drinker, and nearly two decades as a policeman, the culture of drinking in India has undergone a huge transformation. It is a lot less frowned upon, and more acceptable at social events in mixed company. Young women are drinking in greater numbers. Of course all this has evoked a great deal of moral indignation from conservative votaries of traditional Indian culture. In my view to use tradition and history to either support or ban drinking is a mistake. The desire for intoxication in some form seems to be an essential part of human nature and the state must tread in these areas with great caution and reluctance. Concerns over public order and morality remain the primary forces driving our excise laws. However there is another dimension. There is a growing realization in Western countries that alcohol perhaps represents a greater threat to public health than even illegal drugs. This may result in a fresh round of regulations regarding the sale and purchase of alcohol. Perhaps such concerns will eventually find their way into our public policies too. Alcohol may gradually go out of fashion. But till then the theka will remain an important but unacknowledged part of our physical and cultural landscape.

KING OF CLUBS

Jairaj Singh

A few evenings ago, I met Jai at 4S Chinese and Thai bar and restaurant in Delhi's Defence Colony. I hadn't seen him for the longest. After draining a few rounds of beer and churning out the usual pleasantries, our conversation slowly veered towards what was buried deep within the pockets of our hearts and at the tip of our tongues, Arjan.

At seven in the evening, 4S was brimming with people, but Jai and I were fortunate enough to find a table for ourselves. Jim Morrison was singing about breaking on through to the other side from the speakers. We knew Bob Dylan's 'Tambourine Man' was to follow (they have only four playlists, loaned to them by regulars, so you can hear anything from pop to EDM to blues to classic rock, depending on your luck, or if you have something to offer).

Mahesh, one of 4S' friendliest waiters, who always takes it upon himself to decide what I should drink, given the time of the year and the weather, was swiftly replacing empty beer bottles on our table with fresh ones. In between, he would come and inquire how we were. 'With you, I feel, I can openly talk,' he said. 'You are not just customers, you're like guests.'

Mahesh is from Uttarakhand, and over the years, has learnt that I too have a home in the foothills. A few years ago, when he would find me drinking alone, he would come over and gloat: 'Surya ast, pahadi mast' (sun down, man from the hills is merry). Nowadays he doesn't like to talk about his village and the mountain life. He's happier instead to discuss Delhi politics, fashion and culture. He says Kumaon, in the last few years, has undergone an ugly change. People have become conniving and wily as land prices have shot up and farming and maintaining cattle is no longer yielding profits.

On the table next to us was a well-known playwright sitting with a team of creative writing students. They were talking about drinking and kids today. One of the girls was narrating an incident of how a Class 8 student from a popular south Delhi school had recently thrown a birthday party and served liquor to her classmates. To this, there was great outrage at the table. One of her companions stretched her arms above her head, and said, 'Guys, please, I went to a respectable school where we started drinking and smoking in Class 12. Not like kids today, Class 7.'

On the table behind us was a young couple. The girl was softly nudging her boyfriend to leave and drop her home. 'Why do you drink so much, sweets,' she purred. 'You can't even get it up after this…'

~

Almost a year ago, Jai's older brother and my best friend died of leukaemia. Arjan and I went to school together. He was more than a brother to me and perhaps my most faithful and oldest drinking buddy. The first time he and I drank together was when we found ourselves finishing a McDowell XXX Rum quarter, ambling down a dusty lane in Ajmer towards school, unsure if we'd taken to the taste. In the boarding school that we attended, during the late 1990s at least, civilized drinking was like an oxymoron. Once, I recall, shortly after we had our 'first real drink together', a few of us pooled in to buy a bottle of vodka and drank it straight from a water jug mixed with Sprite. We then drifted off to our respective houses and were out for the count for the next fourteen hours. It was the first time we went on a binge. I still cannot stomach vodka.

I have been visiting 4S for more than six years now, celebrated three birthdays here. Arjan and I would catch up here after work after we graduated from school. It was a convenient place for us to meet as he lived in a part of this burgeoning colony, whereas I lived in the boondocks, Gurgaon. Years later, when I would find myself landing at his doorstep, incomprehensibly drunk, he'd open the door for me, even though he was sick and undergoing chemotherapy, and ask me about my evening.

In the early days, 4S was an abysmal dive (it has only marginally improved since). Concealed behind two large wooden doors, it was known by a clutch of alcoholics for its notoriously cheap booze; its interiors suffocated with smoke. The small aquarium on the stairs was—and is—home to a few bloated goldfish, appearing forever frozen out of either death or boredom.

4S was never really my favourite bar, but eventually it became the place where I started to drink regularly.

I remember asking poet Jeet Thayil once what it takes to be an alcoholic. He asked me if I had ever woken up one morning in an unfamiliar room with a splitting headache, no clothes on and no recollection of how I wound up there.

I belong to a family where alcohol has been cited as the death of many family members. When I was growing up, my mother would hold my hand firmly and make me promise her that I would refrain from alcohol. In a lighter mood, she would remark, 'In our family, you don't need to drink, son. Water is good enough. You have enough alcohol in your bloodstream. Dilute it.'

Depending on the mood of early evening conversations, a lot of stories about drinking, which I would overhear, would waver between humourous and macabre.

One such story was that of Uncle Bidhi and Uncle D. The story goes, while driving in the middle of one drunken night in search of liquor in Uttarakhand, Uncle Bidhi parked the car on the side of the mountain to take a leak. Now, no one knows how it happened, but the next thing he knew was that the car had toppled over with Uncle D in it.

'D, save the bottle, save the bottle,' Uncle Bidhi hollered. A few piercing moments later, a bruised voice came hurling back from a pitch black void: 'I saved it! I saved it!'

Uncle D was a jovial man, with bright ruddy cheeks. He was kind, good-natured and generous, but on most days, we would find him sozzled by morning. His face would be swollen and eyes, red and rheumy. It was disheartening to see him looking lost and unintelligible, while we would be at the table having breakfast.

Uncle Bidhi, on the other hand, got his name when he was eight years old and was caught smoking a beedi behind the bushes by his father. He was tall, fair and always full of conversation. He could talk anyone under the table from dusk till dawn with a drink in his hand, be it at the boathouse club or in a tavern with the locals. He was also notorious for being spotted walking barefoot. In one hand he'd carry his shoes, and in the other, there would be a bottle of rum.

Together, Uncle D and Uncle Bidhi were the tail of many a tale. I remember I would laugh unwittingly while listening to some of their stories. But today, both Uncle Bidhi and Uncle D are dead and, well, so are the jokes about them.

As I mentioned, alcoholism runs deep in the veins of my family.

One of my worst nightmares while growing up would be of waiting with a knot in my stomach for my father to get home after work. If he was late, it would invariably mean that he had stopped by somewhere for a drink. There was always the fear of an accident or a car crash and several times he hurt himself irreparably. He was an alcoholic and a depressive, words that were meaningless to me then.

At least, he was not violent or abusive. He had cousins, he would say, who upon drinking could very easily pull out guns from the cabinets, ready to declare war over an argument or a misunderstanding. Either way, drinking doesn't need justification. You don't have to drink every day, or excessively, to find out you're an alcoholic, it always starts with an innocent sip.

It takes that one sip to know, too, that there's no such thing as having just one drink. My grandfather would have a beautiful phrase for it: 'A glass of cold beer is divine. Anything after is plain old drinking.'

~

When Arjan left for Pune to study in 2005, I found myself terribly alone. I started working at a newspaper and all the friends I made were much older than me. Reporting on the nightlife beat for a lifestyle section of a leading national paper also opened doors for me. I could walk into any pub or bar and be offered a drink. On one assignment, in particular, I had so many drinks that I shamefully missed the toilet bowl by an inch while throwing up that night. Understandably, I was chucked out of my uncle's home the very next day. My editor, fearing that she could be questioned for sending an 18-year-old for such events, subsequently forbade me from covering the beat.

In journalism and literature, I found people—living and dead—whose tales of drinking were haunting as well as alluring. Both Arjan and I grew up reading the hallowed and depraved works of Hunter S. Thompson, Jack Kerouac, F. Scott Fitzgerald and Ernest Hemingway. The Victorian poet William Blake wrote 'the road to excess leads to the palace of wisdom'. Could I unlock my doors of perception? I wanted to find out.

Drinking, like any addiction, starts with some form of deception, a lie, and for me, it was that I wasn't my father. I could handle my drinks. But who was I fooling? As Fitzgerald put it before me, 'First you take a drink, then the drink takes a drink, then the drink takes you.'

My visits to the Press Club at Raisina Road were as evocative as those Thompson describes in his lost novel, *The Rum Diary*. You could enter and drink rum from those cheap tumblers till your legs weakened, while you pampered a source, or hobnobbed with an editor, or bickered about the trade and the pay. But the club stank like a ditch of so many who had come here and drowned. It also belonged to an older and another class of journalists, the place stuck somewhere between the 1950s and '80s, dank with melancholy, cynicism, ambition and despair.

I was looking for some place else, with life and stories that were not my own. In 4S, I found acceptance, friends and a few glimpses of love.

In the summer of 2009, I moved to Defence Colony. I had just lost my job. The city tabloid I used to work for had unceremoniously shut down due to the first ripple of global recession. I found myself toying with the self-consuming idea of writing a novel. I would spend the mornings writing in Barista and the evenings drinking in 4S. After which, I would totter home to sleep. Once, on the way back, I found a drunk lying on his belly over the stump of a tree. He was bawling, babbling and cursing in the dark. I tried to imagine what was going on in his head. There was just a thin line of sanity between us.

One of the few things going for 4S then was that it used to play songs from the World Space satellite radio station, never too loud to interrupt one's conversations. Girls wouldn't mind meeting you here given that the bar was magically cloaked in a respectable family marketplace. One could stop by for a drink, without making a plan, and expect to find a familiar face or two. If by chance you didn't, a casual conversation over a smoke could easily ensure an invitation to a table, a welcome opportunity to make new friends. It was also one of the first few places I saw in the city where women unescorted by men would feel quite comfortable spending an evening all by themselves. Most evenings, the six degrees of separation would end in such a way that all the tables would be conjoined. Everyone was a friend after two drinks.

A running joke in those days was that 4S was not a bar, but a club, and we were all lifetime members.

The Happy Hours (one plus one, and now 50 per cent off) and the company of intelligent women made it an attractive place to be. Around the time the original Turquoise Cottage in Adhchini shut down, the city's youth felt as though they were sinking in a void, thirsting for watering holes in the city where like-minded people could trickle in and wobble out. While some veered towards nightclubs and lounges that would play club music, others like me, desperately sought quieter places where conversations were easy and the alcohol cheap.

Over the years, there have been plenty of rumours of what 4S stands for, and who owns it. The popular theory is that 4S is an abbreviation of 'four Sardars', based on the claim that it was owned by a partnership of four Sikh men. Another theory someone floated was that the gent who runs it is an extremely wealthy fellow and lives next door to none other than Rahul Gandhi in Lutyens' Delhi. This, too, seems untrue.

Whatever it is, fact or fiction, I have never bothered to find out further. Everyone has a different theory. On its slick one-page website, we are informed that the bar and restaurant had a new owner in 2002, who renovated and renamed it after taking over two of its branches in Greater Kailash II and Saket. That's all the information I need to know.

Whenever I have spotted the owner—a bald, middle-aged man who seems to be a recluse—he has appeared drunk, uncouth and unfriendly. You know he is around when you see the staff hover around the most assertive person at the bar. If you mistakenly walk towards him, as I once did, the bartender will implore you with his eyes not to engage with him. This comes as a huge contrast, considering everyone else here is always so polite and sincere.

4S boasts of a spectacular cast: PK, the Malayali manager with a goatee, is known for his sumptuous beef curry, though it's not on the menu. And, of course, no one misses out on the irony of his initials 'peekay' (drunk). He is popular and I have seen him being invited for weddings of regulars, couples whose love lives blossomed in 4S. Mohan, who manages the bar, is soft-spoken and enjoys sharing quick one-liners. Every time a pretty girl walks into the bar, he will pull the leg of the waiter serving the table she is sitting on, till the man blushes and delays his orders. Chauhan, the guard outside with a handlebar moustache, has a revolver-shaped lighter (and is most grateful when he is tipped with a cigarette). And there's Mahesh, whose famous story about me is how I spent one cold drunken winter evening looking for my muffler along with him, when it was all the time wrapped around my neck.

'I don't know what it is about this place,' said writer Palash Krishna Mehrotra to me on a recent visit. 'Every time I drink here, we end up so late and behave so badly that they have to kick us out. But every time I return, they seem all the more happy and welcoming.' When I asked him if he remembered what had happened on his previous visit, he said he didn't.

It's true: short-term memory lapses occur if you visit 4S often. Once over a conversation, a girl I met at the bar said she would really like to meet me again. The next day, when I called her, she even refused to believe that she had given me her number.

Unlike other bars in the city where fights are almost commonplace, you rarely find people breaking bottles on each other's heads here. In all my years of visiting 4S, I have never seen a fight but once. A young girl was giving a boy a hard time for making a pass at her. The boy kept insisting that he had not, and added, 'Besides I couldn't have…you're chubby and black as a buffalo.' At any other bar or club or in any hole in the city, this would've been provocation enough for others to invite themselves in, and for a scuffle to break loose. But the argument died with a whimper. 4S' dim environs were bright enough to reveal the bemused you-don't-belong-here expressions of its awkward patrons. The company the boy and the girl were with (some of whom we knew) were mortified; they quietly slipped out, never to return.

The crowd has traditionally comprised journalists working the night shift, publishers and writers returning from a book launch or a poetry reading, lawyers after work from the warren of offices tucked away in the residential colony, feminists and gays, foreigners and backpackers, stoners at work rolling joints under the table, and environment-friendly activists, self-proclaimed intellectuals and Twitter celebrities, hipsters and foreign educated-and-just returned, all vying for the narrow strip near the bar when the tables are taken.

Thanks to them, 4S has seen an upswing in popularity in the last couple of years. Today, its customers are also posh. They come here to sample the 'grungy experience' before they head to a nightclub, where the sum of our entire evening's bill is the price of entry. An occasional family will once in a while also slip inside, fooled by the 'Chinese and Thai restaurant' signage, and suddenly you'll find a child trotting about with a toy.

But a quick glance at the tables and you'll find people mostly drink beer, even the women. You can spot a newcomer, easily, if they're caught ordering a cocktail, or even opening the food-stained menu (which is filled with gems such as 'tea totallers' and 'tit bits'). The most common mistake people make here is when they bitch about someone on their table who has just gotten up and left for the loo: you can hear almost everything as entire conversations get lifted and sucked into the air ducts and played out while you're taking a whizz.

The afternoons continue to be shady. Every hour invites its class of sleaze and misunderstood. Every time you visit, a new legend has just taken birth: these days, I'm told, it is an American in his mid-40s who has a massive potbelly and drinks at least ten-fifteen bottles of beer every evening.

Today, 4S isn't even cheap anymore.

~

I have stopped being a regular at 4S (some friends may disagree). Recently, they were closed for renovation. Unlike the last time, when the only change after a two-week closure was new giraffe print upholstery, this time it was not because they wanted to fix their menu, as we hoped, but because the kitchen wall had caved in.

I still feel though, that in this ruinous city, it is one of the few places where you can go and drink alone and come out with happy memories.

Every other Thursday, five of my friends—four journalists and one conflicted PR professional—collect and discuss stories, offer unsolicited leads, muse about the trade and attempt to unravel some of life's many unravelling mysteries. I don't make it so often. But every time I do, I miss Arjan. I am also reminded of what an old loved one would say, no matter how down and out you get: 'May the 4S be with you.'

The Bootlegger and the Bandicoot

Arunabh Saikia

'The fog has come to Delhi from Calcutta, via Benares—it was never there when I came to Delhi from Pakistan in 1947. I was twenty-two, fair and fat then.'

The latter bit of information is not new. Shanti Devi repeats it verbatim each time I am at her house, drinking Murthal No. 1, diluted by copious quantities of Lemon No. 1, from a chipped chai glass, sitting on a broken chair that defies all possible laws of physics—much like Shanti Devi's one-room house itself.

The first part, though, is new—and, it turns out, fairly accurate too.

A 2011 *New York Times* report titled, 'What's Behind Delhi's Fogged In Flights?' quotes 'the top official' of the Directorate General of Civil Aviation saying that Delhi's annual fog mayhem is a recent phenomenon, perhaps as recent as 1999.

But then I should have expected it. Accuracy is never much of a concern with Shanti Devi.

She remembers the chronology of the Gandhis' (or the Nehrus, if you like) deaths—*first badmash Sanjay, then Indira and then Rajiv*. She remembers Rajiv Gandhi's blood-soaked shoes (the Lotto sneakers he was wearing when he was blown up by a suicide bomber, continue to be on display at the Indira Gandhi Memorial Museum at Safdarjung Road). 'We had taken the 212 to attend the cremation. He had big feet, I cried when I saw his shoes—the blood was still fresh.'

Shanti Devi, though, is not willing to accept that Indira Gandhi died in 1984, and not 1987—'What do you know? You were not even a thought then.'

It's wiser not to persist. Shanti Devi is proud of her memory—*I can't see and hear properly but I remember everything*—and I could live with Indira Gandhi dying three years later than she actually did. Particularly, when it's past 10 p.m. and Shanti Devi's fuse is shorter than Virat Kohli's.

'Don't come here so late. The cold makes my fingers hurt.'

They must really do, for Shanti Devi's hands with their long frail fingers are a wobbly mess when she drains the full bottle of Murthal No. 1 into a quarter bottle through a funnel for me. The whisky spills all over, and Murthal No. 1's peculiar smells—it is one of those smells, like fresh paint, which is not offensive as such, but you can only stand it for so long—is all over the Shanti Devi house bar. But it's a minor glitch. Shanti Devi is in control otherwise. She has been in control since 1996—the year the Shanti Devi house bar was set up, after Pradhan-ji, Shanti Devi's husband, died in his sleep.

~

It is on a bright autumn morning, a day after Diwali, that I first go to the Sansi colony near Majnu Ka Tila in Delhi's northern district. There are stray news reports about 'communal violence' in two localities of the city—Trilokpuri and Majnu Ka Tila—the previous night. My editor at the news website I work for, wants me to go find out what's happening. I head to Majnu Ka Tila first and after some asking around, find myself near the Mother Dairy booth, where the alleged 'communal violence' had taken place. Except for a few broken bottles, there's nothing much to suggest any turbulence, and one of the cops stationed there, tells me what the *Times of India* also said—'Situation under control now.'

Situations-under-control don't augur well for the kind of comprehensive follow-up report my editor wants. The beat constable, though, is in no mood to recap a narrative he must have repeated ad nauseam, and directs me to the Valmiki colony skirting the main road.

The Valmikis are having a post-mortem community meeting. I get easy access to it, courtesy my press card. From what I gather after more than half an hour of listening and nodding my head to everything they say, it is a classic street fight.

A bunch of firecracker-bursting kids from the Valmiki community annoy a set of drunks from the Sansi colony across the road. The Valmiki kids get roughed up, they come back and complain to more powerful friends, who then set out to avenge. There's some stone pelting from both sides, but soon better sense prevails, and things calm down on their own accord.

Standard North Indian Diwali fare.

The fact that the Sansis too are a Scheduled Caste like the Valmikis, it seems, helps the situation cool down faster (in Trilokpuri, clashes had begun in similar fashion, but ended up in a whole week of Section 144, because it involved two different religions).

However, the Valmikis are still annoyed. 'We are honest hard-working people. Look at the Sansis—their women sell alcohol and their bodies. That's the only thing they know. We can't keep cleaning up their shit, we have had enough,' says a young man who teaches in the nearby government school.

Although the portrayal is unfairly exaggerated, the young teacher is hardly to be blamed.

The Sansis are a victim of one of the most barbaric legislations of the British—the Criminal Tribe Acts of 1871—the unfortunate legacy of which continues to distort perceptions of entire tribes even now.

While introducing the act, a government official by the name of T.V. Stephens had famously said, '…people from time immemorial have been pursuing the caste system defined job-positions: weaving, carpentry and such were hereditary jobs. So there must have been hereditary criminals also who pursued their forefathers' profession.'

It was ridiculous oversimplification of India's caste dynamics but it went well with the British obsession then—administrative ease.

The Brits wanted loyalty and it was difficult to get it from people who didn't follow conventional practices, like many of the nomadic tribes such as the Sansis (who by then were scattered around Rajasthan, Gujarat and undivided Punjab). The easiest way to keep track and tab was a stringent law that mandated every nomadic tribal to register with the local police. So, for the sake of administrative ease, was born the Criminal Tribe Acts, which criminalized almost 150 tribes.

The Indian government repealed the Acts in 1952. The Sansis were no longer 'criminal'. Instead, now they are a vimukta jati—a denotified tribe.

Eighty years of baggage, though, doesn't go away with a change of name. It keeps coming back, often in unexpected ways, as it just did, almost innocuously, in the form of the teacher's description.

It is perhaps this stigma of years that has resulted in men taking to the bottle and cheap drugs like low-grade smack, and turning into unproductive louts in the Sansi colony of Majnu Ka Tila.

And as the men while away their time getting high, the women get other men high to bring food—and more alcohol—to the table.

The current headman of the colony, who I meet to get the 'other side' of the story, agrees. 'Yes there's a problem, there's too much of nasha here.'

It is the headman's son, who, a few days later, introduces me to Shanti Devi. He calls himself an Aam Aadmi Party volunteer. 'I want to rid this colony of nasha,' he tells me, as he leads me to her house

~

Shanti Devi is severely underdressed the first time I meet her. It's a cold December night and Delhi is in the middle of what they call a 'cold wave'. Wrapped in a light shawl that could do well with a wash, she is shivering, as she asks me what I want. The first thing I notice about Shanti Devi is her height. In spite of a pronounced hunch, she is almost as tall as me—and I am an inch or two taller than the average Indian male. She has big eyes and prominent cheekbones accentuated by the lack of flesh on her face. She wears big earrings (silver, which has turned black) that make her earlobes hang. Shanti Devi, at twenty-two, 'fat and fair', must have been an attractive woman.

Now, at eighty-nine, she has a body many 22-year-olds would kill for. Only that, I suspect, she'd rather be fat and fair, and have some more flesh around her long frail fingers so that the cold didn't hurt the bones so easily.

During the first few drinking sessions at Shanti Devi's, communicating is a problem. She can't hear most of what I say. Her hearing-aid machine has broken, and the chemist, she tells me, wants an advance of Rs 1,200 before he orders a new one. 'I've told him to bugger off; get the machine first, and then I pay. As it is, there is very little I want to hear from people,' she says disdainfully.

From then on, I stick to what seems like a behavioural brief from Shanti Devi—*Talk less, I'll do the talking*. Shanti Devi talks, I listen and only occasionally interrupt her for a refill of the Murthal. It works really well.

Later, I realize that this is, in fact, the USP of the Shanti Devi house bar. It's one of those places where you go when you want a drink and nothing else. Partly because it is small, and partly because Shanti Devi doesn't expect any reciprocation in terms of conversation, the Shanti Devi house bar is popular with people who just want to have a drink or two and do their own thing (mostly truck drivers from the nearby depot, who want to unwind after a long journey). If you want loud and fun, you go to one of the younger women. Shanti Devi's is when you want to have your Murthal No. 1 in peace, with perhaps a plate of momos bought from the adjacent Tibetan refugee colony.

~

When Shanti Devi's husband dies in his sleep in 1996, and his Rs 450 monthly pension that he is entitled to by virtue of being a former Indian Railways coach cleaner suddenly stops, she decides she'll start doing what all the other women around her did—sell alcohol.

However, getting the logistics in place is an issue. Shanti Devi doesn't have the male support system that the bootlegging business worked around in the colony.

The modus operandi is simple: the men in the family work out an arrangement with the government theka near the truck depot on the bank of the Yamuna to procure booze in large quantities at rates marginally less than the retail price. The business model runs on an extremely tight margin—the alcohol is sold by the women at only slightly higher rates than the theka in the house bars of the Sansi colony—and since successful business entails loyal patronage, courtesy calls for some free munchies to customers too.

Shanti Devi doesn't know any men who would do that for her. She didn't bear Pradhan-ji any children.

Pradhan-ji's sons (one of whom stays next door with his wife) are from another woman. Her step daughter-in-law runs a similar establishment next door and is direct competition.

Shanti Devi pulls it off nonetheless.

There is always someone who does the procuring for her. Now, it's one of her step grandsons—a quiet young boy who doesn't look a day older than twenty. He is protective of his grandmother and doesn't like me hanging around with her beyond 10 p.m. He is suspicious of me—and I return the favour.

One night, when I overstay, he is particularly annoyed. It's well past 10.30 when he arrives to see me and a friend nursing a drink each. He has got something for Shanti Devi, wrapped in a polybag, which she is eager to check out, but he makes it amply clear that she shouldn't in front of us.

Shanti Devi throws us out soon.

I am cursing both grandmother and grandson on my way out, telling my friend that the guy probably wants to poison the old lady, and rob her. Just as I step out of the narrow lanes of the colony to the Outer Ring Road, I realize that my wallet is missing. 'That's why the bastard wanted us out so desperately,' I swear.

As we rush back into the dark lanes of the colony, we are face to face with Mr I-am-perpetually-grumpy. He has come running behind us with my wallet, which had evidently fallen out of my jacket pocket. 'You should be more careful,' he says in the most matter-of-fact manner. I mumble a thank you and head out as urgently as I had come.

The next day, Shanti Devi tells me it was his birthday the previous day. In the polythene, he had saved her some of the birthday cake his friends had gotten him. 'He was too embarrassed to let you guys know that it was his birthday.'

No, we don't raise a toast to him, but we could have, in hindsight.

~

Drinking is a ritual—every serious drinker knows it. Going to a South Delhi pub that furiously switches between Dire Straits and Lady Gaga, and sharing a pitcher of watery beer among four people with French fries is not drinking. It's at best an attempt, but it is far from the real thing. *Ambience* drinking—where you care for the surroundings more than the poison—can never be.

Serious drinking involves a certain method to the madness—you break the seal of the bottle, rotate the now loose cap anti-clockwise and pour the alcohol into each of the glasses with clinical precision. Measures are important; it lends a sense of equality and democracy to all drinking partners.

Shanti Devi, of course, plays by the rulebook. Each time I go, she brings out a new bottle of Murthal No. 1, but is careful to ensure I don't get to see her reserve stock. She uncorks the bottle with a rusted kitchen knife, pours a drop of the pale golden liquid onto her index finger, and then touches her forehead with the finger. Following that, she pours some more into the cap of the bottle and sprinkles it on the floor—a mark of obeisance to the holy liquid. Then she produces a funnel to drain a quarter bottle's worth of alcohol into another bottle for me. The last step is perhaps somewhat futile, considering her shaky hands defy the point of the funnel, but it's a ritual. When she had stronger hands, and Delhi's cold was not so harsh, the funnel would guarantee no wastage. But that's the point of a ritual—you follow it, without questioning frivolous things like practicality. It adds a sense of seriousness to the drinking exercise that a drinker appreciates.

Drinking at the Shanti Devi house bar is not ambience drinking. There's no music, no mood, none of that flippant nonsense. The walls don't have anarchist graffiti or life-size cutouts of Jim Morrison and Bob Marley. There are no fancy comfortable colourful couches—you sit on the floor or on a single broken chair. One of the walls, which I once dream about giving way and crushing all of us, has two framed photographs though—one of Rajiv Gandhi, and the other of Guru Nanak and Guru Govind Singh. All three look solemn. Also, there are no French fries or cheesy nachos.

But then if you think munchies too are an imperative for a rounded drinking experience, Shanti Devi will give you that too—and without you having to pay anything extra.

When you're nursing your first drink, Shanti Devi will give you namkeen (which would usually be flakes of fried gram flour). The first serving is voluntary, and any refill is strictly contingent on Shanti Devi's mood—but then she is a generous woman and you'll rarely be refused. So I was surprised—more so because it was not even 10 p.m.—when one night she says she doesn't have any more namkeen.

It isn't that Shanti Devi is being uncharacteristically stingy; it is a bandicoot wrecking havoc. 'It eats up everything; I have stopped keeping anything edible in the house,' she tells me in her most distraught voice. She has bought two traps, but our Delhi bandicoot is smarter than that. Shanti Devi is a defeated woman when she tells me about the bandicoot's exploits.

I think to myself that it is unfair that Shanti Devi should get beaten by a sly rodent, when she's trumped much stronger opponents to remain, at eighty-nine, more independent than most of my 'I'm an independent young woman' friends. But then you win some and lose some—and Shanti Devi, I decide, needn't lose this one.

~

The next time I go to Shanti Devi, I buy 'Rat Kill' from a shop in the DDA market near office. When I ask the retailer how to use it, a middle-aged lady, doing her monthly groceries, generously fills me in. 'Just keep it under the bed, and you shall see the little rascal dead outside your door tomorrow.'

When I repeat that to Shanti Devi later, she is initially apprehensive. 'What if it shits all over?' I assure her, over a particularly strong drink, that it'll be all fine. Shanti Devi sounds convinced. Convinced enough to let me stay on for a few more drinks at least.

Then Shanti Devi begins a bizarre story, about smuggling gold from Patna to Mumbai, and feasting on puri-kheer to celebrate the successful delivery of every consignment. 'We'd wrap the golden threads all over our body, and take the train from Patna to Bandra. It was risky business, but the Sardars paid really well. I was rich, fair and fat then.'

It's past 10.30 but Shanti Devi doesn't ask me to leave that day.

Egged on by Shanti Devi's sudden exuberance, I drink too much and too fast. I can see Shanti Devi in her golden thread suit, her frail body covered by nothing but threads of gold.

Shanti Devi is Gold Woman. I don't like superheroes. I should leave the Gold Woman with her flying bandicoot.

On the way back in the metro train, I call up a friend. She is on another train, on her way from Mumbai to Delhi, wading through the thick fog of Uttar Pradesh. She is coming back from a conference on cyber law and gender in Goa.

I ask her if there's an old lady smuggler on the train. 'You're drinking too much again, but never mind I'm back tomorrow,' she tells me sympathetically.

I can hear Shanti Devi laughing at her. *Little fool.*

ON DRUNKENNESS

Henry Derozio

Editor's Note: *Published in 1824 in* Helter Skelter *under his pen name Leporello, Derozio's classic essay, 'On Drunkenness', is one of the first on the subject of drinking written in English by an Indian. It is taken from* Derozio, Poet of India: The Definitive Edition *(2008) edited by Rosinka Chaudhuri, who in a headnote to the essay says: 'The personal accounts of occasions of drunkenness and the descriptions of progress through numbers of bottles add a captivating dimension to the text, as the picture that is so vividly and humorously presented here, attains, with hindsight, a certain poignancy in view of the notoriety of Young Bengal's tendency towards drink. The glorification of drunkenness among Derozio's students was legendary, and it is this addiction towards brandy and beer that was censured in the newspapers years later, as well as satirized mercilessly.'*

Sumanta Banerjee in his essay in this anthology tells the story of one of Derozio's students at Hindu college, Calcutta, who turns out to be a teetotaller: 'Typical is the following story about Ramgopal Ghosh (1815-68), one of the brilliant pupils of Derozio, who rose to become a famous Bengali social leader and philanthropist. When one of his nephews graduated from the same college, and yet admitted to being a teetotaller, Ramgopal was said to have expressed his shock and rebuked him: "What a shame! How can I introduce you to respectable social circles?"'

The gaps in the essay are as in the source text.

'Man, being reasonable, must get drunk;
The best of life is but intoxication.'

        —Byron

'Would I were drunk, dog drunk.'

      —Beaumont and Fletcher

I have heard that Drunkenness is a vice, it, if it be, it is one so nearly allied [*sic*] to virtue, that (I have done with Mr Phillips,) I, poor bad mole as I am, have often fallen headlong to the sin, at the very moment that I thought myself approximating to Sainthood; and have been fairly half-seas-over before I knew that I had left the strand. I scorn all palliation, and do not desire to be thought a whit better than I am. I love wine for its abstract and intrinsic excellence; and firmly believe that nine-tenths of the Apothegms that have been written against it, were penned in maudlin sorrow, under the inspiration of sick headaches, and qualms at the stomach. I am a firm disciple of Madame De Stael, as far as her theory of the perfectability of human nature goes, and with reason; for I have arrived at such a state of comparative beatitude, as to be able to discuss any given quantity overnight, and to rise the next morning as fresh as any one-pint-man in the universe. With men, whose unhappy constitutions may be so infirm that they suffer from the effects of any extraordinary deep potations, the case may be somewhat different; unless supported, they may become backsliders; and they doubtless require a few cogent arguments to expose the weakness of their scruples, as well as some exhortations to confirm their frail humanity in the right way. They shall have both. It is a sight to make Angels weep to observe the lamentable ascendancy of matter over spirit in the majority of our species. I know many a big, raw-boned fellow, with thews and sinews that might qualify him for the model of a Statuary's Hercules, but with no more energy over a bottle than 'it had been any Christian child.'

'Claret for boys—port for men—but brandy for heroes,' said Johnson, but I will not pin my faith to the 'ipse dixit' of any man, more especially as I remember that the great Moralist also asserted that the * * * liquor, would drown before it could intoxicate you. So far is this theory from holding good in practice, that I have a distinct recollection of having, in my younger and uninitiated days, fallen down stairs, and inflicted severe injury upon my nose one evening upon which I am positive that I had not drunk more than six bottles. In fact, however, all that I now complain of is an inability to get drunk as fast as I could wish. I drink out of tumblers, whilst the rest of the company are using wine-glasses; but 'tis to no purpose—they are invariably in Elysium before me. Whilst they are gay, I am sombre; and by the time I am beginning to get into spirits, they are all under the table. Amiable readers of the *Helter Skelter*, sympathize in my sorrows! I stand alone in the world. Like Godwin's St Leon, there is a gulph fixed between me and my species; for since Harry Norman married and grew steady, I have not met an individual who can advance, as it were hand in hand with me, from the first glass to the last—from Zero to blood heat—and from thence progressively upwards, bottle by bottle, until we arrive at that happy stage, where as the Thermometer impressively informs us, spirits boil!' Poor Harry! He took to a wife, and to drinking toast and water upon the same day and has never held up his head since. Whether it be the wife or the water that has affected him, I cannot presume to say. 'Much,' as Sir Roger De Coverley observes, 'may be said on both sides of the question.' We were so nicely and equally matched, that by the time the evening was well advanced, I could tell to a certainty how many glasses of Madeira he had drunk at tiffin. I could see if he was one-twelfth of a bottle drunker than I was. He was a nine-bottle man: there are few of his kidney left now. And yet, with all this he never wanted more than two hours' sleep. He breakfasted regularly at nine, and if his appetite was not so good as usual, that is to say, if he could not finish a beef steak and a bottle of French claret, besides fish, bread, rice, eggs, &c, he would say, 'what can be the matter with me? I couldn't have been properly drunk last night!' Excuse me, gentle reader, if I hang too long and too fondly upon these reminiscences of days gone by. I will tear myself from the melancholy contemplation and proceed as I have promised, to offer some advice to those whose powers are not equal to their wills, and who tho' possessing the best intentions, are unfortunately unable to carry them into execution; as well as to others who suffer their immortal essence to be clogged by the weight of the sordid clay in which it is pent up; and where fears of the bodily pain of tomorrow prevent them from participating in, or, at least, from enjoying with zest, the festivities of tonight.

To the first I would say, persevere with resolution in so good a cause. Your heads are weak; time and custom will strengthen them. The porters of Bagdad begin when children to carry mimic burdens. As their years and strength increase, so do the loads which they voluntarily impose upon themselves, until, if like Archimedes they could find any other world to stand upon, they might walk off with this upon their shoulders. Profit by the example; but be careful not to commence **ly or hastily; let a single bottle be the starting post and drink an additional glass at the end of every week; by the 1st of April 1825, you will drink one bottle and fifty-two glasses per diem. There are about eight good glasses in a bottle. * * *until you can drink a dozen of claret at a sitting with ease and satisfaction. It would be useless to go * * *one dozen with comfort to himself, might dispense of six bottles more without inconvenience, and the nights are unfortunately too short in this country to admit of any more serious debauchery. The whole moral beauty, the very pith and marrow of what Philosopher Square would call 'the eternal fitness of things' in conviviality, consists in simultaneous and contemporaneous intoxication; and nothing is so complete a wet blanket to all good fellowship as the unique and unaccommodating sobriety of an individual. I remember being some years ago, at a party in which every member applied himself with laudable diligence to the great business of the evening—the discussion of what a mathematician would designate as 'an unknown quantity' of claret. After some hours of serious devotion to the object in view, we had just arrived at that happy oasis in the dreary desert of human existence, that vision of an El Dorado too bright not to be transient, the state of vacillation between drunkenness and sobriety, when a friend of our host, who had escaped from some less jovial party, came in. We were all in extravagantly high spirits; bad jokes and worse puns were circulating with as much rapidity as the wine; and not an angry, or even a pettish word had passed from the moment that we sat down to table. Yet within a quarter of an hour after the entrance of the newcomer, the whole company were together by the ears. He commenced by quarrelling with every individual in the room, and then involved us all in a civil war. The stormy dinner-party of the Centaurs and Lapithae, recorded by Ovid, was a very jest to it. I, who detest all objurgations, and agree most cordially in the sentiments expressed by Horace—

'Natis in usum laetitiae scyphis
Pugnare, Thracum est; tollité barbarum

Morem, verepecundumque Backhum
Sanguineis prohibete rixis.
Vino et lucernis Medus acinaces
Immane quantum discerepat!'

I remained silent, and endeavoured to avoid becoming an actor in the broil. All would not do; they quarrelled with me for my very taciturnity. Yet the man, with whom all this pugnacious spirit originated, was not in fault. He was, I believe, a very good-natured fellow, and a remarkably pleasant member of society, but his mind and blood were not up to 'concert pitch.' [...]

A few words, in the way of exhortation, must now be addressed to those 'sons of little men who abjure conviviality, because, forsooth, they find that their heads ache when they wake after a debauch. 'Tell it not in Gath, speak of it not in Ascalon!' Are ye so infirm of purpose as to be diverted from the pursuit of what all men hunt in some shape or other; pleasure to wit, by the sordid apprehension of a little temporary bodily pain? I have forgotten, as I have said elsewhere, all my Greek, or I could tell you the words which Homer puts into the mouth of Hector, when he reproaches his army, for their pusillanimity—'Ye,' says Hector, (but *he* talks pure Hellenic,) 'are Trojan women not men.'

'Mutato nomine, de te
Fabula narrator,

Pluck up a little courage, and return to the right way. Make a fair, Algebraic equation of the pain and the pleasure. The deuce must be in it if the satisfaction of swallowing half a dozen of claret is not = to the affliction of a little squeamishness the next morning. But you reason fallaciously. You foolishly imagine, like the silly fellow who is always convinced by the arguments of the last speaker, that because the pain is posterior to the pleasure, it must necessarily overbalance it. In the name of all the Gods, what would you have? 'If two men ride upon one horse,' says the sage Sancho, 'one *must* ride behind'. You cannot be hot and cold at the same instant; happiness must either precede misery or follow it. But if you listen to my advice, you may obtain the former almost unmixed. If your heads ache after three bottles, drink four, and follow my Lord Byron's instruction with respect to hock and soda water as a matin beverage after inebriation. 'There is much virtue' in the recipe—it corrects the acids, and restores the equilibrium of the system. Give it an honest and patient trial; when I was greener in the trade it served me in good stead. Like the worthy Doctor Kitchener, I never recommend anything to the gastric faculties of another, which I have not personally tried, and found beneficial. My friend Jack Nightshade used to drink soda-water at the rate of nine bottles per diem. But then he had more acidity to correct than most men, seeing that he swallowed, with the most praiseworthy regularity, at least as many quarts of claret, to say nothing of a quant: suff: of beer and madeira. *He* was never troubled with headaches; which I attribute partly to his regularity in his habits, partly to his never polluting the neat, genuine liquor by any deleterious dilution, and partly to those diurnal potations of soda-water. He was seduced one day poor fellow! by bad example, into drinking a tumbler of water, and we laid him underground in a fortnight. The Doctors, ignorant coxcombs! swore that he died of a claret-fever; but he always said it was the water, and surely *he* must have known best. There are, however, several other excellent nostrums for obviating the bad consequences of an overfree indulgence in liquor; which pernicious effects are, I believe, to be attributed entirely to the wicked practices of the London wine-merchants in infusing large quantities of filthy Thames water into the unsophisticated creature. The famous George Falconer, of Dublin notoriety, some fifty or sixty years ago, always kept a strawberry in the bottom of his glass; which had been recommended to him, he said on account of its cooling properties, and filled upon it from three o'clock in the afternoon, (they dined earlier in those days,) to the same hour in the morning, not only without experiencing any inconvenience from the freedom, but with infinite comfort and satisfaction.

If the use of wine were a mere invention of modern times, I who am a great 'laudator temporis acti,' should be ashamed to recommend it so strongly. But it is as old as the hills, or older for anything I know, since Job praises it quite con amore. The great Kings of Persia, not of the present or any late dynasty, who are about as mendacious as the generality of Potentates; but of that race who taught their children to speak truth, and to use the bow, (not the *long bow*, I presume, or there would be rather a contradiction between the members of the sentence, a fault especially to be shunned in composition and oratory—an error religiously avoided by my Lord Castlereagh;) were stout men at the bottle, and had very pretty notions of the true and liberal rules of the symposium or drinking-bout. I have a brief, but withal a very sufficient authority for my assertion. 'And the drinking was according to the *law;* none did compel—for so the king had appointed to all the officers of his house that they should do according to every man's pleasure.' Nothing could be fairer, or display a deeper knowledge of the real principles of conviviality. The king did not shout out, 'Mr Cyrus, I'd trouble you to take off your heeltaps:' or 'Cousin Darious, I can see daylight in your glass.' No such thing; they filled and drank as they pleased. But mark I beseech you, the clinching expression of the whole sentence—the word *'law.'* Their proceedings were, doubtless, regulated by the code of the Medes and Persians, 'which could not be changed.' Wise and beneficent Legislators! It will be long enough, I fear, before we see so excellent a regulation promulgated by the Governor-General in Council! But, fortunately, such a statute would be but a dead letter in Calcutta, as there are but few much addicted to any troublesome earnestness in pressing their guests to consume their claret. The good old times are gone by—vanished, 'Like Ajut, never to return,'—when the six-dozen chest was brought into the room, the door locked, (no sober intruders, observe you,) and the key thrown out at the window. To revert, however, to my theme, the customs of the Ancients. The Greeks, both of Homer's and of later times, were excellent boon companions. When the deputation (to use modern phraseology) waited upon Achilles to persuade him to show fight, he called lustily for wine before they were well seated. The hero knew well what was right and proper. Socrates and Alcibiades passed many a jolly evening together. There was no shuffling there, if Plato and Xenophon are trustworthy chroniclers. The Roman law, like the Salic, excluded the women from the cellar as the latter did from the throne, but the men kept the key, and the wards of the lock were not suffered to rust. There Proverb speaks their opinions; 'in vino veritas.'

> 'Wise were the kings who never chose a friend,
> Till with full cups they had unmark'd his soul,
> And seen the bottom of his secret thoughts.'

The words are my Lord Roscommon's but the original is in Horace, tho' I cannot lay my hand upon it at this moment, and I write in a hurry to be in time for the press. It is something about 'torquere mero,' to twist a man about, to turn him inside out (rather equivocal that) with wine, till you could see his very heart. Wise fellows those Romans! But I must pause here for the sake of an argument; tho' arguments in general are things that I hold in especial detestation, because, like the Bank Restriction Bill, they impose a restraint upon the genuine 'circulating medium,' and give us nothing but flimsy paper— or what is still worse, frothy words in its stead. The truth of the Proverb 'in vino veritas' being once granted me, I will undertake to demonstrate upon that sole datum, the superiority of wine to everything under the Sun. No one I think, will be hardy enough to deny, that truth is an eminent virtue; perhaps the most eminent, since without its constant exercise Society would not exist, and we should be driven again into that state of dead-existence in which 'Wild in woods the naked Savage ran,' when the grape was not cultivated, and consequently no wine was made. Euclid informs us that the whole is greater than a part. Now since truth is in wine, wine must contain truth, (besides other excellencies which I will not detain my readers by particularizing) and being the whole, of which truth forms only a part, must, or Euclid has fallen into a very unphilosophical error, be greater than it. There is no quibbling here: a man who runs must read, and I flatter myself that I have made my reasoning lucid even to the intellects of childhood. Let me, however, state the question Algebraically:

A, truth, = virtue. But A is included in X, wine, ('an unknown quantity' mark you) I will allow, tho' merely for the sake of argument, that X, in itself, is valueless;

> but it would be very monstrous if X+ virtue,
> or A, which is synonymous, be not something
> very excited indeed, since it comprehends A.

To revert, Our German Ancestors were not a whit behind their more polished contemporaries of Italy. They always, so Tacitus says at least, debated upon the most important affairs of State over the bowl, and reconsidered them in sobriety. I might, if I chose, (for my classical learning is prodigious) deluge the Magazine with quotations; but I have, I trust, said enough to demonstrate to candid readers, the vast antiquity of the love of wine, and the respect in which it was held by the ancients. Modern times might furnish me with as many illustrations. Blackstone composed his commentaries over a bottle of port; Johnson's affection for good liquor is well known, and *he,* you all know, was a moralist, if I am not; and Addison, another moralist, did not, it is said, reckon sobriety among the number of his virtues (Mr Philips again), if it be one. But a word is enough to the wise. Wine, like Saint Cecilia, could 'draw an angel from the skies;' so at any rate the Mahomedans maintain; and I have a respect for all creeds, that of the Athenian Philosopher included, who believed that 'the glorious Sun himself was (not like Falstaff, 'a wench in flame-coloured taffeta') but a ball of red-hot iron as large as—Attica. Hear Moore speak 'ore Mahommediaco.'

> 'Here sparkles the goblet, that hallow'd by love,
> Could draw down the Angels of old from their sphere;
> Who for wine of this earth, left the fountains above,
> And forgot Heaven's stars for the eyes we have here.'

But I have done: not, believe me, from lack of matter, but from its too heavy press, and inability to arrange it, systematically; for I love all systems, from Newton's of the Planets, to —'s of the Resources of British India. Adieu, au revoir.

—Leporello

ALCOHOLICS UNANIMOUS

A HISTORICAL TALE OF THE FRATERNITY OF AFICIONADOS OF ALCOHOL IN CALCUTTA

Sumanta Banerjee

Let us first disengage the term 'alcoholic' from its rather pejorative medical and socio-criminal associations. While medical practitioners tend to attribute almost every physical ailment to consumption of liquor, the police are obsessed with linking every crime with booze. Yet, both the assumptions have been proved to be fallacious. There are numerous cases of cirrhosis of the liver (an ailment which is usually attributed to alcohol consumption) occurring among patients who had never touched alcohol. Similarly, official statistics indicate that not all criminals are driven by alcohol, just as not all alcoholics are criminals.

Still, a social paranoia has been created about a beverage, which for ages had been enjoyed as an occasional stimulating drink by the common people, and celebrated by poets for quenching their creative thirst. One such poet was Mirza Ghalib, who expressed his desire in the following couplet:

> *Masjid mein baith kar peene de Ghalib,*
> *Warna aisi jagah bata jahan Khuda na ho.*

Please permit me to drink wine in mosques,
Or direct me to the spot where God is not present.

Ghalib found his desired spot in Calcutta, which he visited in 1827. This new-grown metropolis offered ample opportunities that brought together people, not only from various parts within India, but also from different corners of the world, to form a multi-lingual, multiethnic and multi-national society. Ghalib was to write later to a friend, recalling his days in Calcutta—'One should be grateful that such a city exists…To sit in the dust of Calcutta is better than…the throne of another dominion…How excellent are its pure wines and ripe fruits.'[1] In fact, wine was the means of urban conviviality. Among the rich, communal drinking became fashionable within their houses, like the mansion of the Shobhabazar Raj family, or the Belgachhia garden house of Dwarkanath Tagore (Rabindranath's grandfather), where the British officials of the East India Company sat with their Bengali hosts to guzzle sherry and champagne. But one of the earliest institutions of public fraternity among the common citizens of Calcutta was the street tavern. It was open to anyone who could walk in and afford to buy a bottle, and spend hours. Taverns offered a variety of liquors, ranging from the strong indigenous arrack (made by distilling fermented molasses or raw brown sugar) and toddy (palm wine) to the imported claret and Madeira.

Although alchohol had been primarily a man's drink, curiously enough it was a woman who was one of the earliest tavern owners in Calcutta. Her name was Demingo Ash (probably a European or Eurasian). She obtained a license from the East India Company administration to run a shop selling arrack, combining hotel accommodation, sometime around 1710.[2] Taverns in those days, like inns in England, served the dual purpose of a pub and accommodation on a rental basis. One J. Tresham, for instance, established a tavern in Meredith's Lane, in Kasaitala (which is today known as Bentinck Street) in 1758. This was followed by the famous Harmonic Tavern in Lalbazar and a string of similar establishments all around—like Union Tavern and Parr's Hotel among others. Lalbazar in those days was known as Flag Street because of the strings of flags across the road that led to the eating houses and grog shops.

Alcohol Abuse and Criminalization of Alcoholism in Colonial Calcutta

The hospitality and cordiality that the Lalbazar taverns offered were soon to be abused by European soldiers and sailors who gathered here, boozed and fought among themselves. What used to be a congregation of the goddess alcohol's true devotees, who knew how to respect her, and recognized the boundaries beyond which she should not be approached, soon degenerated into a den of drunken criminals who dragged her into the gutters. Sometime in the 1780s, a Governor went personally to Flag Street to investigate into complaints of drunken brawls by the soldiers, and discovered a group of Spaniards, Portuguese, and Italians selling arrack to the soldiers. They were arrested and taken to Fort William.[3] Over the next decades, most of these taverns around Flag Street turned into seedy little joints run by fly-by-night European operators with the help of local touts, who used to lure to these places the unwary young English clerks looking for shelter in the strange city. One of them arriving in Calcutta at the turn of the nineteenth century complained about his plight in Parr's Hotel, where he was served '…a most abominable compound of villainous Madeira, sugar and lime juice, called Sangaree all day.'[4]

Such happenings led the British administration to criminalize drinking. In the pre-colonial days, alcohol was brewed in the rural environs (that came to constitute Calcutta) from a variety of sources— fermented rice, palm juice, molasses, etc—and was consumed mainly during festivals (and not as an everyday drink). These modes of manufacturing alcohol were brought under the strict surveillance of the British administration's excise department, which enacted a number of rules to control the distilleries that produced liquor and the outlets that distributed it. In 1790 it took over the right of collecting duties on spirits from the Bengali zamindars on the moral ground that 'the immoderate use of spirituous liquors and drugs….had become prevalent among many of the lower orders of people owing to the very inconsiderable price at which they were manufactured and sold…'[5] Intent on increasing its revenue through a centralized system, the government first granted licenses to local entrepreneurs to set up distilleries in large towns and fixed high rates of taxes and high prices of liquor. Brewers and consumers who could not afford to meet the stringent financial demands of the administration were forced into the underworld and became branded as criminals. A latter day

British official was to admit that the centralized system of distilleries 'had been found in practice to lead to fraud, to loss of revenue, and to the demoralization of the subordinate officers, without affording any check on consumption.'[6]

The colonial administration was thus trapped by its own excise policies. It did not want to give up its monopoly over alcohol which yielded revenue, but could not prevent its manufacture and distribution through the subterranean channels of Calcutta's underbelly. Yet, firmly convinced by its racist belief that alcohol bred criminal tendencies among the indigenous population, it continued with its self-defeating stringent laws. For instance, in 1863, Calcutta's Police Commissioner, alleging that 'a very large proportion of all crime is caused by drunkenness…(and that) liquor shops are frequented by every class of criminals,' announced: 'In Calcutta no house can be licensed, and no person can obtain a license to sell liquor without any (police) sanction…' He then bragged: '…in Calcutta, the keepers of licensed houses look to me, and not to the Revenue Authorities, as the controlling power….'[7] He was however proved to be wrong—as evident from the next part of this narrative.

The colonial administration's tendency to stigmatize alcohol as a source of crime among Indians, could have been a strategy to divert attention from the basic problem. The problem was the miserable working and living conditions of the city's labouring poor. After migrating to Calcutta, the peasants-turned-labourers, to cope with the back-breaking toil in alien occupations in a hostile city, needed opiates, sedatives and hallucinogenic drugs. They found them in the hemp-joints and liquor breweries that proliferated in the murky alleys of the Black Town. Alcohol served a two-fold purpose. One, it offered them an avenue for escaping from their physical weariness at the end of a hard day's work, and inuring themselves to the toil, tedium and utter helplessness of their quotidian existence. Two, it helped them to reinterpret their surrounding reality through visions and hallucinations—taking flight into wishful dreams. Artificial sanctuaries of pleasure were opened up to them, which they could inhabit as long as the intoxicants allowed them to fantasize, before the euphoria slowly sank into somnolence.[8]

Alcohol in the Social Life of White and Black Towns

Meanwhile, taverns had begun to stretch from Lalbazar in the centre of the White Town to the south near the dockyard in Khidirpur. The Lalbazar taverns, as mentioned earlier, provided the European sailors and soldiers with the hot indigenous arrack, and the Khidirpur grog house-cum-bordellos offered them an equally hot spread of women from all parts of the world. These women came in search of fortune, but unlike their more fortunate sisters (who found husbands among the city's European residents), ended up as barmaids-turned-dockyard prostitutes. A song of apocryphal origins, invented later as a variation on an old Gaiety song, celebrated the charms of these women who converged from all over the world at Khidirpur, in the following lines:

> Gone away are the Kidderpore girls,
> With their powdered faces and tricked up curls;
> Gone away are those sirens dark,
> Fertile of kisses, but barren of heart—
> Bowing alternately cold and hot—
> Ste(a)dfastly sticking to all they got—
> Filling a bevy of sailor boys
> With maddening hopes of synthetic joys.[9]

These taverns of old Calcutta primarily catered to the needs of the British and European cosmopolitan crowd of the White Town (the central part of the city where they lived). But among the Bengali aristocracy and middle classes of the Black Town, alcohol acquired a new importance with the introduction of imported European varieties like wine, whisky, brandy, with which they entertained their British guests. This was a part of their attempt to emulate the colonizer's social habits and gain entry into their society. Meanwhile, the Bengali middle-class youth were also getting educated in the Western values and lifestyle that were imparted through lessons in the Hindu College (set up in the nineteenth century in what is known today as College Street). They imbibed the taste for foreign liquor, consumption of which often became socially mandatory, as an advertisement of their 'emancipation' from the conservative norms of their traditional society. Typical is the following story about Ramgopal Ghosh (1815-68), one of the brilliant pupils of Derozio (the radical Eurasian teacher of Hindu College), who rose to become a famous Bengali social leader and philanthropist. When one of his nephews graduated from the same college, and yet admitted to being a teetotaller, Ramgopal was said to have expressed his shock and rebuked him: 'What a shame! How can I introduce you to respectable social circles?'[10]

To meet the demands of this new generation of Bengali middle-class youth of the Black Town, liquor shops cropped up in Calcutta. As mentioned earlier, in order to earn revenue by controlling the brewing and sale of alcohol, the colonial administration had granted licenses to some local distillers, who manufactured Western-style beverages like whisky, rum, gin and brandy to be sold to the middle class clientele (who could not afford the more expensive imported stuff).[11] To be termed later as Indian Made Foreign Liquor (IMFL), it yielded enormous revenue to fill the coffers of the government's excise department. The availability of affordable liquor through these licensed outlets encouraged alcohol abuse among the middle-class youth. Their addiction—unlike that of the lower orders—was motivated, among some sections by the desire to climb up the social ladder through aping Western manners, and among other sections by a sense of frustration at their inability to cope with the pressures of the rat race that gripped the metropolitan psyche. With the latter, it became a means of self-flagellation which led to self-destruction. The classic representative of this latter type of nineteenth-century Calcuttan who had been immortalized in Bengali literature, is Nimchand—the charming hero of Dinabandhu Mitra's play *Sadhabar Ekadoshi* (1866). A bright product of an English-medium school of nineteenth-century Calcutta, fond of quoting Shakespeare, and lashing out at both the hypocrisy of the conservative Hindus and the opportunism of the British-trained Bengali bureaucrats, Nimchand makes a virtue of his addiction to liquor. Barring a few moments of indulgence in self-pity which hark back to his past that held a promise of a better future, he mainly follows the daily lifestyle of a 'deviant'—reconstructing himself in terms of the attitudes, feelings and cultural affinities of a decadent fop who both entertains and battens on his rich friends.

Aficionados of alcohol in nineteenth-century Calcutta therefore could be categorized under a three-tier order, each group differing in their respective impulses and the brands of liquor they preferred. At the bottom, the lower orders visited the grog shops in the lanes and alleys of the city, which served cheap indigenous spirit that helped them to escape from their daily drudgery. At the top, the urban upper classes shared a private and exclusive domain of parties in their residences or elite clubs, where expensive imported liquor was served. The middle-class Bengalis who occupied the second tier between the upper and the lower, sought solace in IMFL, mainly available in the liquor dens of the city's disreputable backyard, from where they used to come home roaring drunk at the dead of night (a middle-class habit that had been the staple of Bengali novelists and short story writers for ages).

Bacchus Versus Shiva—Alcohol Vis-a-Vis Drugs

In colonial Calcutta's world of intoxicants, this generation of middle-class neophyte Bengali worshippers of Bacchus emerged as rivals to the traditional Bengali devotees of Shiva. In Bengali folklore, Shiva had been depicted as a lazy hemp addict who is absorbed in his own thoughts, while his wife Parvati has to bear alone the burden of domestic chores.[12] In pre-colonial Bengal, although rice and palm-based alcohol was in use, drugs like hemp and opium were more common as intoxicants, and their consumers recreated Shiva in their own image as their favourite deity. The reappearance of alcohol in the new form of imported whisky and brandy in Calcutta posed a challenge to the drug addicts. They demarcated areas in the city to separate themselves from the alcohol-lovers. A street rhyme described these spots as

> *Bagbajare ganjar adda, gulir Konnagare.*
> *Battaley madder adda, chondur Bowbajare.*[13]

Bagbazar is the centre of hemp-smoking,
Konnagar of opium pills.
Battala is the den of boozers,
And Bowbazar of chondu-smokers.

The territorial segmentation of the respective dens of boozers and junkies in colonial Calcutta and its suburbs, as indicated in this verse, has a sociological connotation. Battala which covered the nearby College Street area, was identified with the drinking habits of the students of Hindu College there, while Bagbazar in the north was the traditional centre of hemp-addicts.[14]

The other popular haunt for tipplers was the Black Town's red light area in Sonagaji (now known as Sonagachhi). The unsurpassable chronicler of nineteenth-century Calcutta's street life, Kaliprasanna Sinha, while describing the night scene there, animated by a variety of sounds and sights that heralded the arrival of the customers to the whorehouses, added: 'Under the excise rules, the main doors of the grog shops are closed, but no customer ever goes back empty-handed...'[15] Contrary to the Police Commissioner's claim (quoted earlier), liquor was available in this area even at the dead of night. Another contemporary account narrates how a Bengali host, when entertaining his guests in his house in that neighbourhood, suddenly ran out of alcohol at midnight:

> The babu said that he didn't have any liquor in his house, but if it could be procured, he had no objection. A couple of his hangers-on cried out together—'No problem, Sir, as long as you have money? If you shell out the money, we can bring here as much liquor as you want even at this time of the night.' The babu said—'But how can you do it ? I hear that the government is very strict about violation of excise rules. It fines wine shop owners if they keep open at night'...The babu's sarkar (housekeeper) reminded him: 'Sir, they shut their main doors, but keep open their little doors at the rear... (We) cover our faces while entering the shops from the rear doors, finish a bottle standing there, or carry two bottles under our armpits and come out hiding them under our cloaks.'...After this, some of the old hands among his hangers-on...took the money and...at one o'clock at night came back with bottles of indigenous rum...[16]

Alcohol as a Leveller in Today's Kolkata

This tale cannot be complete without touching upon the continuity of the three-tier order of 'alcoholics unanimous' in modern Kolkata.

Alcohol in twenty-first-century Bengali society has been reconstituted in the same class-based hierachical order—from imported and expensive wines (for the rich), to the intermediate IMFL, and down to the poor man's desi sharab. It also continues to be a common source of abuse. The drunken European soldiers and sailors of nineteenth-century Flag Street have been replaced by rowdy Indian upper-class predators in posh Park Street, while the lower-class labourers are driven to drink cheap liquor from illicit distilleries and die in the city's underbelly.[17] Alcohol thus acts as a great leveller. It cheers up its addicts—and distorts and destroys them also—irrespective of class and religion.

We observe a new class of rich Indian industrialists, CEOs of multinational companies and big business houses and politicians, patronizing the bars of five-star hotels like Sonar Bangla Sheraton and Taj Bengal which have superceded Grand Hotel and Great Eastern of the old White Town. The middle-class clientele of journalists, college teachers, executives of commercial firms and advertising agencies, among others, do not have to sneak into the backyard, but frequent bars in the respectable Park Street and Esplanade neighbourhood— Trinka, Olypub, Amber, Elfin, which along with the expensive imported Johnnie Walker and other brands, serve the more affordable IMFL. For the less privileged classes, there are licensed dens of desi liquor spread all through the city's alleys, the best-known among them being Khalashitola on Wellesley Street. It still carries the aura of the 1950-60 period, when some of the city's leading writers and poets like Kamal Majumdar and Shakti Chattopadhyaya used to jostle here with the commoners over bottles of Ma-Kali (the name of Calcutta's cherished goddess with which they had sanctified the desi alcohol). Drinking in such gatherings becomes a ritual of transcendence through long conversations on contemporary culture and politics, as well as jokes, that make the participants feel that they are a happier lot occupying a better space in an otherwise dismal world.

Notes

1. Ralph Russell and Khurshidul Islam—*Ghalib, Life and Letters*, OUP, 1994, p. 48.
2. Harisadhan Mukhopadhyay—*Kolikata Shekaleyr O Ekaleyr*, 1915. Reprint 1991, P.M. Bagchi. Calcutta.
3. Major H. Hobbs—*John Barleycorn Bahadur*, Calcutta 1943.
4. Ibid. p. 195.
5. C.E. Buckland—*Bengal Under the Lieutenant Governors*, Vol. I. (Reprint) New Delhi,1976, pp. 19-20.
6. Ibid. Vol. II. p. 721.
7. Despatch from S. Wauchope, Commissioner of Police, Calcutta, to Secretary, Government of Bengal, 3 September 1863, Judicial, October 1863. No. 92.
8. Explaining the need for intoxicants among the poor to build up a temporary hallucinatory world of escape, the modern Italian scholar Piero Camporesi wrote about the drug habits of the labouring class of medieval Italy: '(Their) nocturnal deliria were piled together with the daytime intoxications and obsessions in order to build a particularly adaptable dream machine...' (*Bread of Dreams*, Cambridge, Polity Press, 1989, p. 128).
9. Major H. Hobbs, op.cit.
10. Re: Reminiscences of Lalitchandra Mitra, in his introduction to his father Dinabandhu Mitra's play *Sadhabar Ekadoshi*, (1866). Reprint, Basumati Sahitya Mandir, Calcutta.
11. In later days, some of these shops were turned into bars, like the one which is situated today in a narrow lane behind Dharmatala Street at its crossing with Esplanade, known as Moti Sheel, recalling the name of an ancestor of the family which still runs the establishment.
12. The domestication of Aryan gods like Shiva, in the Bengali popular psyche and practices, has been explored by the present author in his book: *Logic in a Popular Form*, Seagull, Calcutta, 2002.
13. Quoted in Harihar Seth—*Pracheen Kolikata Porichoy*, Calcutta, 1934, p. 322.
14. For a description of the famous club of hemp-addicts set up by the Bengali grandee Shib Chandra Mukhopadhyay in Bagbazar in the early nineteenth century, *see* Purnachandra Dey Udbhatasagar—*Kolikata Bagbajarer Pracheen Itihas* in *Desh*, 20 January, 1940.
15. Kaliprasanna Sinha—*Hutom Penchar Naksha*, 1861. Reprint 1991, (ed. Arun Nag), Subarnarekha. Calcutta. p. 35.

16. Bholanath Mukhopadhyay—*Aponar Mukh Apuni Dekho.* 1863. Reprint 1982. Pragmya Bharati. Calcutta, p. 15-16.
17. The most infamous instance of the first is the gang-rape of a woman in Park Street in February, 2012, and of the second, the death of more than 100 consumers of hooch in the city's impoverished outskirts in 2011.

On An Odyssey Through Toddy Shops

Samanth Subramaniam

If you ever find yourself on one of Kerala's highways with an hour or five to spare, keep your eyes open for a distinctive black-and-white signboard by the side of the road. This board will have, in its centre, the single word 'Kallu' in Malayalam, and above it, a legend like 'T. S. No. 189', the number being subject to change. If a few kilometres go by and you spot no such board—which in itself would be remarkable—you should flag down the first passing male cyclist or pedestrian and say just one word with a questioning drawl: 'Shaaaaaap?' If it is particularly early in the morning, throw in a sheepish smile for good measure. You must note here that the drawl is everything. If you simply say 'shop,' you will get either an indifferent shrug or a vague gesture towards an establishment selling soap, toothbrushes and packets of potato chips. If, however, you get it right and say 'Shaaaaaap?'—like 'sharp' but without the burr—you will get an animated nod and detailed directions to the nearest toddy shop.

More often than not, you will then drive up to a walled-off compound that has one little structure easily identified as the kitchen, another little structure with bicycles parked outside it, and a number of individual little cabanas. There is, unfortunately, an explicit social code that kicks in at the shop's gate. If you happen to look like a local or a paddy field worker, you will be led towards the common bar area; if you don't, you will be requested, equally firmly, to take any of the cabanas that are free. Mixing is discouraged. If you insist on the common bar for yourself, you will get nothing more than a dirty look, but it will be a very dirty look indeed.

The more upscale cabanas, you will find, are furnished with a small ceiling fan, thinly padded benches around a table, an asbestos roof, and chicken wire windows. Curtains are optional. The toddy will be brought to you either in a pitcher or in tall Kingfisher beer bottles, with glasses or earthen tumblers on the side. And then, inevitably, you will ask for something to eat with your toddy, and thus wander into a whole new subculture of food. The best toddy, toddy that is fresh and untouched by base additives, should taste only marginally less mild than milk, with a slight sweetness, a faint note of ferment, and the occasional granule of coconut husk. When it is collected as sap from the palm tree, the toddy is entirely non-alcoholic, and it is thrown into ferment only when it picks up tiny residues of yeast from the air. Tapped early in the day or late the previous night, it would have barely begun to turn into alcohol, so stories of how, in the olden days, the rich owners of coconut groves would knock back five or six glasses every morning for their health seem entirely plausible. As much as it sounds like an invitation into dipsomania, the best toddy at a toddy shop is to be had at around eleven in the morning.

By lunchtime, the toddy's sweetness will begin to fade, and a few hours after that, questionable practices slip into operation like well-worked gears. A shaaaaaap owner will dump sugar into his toddy to make it more palatable. He will ramp up the kick of the drink, pouring in cheap vodka or dubious arrack or country liquor. Some owners, I was told, powder dried marijuana leaves, tie them into a bundle of thin cotton cloth, and soak the bundles in the toddy. Mahesh Thampy, a friend living in Trivandrum, has heard even more horrific stories, of old batteries dropped into vats of toddy, for the acid to mix slowly with the alcohol. 'You have to remember, most of the people who go to these shops just want to get high as fast as possible and leave,' said Thampy. 'Nobody wants to sit around and drink the good stuff. Which is why there is so much bad liquor floating around, so many newspaper headlines of blindness or even death because of illicit alcohol.' He told me one fantastic story of sitting in a bar in Trivandrum. 'Suddenly there was a power cut, and the lights went out. In the silence, one agonized voice cried out: 'Oh my god! I've gone blind!'

The arrack-mixed toddy, in local parlance, is called 'aana mayaki,' which reassures its drinkers that it is strong enough to addle an elephant. 'It's all controlled by the liquor mafia here in Kerala, of course,' Thampy said. 'Two or three years ago, somebody calculated that even if every coconut tree in Kerala was tapped, you wouldn't get the volume of toddy that is being served in the state.' Trivandrum has its share of liquor plenipotentiaries, including one gentleman who goes by the zippy label of Yamaha Surendran. Thampy promised he wasn't making that name up.

Meeting Thampy was my introduction to a world where, I was told, work stops for toddy. Thampy is a clean-cut, neatly moustachioed man who runs a thriving real estate business in Trivandrum. He has an MBA, and he is intelligent and earnest about his work. But on a Monday morning, he was still eager to troop out of town, onto the highway, in search of a good toddy shop. Indeed, the only person who showed any alarm at all at our agenda was our peach-fuzzed young cabbie, smiling nervously as he examined the prospects of an afternoon of driving drunks around the countryside.

We began inauspiciously. When we entered our first toddy shop, the owner personally came out to discourage us with vigorous gestures from staying, claiming that he had no good toddy on hand. For a barkeeper to turn away paying customers seemed astounding, but it confirmed what Thampy had told me about the rigid product differentiation—about how certain types of toddy are only sold to certain types of people. I had exactly five minutes to mull over that nugget of economics in the cab before we stopped again, at a 'toddy garden' further down the same road.

In one of the seven cabanas with wine-red curtains and blue wooden benches, we were brought our toddy, as pale white as diluted buttermilk, served in earthen pots. On the tongue, the toddy fizzed gently, a mild and lazy alcohol that sauntered down your throat. Thampy sipped twice and proclaimed it fresh and 'very decent' compared to some of the toddy he'd had before. I wasn't going to point out that, in comparison to battery-acid toddy, that was no great accreditation.

Toddy-shop food is strategically kicked into a high orbit of spice, so that customers constantly demand more toddy to soothe their flaming tongues. Our mussels, which arrived first, had been quick-roasted with coconut, curry leaves and coriander, and then buried under lashings of chilli powder. Done differently, in another dish, the mussels looked like giant spiders that had waded heroically through batter only to then accidentally fall into hot coconut oil.

But the staple of every toddy shop is its kappa-meen curry combination. The kappa—bland, steamed lumps of tapioca, tempered with coconut and chillies—is such dense starch that, according to the laws of physics, light should not be able to escape it. It would be inedible without its thin, oil-slicked fish curry that, in happy symbiosis, would in turn be inedible without the kappa. All toddy shop meen curries come furiously red with industrial dosages of chilli powder. In the average curry, the fish is incidental, a temporary tenant in, rather than the owner of, its overwhelming gravy. The question of which fish you would like in your curry is perfunctory and academic; you won't be able to tell the difference.

At the toddy garden, Thampy also ordered a karimeen, a perfectly shaped pearl spot fish that was hollowed out, stuffed with masala, fried to a fantastic crisp, and served whole. 'But this,' he intoned, after two bites, 'This is a fake.' Made in China, did he mean? In a sweatshop, to a template exported from Kerala? 'It isn't karimeen. It's some other fish that they're passing off as pearl spot, and charging pearl spot prices for it.' The dastardliness of it all seemed to move him deeply, and he buttonholed our waiter to ask where our fish was from. 'The river fish is from Quilon,' the waiter offered. 'And the sea fish—that's from just down the road.'

By 'just down the road' he meant Vizhinjam, a port of ancient, ancient vintage, and one of the deepest natural harbours in India. In a smooth crescent of water and shore, watched over by an incongruously new beige-and-white mosque and a church of Portuguese construction from the 1500s, was a swarm of anchored fishing boats. On the quay, outboard motors, pulled out and oiled, were racked methodically like black metal carcasses. Intriguing clusters of cleaned, empty cans of Servo engine oil sat near the waterfront. An auto-rickshaw puttered around, wheezing, while a loudspeaker mounted on its top shouted out the dates of a speaking tour of a roster of Christian priests. It was quite by accident that we ran into Mariadasan and heard his story. In plastic red-and-black slippers, a blue shirt, and a flawless white mundu edged in gold, he was standing at the edge of the quay, looking out to sea and gorging himself on the delicious, salt-flecked breeze. He must have seen us poking curiously at one of the giant clumps of palm and coconut fronds on the quay, because he walked over to us, stood there patiently until we had poked to our satisfaction, and then said: 'It's for the GPS.'

We pretended to understand, but only for a few seconds. So he explained: 'When we go out to sea, we plant these in the ocean, and we track their coordinates on the GPS.' In these bobbing tangles of vegetation, the fish would lay their eggs and begin to lead a comfortable middle-class existence—until, a few months later, the fishermen would return, guided unerringly by their GPS, to simply scoop these residents of suburbia into their holds.

Every single boat in this harbour had a GPS system in its cabin, Mariadasan said, and he invited us onto his craft, the *Julymol*, to take a look. Swaggering a little now, enjoying the interest, Mariadasan hitched up his mundu and began to show us around his compact boat—the yawning mouth of the hold; the giant wad of orange nylon net, as thick and wide as a queen-sized mattress; long bamboo poles with Servo cans tied to them as flotation devices. 'We plant those poles in the water where we have our underwater nets,' Mariadasan said. 'In the daytime, there's a flag at the top, and at night, a flashlight. That way, other approaching boats know exactly where they shouldn't go.' Inside the cramped cabin, Mariadasan pointed lovingly to his GPS, and then in succession to an echo sounder, a wireless, and a CD player. 'Look, listen,' he said, and switched the player on. From tinny speakers poured an approximation of 1980s British pop, garbled but insistent. When Mariadasan wasn't looking, I pressed the eject button on the CD player, eager to find out who the band was. Out popped the CD, pasted over with a label of a naked woman, hands demurely covering her nipples. Very efficient, I thought to myself—two forms of entertainment in one.

The *Julymol* sails with a crew of between eight and ten, Mariadasan told us. 'We sail for about twenty-four hours, to find our spot. Then we drop anchor and fish.' The boat remains at sea for as many as twenty days at a time, by which time, Mariadasan admitted, the first day's catch begins to smell somewhat rank. Then they set off for home, with fish worth about Rs 4 lakh in their holds.

On one trip in 2004, Mariadasan, who lived in Mumbai at the time, strayed into Pakistani waters. At the time, he was thirty-five, and he had two sons in school. 'I didn't even know if I'd ever see them again.' Mariadasan and eight other fishermen were imprisoned in a Karachi jail, and fed almost exclusively on five rotis and three cups of tea a day. 'We were beaten a little when we were first caught, but luckily, we'd just managed to radio out for help before they picked us up,' he said. Ten months later, with some new wounds and scars, all nine were released. Mariadasan packed up and returned to Kerala—just in time for the Indian Ocean tsunami to hit the state's coast that December.

That year, travelling down the coast of Tamil Nadu in the aftermath of the tsunami, I had seen something of its pitiless impact on fishing villages and harbours. 'Was there much destruction here?' I asked, already prepared to commiserate and condole with him and his inevitably woeful story. 'Did many fishermen die?' 'Oh no,' Mariadasan replied. 'It was the day after Christmas. Nobody here was at sea. We were all still sleeping off the previous day's toddy hangover.'

In Kerala, where toddy is as much of a state passion as football or Communism, canvassing views about the relative merits of various toddies is a thankless venture. Every man will have an opinion, for starters, and he will not be stopped until he has expounded every facet of it, accompanied wherever possible by proof of a practical nature. The only vote that approaches anything resembling unanimity is about where in Kerala the best toddy is to be found. That would be in the Alappuzha district, which has long operated under the alias of

Alleppey, drawing tourists to its backwaters as a siren would Ithacans. Alleppey is the toddy shop mother lode, where shops glint like nuggets every few metres.

The town of Alleppey is only a few hours away from Trivandrum by train, but that brief trip may as well have taken us into a different quadrant of the world altogether. Trivandrum was dusty and, even at 5 a.m. on a February morning, sticky and airless. Alleppey, at half past eight the same day, was fresh and cool, newly washed by rain, its waters and trees gleaming silver and gold. It was a perfect time to be outdoors. Purely in the interests of research, though, we were in a toddy shop cabana an hour later, by about 10 a.m.

There is a word to be said here about rooting out the best toddy shop in an unfamiliar town. We stumbled onto the most ideal method by chance—to commandeer an auto-rickshaw and solicit its driver's guidance. The auto-rickshaw driver will be immediately so struck by the appearance of people after his own heart—people, in other words, who will get out of an early morning train, exit the station, and ask for a toddy shop—that he may even forget to inflate his rate. Our man steered us unhesitatingly to T. S. No. 86, calling it one of the most highly recommended toddy shops in Alleppey—thirty years old, plying four hundred customers with toddy every day. It sits off a narrow stretch of a highway, opposite paddy fields with water lilies growing out of their banks of water. Its nerve centre is a two-room affair of kitchen and pantry, and it has four or five cabanas in its yard. It would be too much to say you can't miss it—you can very easily miss it, in fact. But you shouldn't.

This shop's prep kitchen consisted of a couple of tree stumps out back, near a small stream. Having ordered what I hoped was un-faux karimeen, I was shown the gills of the fish, still red, proof that it was fresh. Then our sous chef peeled the fish like a potato, hacking off the scales with a knife, revealing flesh the colour of pale twilight. For the tougher scales on the top and the back of the fish, he used scissors. From a slit, he felt around with a couple of fingers and pulled out the innards, like a magician extracting streamers from his sleeve. The karimeen then moved into the kitchen, where on a ledge of stone, a wok full of coconut oil was already sitting on a stove. Next to it was a colander, bearing what I was told were turtle parts. On an open wood fire in another corner, a heavy pot of rice muttered quietly away to itself.

In this kitchen, I finally had a chance to see exactly how much spice went into toddy shop food. The most reliable measure seemed to simply be: A lot. In a little stainless steel bowl, our chef mixed red chilli powder, black pepper, garam masala, salt, turmeric and water, making a paste that was a dark, brooding vermilion. Into this went the karimeen, the paste worked into its slits with a finger; it marinated there for a while, and then slipped into its jacuzzi of coconut oil.

Coconut oil is a funny thing. Outside Kerala, it is known, thanks to the Parachute brand, as primarily a hair-care product, to be taken off the bathroom shelf on Sundays for a ritual oil bath. In Kerala, it is the frying medium of choice. The mind, of course, knows this vital difference, but as I discovered, the nose does not. When that karimeen hit its wok of oil, there was an overwhelming burst of smell, like an explosion in the Parachute factory. And somehow it smelled very familiar and yet very wrong, as if somebody had decided to make tea with Head & Shoulders or salad dressing out of Brylcreem.

Eyes streaming, I escaped the kitchen into the pantry next door, where, as fortune would have it, the toddy was just being brought in. In most shops, the toddy is stored in huge, black plastic cans that look suspiciously like former containers for kerosene. Here, the toddy was strained through three separate filters, to catch bits of husk and other impurities, caught in white plastic jugs and then decanted into old Kingfisher beer bottles. This toddy had been tapped just a couple of hours earlier, still so sweet that, when it was brought to our table, it managed to attract fruit flies out of nowhere. It was thicker and fizzier than at Trivandrum, backed by the unmistakable aftertaste of fresh coconut, and with only a sotto whisper of alcohol.

The karimeen arrived soon after, brown as toast, wrapped inside its greatcoat of masala, and dressed with black pepper and raw onions. It was a bony fish, but its meat was soft, picked apart by fingers almost as easily as cotton candy. This was magnificent eating—crisped masala, cut by the sweetness of the fish and the tartness of a squeeze of lemon. Mahesh Thampy, it turned out, was right. If this was real karimeen, the fish at the toddy shop in Trivandrum was a certain imposter.

The fish curry, on the other hand, was beginning to increasingly seem to me like an acquired taste. As at Trivandrum, it arrived in seething red attire, and more mystifyingly, it arrived cold—yesterday's curry, with hunks of fresh-fried kaari fish slipped in. The kaari was dense and chewy, its flesh looking like boiled potato. I closed my eyes, dunked a piece of kappa into the curry, and concentrated on really tasting it—and I could still taste nothing but the aggressive rawness of the chilli powder. When I opened my eyes, my Malayali friend across the table had his eyes shut as well. Then he opened them, looked at me, and said: 'That was heaven. That tasted like my childhood.'

Our auto-rickshaw driver insisted that we try one more toddy shop nearby, where we stayed away from the toddy and just asked for any fish that was fresh from the backwaters. We got, first, a plate of fried chembelli, a small, inexpensive fish that tasted chewy and fibrous, like a better class of cardboard. Then we got a hideous-looking fish called the beral. Deprived of its fins, the beral's long, thick body looked almost snakelike, and its face was thuggish—definitely the sort of fish to avoid meeting in a dark, deserted bend of the river. But I had maligned the beral too soon. Its homely features concealed, if not a heart of gold, at least fresh, smooth meat and a crisp skin.

By lunchtime, we were in the poignant situation of already having eaten the equivalent of three lunches. It had grown suddenly warm, my friend's head began to loll in sleep, and I was shuddering at the thought of meeting another masala-heavy product of the backwaters. All three issues were simultaneously addressed by that marvellous mode of transport: The Backwaters Bus. The Backwaters Bus seems to have been created, in some part, as an exercise in voyeurism. With around eighty passengers on board, at Rs 10 a head, it ambles from Alleppey to Kottayam in four hours, through a maze of vegetation-clogged creeks that appear impossible to remember or navigate. But the only time it really slows down from its amble to a shuffle is in relatively open waters, apparently to give every passenger a view of the bizarre houseboats all around.

The most basic houseboats were the most logically constructed ones—long, with a single cabin, and extensive deck space. One level up, the slightly larger houseboats warranted a raised sun deck of sorts, where a couple of lounge chairs could sit on either side of a table of drinks. So far, so good. But then, in a single, befuddling leap, came the top-of-the-line houseboats—raised sun deck, extensive hardwood furniture, baroque cabinets, satellite dishes, and plasma TV sets. It was in one of these that I saw a group of four people, sitting with their backs to the water, watching a golf game on television. Behind me, from the commuters on my Backwaters Bus, there were titters at that surreal vision, and nudges to neighbours to look-look-look. In one stroke, the sightseers had become the sightseen.

It would have been only too easy, I thought, for the residents of this gorgeous district to resent intruders, to be reluctant to share their gold-dappled green waters with anybody else, much less with eyesore houseboats and plasma TVs. But I sensed that nowhere in Alleppey, and it wasn't just the dry logic of capitalism, of how tourism had improved everybody's standard of living. Instead, it tended more towards the sort of benevolent tolerance with which grandparents regard grandchildren with wayward minds. As the Backwaters Bus cleared the open waters and entered a tributary on the other side, a few people exchanged amused smiles, shook their heads in mock wonder, and returned to their newspapers for the rest of the ride.

Later that evening, at Kottayam, our palates rebelled furiously, wanting something other than fish fried in coconut oil. It was a notable meal, if only to observe, in the interests of science, what we ordered instead. My friend, the Malayali, ordered beef fried in coconut oil. And I? I ordered curd and rice—soothing white, free of belligerent masala and pools of silvery grease and shards of bone and the arresting taste of fish. It was heaven. It tasted like my childhood.

The quintessential toddy shop in Kerala is still a male bastion— unsurprisingly, in a state that its residents say is still a deeply conservative one. 'Just yesterday afternoon,' Mahesh Thampy had told me, 'I saw three local women standing at a pushcart, eating a few dosas off paper plates. And people stared incessantly, very unused to even that simple sight.'

But in the last few years, two elevating things have happened. The toddy shop, long a part of authentic Kerala, has now become a part of Authentic Kerala, the tourist-brochure version of the state, and female visitors will not be denied their right to sit in cabanas and order toddy and karimeen. Also, the subculture of toddy shop food has begun to be celebrated, and the food desired not merely as incendiary accompaniment to liquor but in its own right. Enter, then, the toddy parlour. Even its nomenclature is such a far cry from that of the toddy shop that it deserves commentary. The toddy 'shop' indicates the most basic of transactions, where money changes hands, a product is sold, and the customer heads for the exit. With toddy, the process is only slightly less rapid. Few of the paddy field workers, itinerant cyclists or other local drinkers wish to actually tarry in a toddy shop longer than it takes to knock back a few glasses, so that the alcohol can hot up the blood faster and cheaper. The toddy 'parlour', on the other hand, carries the weight of both etymology and custom. The word 'parlour' comes from the French 'parler', to talk, and a room thus dubbed becomes an open invitation to shoot the breeze. But the genteelness and almost Victorian delicacy we have come to associate with a parlour sits amiss with the grime and the focussed alcoholism of the toddy shop.

The two most famous specimens of these toddy parlours, known as far away as Cochin and Trivandrum, sit on the road from Kottayam to Pallom, barely a kilometre from each other, and are bitter rivals in court to boot. The original, Kariumpumkala, started life as a genuine toddy shop in 1958, and although it became known for its superior food, it held on to those roots. But in 2001, when the Kerala government suspended all toddy shop licenses in a brave, and vain, attempt to discourage drinking, Kariumpumkala won through that awful year solely on the strength of its food. When the licenses were restored, one year later, Kariumpumkala didn't even try to apply for one; it had found its new direction.

Kariumpumkala today is a slightly ghastly brick-and-mortar structure, painted in shades of green and pink. Its top two storeys are air-conditioned, every floor is tiled, and the tabletops are made of granite. Over the billing counter is a shelf full of trophies that Kariumpumkala has won in something called the Philips Food Fest. But most heartbreaking of all is a perverse remembrance of times past—a sign that says 'Smoking, alcohols strictly prohibited'.

Kariumpumkala's present owner would talk of none of this. He was obsessed, instead, with his legal battle with Karimpinkala, the upstart establishment down the road that, he claimed, had stolen and only slightly modified his restaurant's name. 'That isn't the real one,' he said repeatedly. But Karimpinkala still serves toddy, and Kariumpumkala does not. That little edge makes all the difference in the sweeps to win Kerala's hearts and minds.

In the leafy parking lot of Karimpinkala, a 'Toddy Shop and A/c Family Restaurant', we found Maruti Swift cars and gleaming SUVs, and cabanas that were closer in size to mid-level dorm rooms. We sat under fans, on plastic chairs that skidded on the tiled floors, and drummed our fingers on a glass-topped table. We were handed a menu, laminated in clear plastic. Apart from the 'Sweet and cold coconut toddy', we could have ordered Diet Coke, Fanta, the enigmatic 'Soda B & S', or ice cream. We could even have asked for that most pan-Indian of dishes, Gobi Manchurian. As we sat staring a little disbelievingly at that menu, another SUV pulled up outside. A family dismounted—parents, little children, and even a grandmother—and stormed into one of the other cabanas. We were, most definitely, not in Kansas any more.

Karimpinkala's toddy, served in small earthen jugs, was thick, faintly stale, and tasted of sediment. But its star turn came in the form of its karimeen polichchathu—fish that was steamed in its marinade rather than fried, wrapped in a banana leaf, and served under a canopy of curry leaves, onions and red pepper flakes. And so I finally managed to grasp the flavour of the pearl spot itself—a tart, citrusy tang, but warmed with the heat of spice, as delicious as a mildly sunny sky. Jijin, our auto-rickshaw driver for the day, had by now cottoned on to our routine, and when we left Karimpinkala, he said: 'But you should also try mundhiri kallu'—literally, raisin toddy—'because that's a specialty here.' Between the months of November and March, Jijin explained, toddy-shop owners slipped raisins into the evening toddy and served it the next morning, when the raisins had drunk their fill and fattened into triple their size. 'Although these days,' he said, as he started to scour the sides of the road leading to Kumarakom, 'people get cheap and just add grape juice to give it the same flavour.'

We found no mundhiri kallu at our first stop, a whitewashed toddy shop set back so far from the road on its dusty little plot that it looked like a Last Chance Saloon in the American West. By this time, it was noon, and hot outdoors, but the shop was dark and cool inside. The day's toddy had lost some of its sweetness by then, and it was bubbling energetically as it fermented. We still managed a few glasses each, Jijin included— which may well have explained his subsequent, intemperate willingness to let us have a go at driving his auto-rickshaw in turns to the next toddy shop.

In our cool, dark shack-cabana, we ordered a couple of bottles of mundhiri kallu, which turned out to be a pale pink concoction, reminiscent of Pepto-Bismol. At the bottom of the bottles were thick layers of white sediment, and the swollen corpses of raisins bobbed in the toddy. It tasted, to my mind, just the same as regular toddy, although the raisins served as occasional happy surprises, bursting with a concentrated blast of sweetness.

'In the villages, the sediment is very important,' Jijin said. 'They add water to it and then mix it into the batter for appams, to make the appams soft.'

'I see,' I said.

'So people come to the toddy shops and take this sediment away. In the cities, of course, they just buy yeast.' Jijin paused here and mulled. 'Yeast works too.'

There was a further comfortable silence. Then Jijin, expounding further on the sediment, said: 'They make a type of vinegar from it as well.'

'How?' I asked.

It was the wrong question to pose. Jijin lapsed into deep thought, emerging only after many minutes to drink more mundhiri kallu. I drank more mundhiri kallu as well. At some later point, the three of us may or may not have sworn to each other to never forget this moment, and that we were all brothers, man, whatever our differences, we were all brothers, well, in a manner of speaking, and that it was important not to lose this— *this,* you know, this connection—never lose that, man. And then we tripped our way back towards the auto-rickshaw, and Jijin drove us to Kumarakom and bundled us onto the bus to Kochi.

Accepted wisdom has it that only in the south of Kerala is the food so fiery, because of its insistence on wading into the chilli and kokum. In the north, curries are tempered with more coconut or coconut milk, taking the sharp edges off the spices. I was curious to see how that principle worked in toddy shops in the north, around Kochi or Kozhikode, but first we had to find some. If Alleppey was the mother lode and the area around Trivandrum was a vein of dubious quality, north Kerala resembled an abandoned shaft, mined clean of all ore. In Kochi, we found one toddy shop purely by accident—in the Jewish Quarter near Fort Cochin, an open-fronted establishment that was very obviously a tourist hook but that nonetheless served some good toddy. Driving out of Kozhikode, we had to look for forty minutes before we found a toddy shop. In that time, in Alleppey, we would have found ten.

The mechanics of toddy shop commerce, we discovered in Kozhikode, changed for no man, not even for a north Keralite. The karimeen curry—or as it was known in these parts, the erimeen curry—still came to the table as bellicose a red as in the south, still singeing the back of the mouth on its way down. The chembelli was still fried in the same masala, and it still tasted of cardboard. The coconut-heavy cooking of the outside world had been stopped and turned away on the threshold of the toddy shop kitchen. The food still left you gasping and sweating, the glasses of water—tinted pink, as always, by a purifying tree bark called Pathimukam—were still laughably inadequate, and I still found myself hollering hoarsely for toddy, for its milky sweetness to put the fire out.

My original rationalization for the sparser occurrence of toddy shops in this region had been the most obvious one: This was an area with a much higher concentration of Muslims than the south, and so consequently a higher concentration of firm teetotallers. But our guide, Madhu Madhavan, a young Kochi-based radio producer of great spirit and enterprise, was not so sure of our theory, so he undertook to interrogate the toddy shop proprietor about it.

'Nonsense,' our host said brusquely. 'The Muslims drink just as much as the rest of us. More, probably.'

As our theory melted into puddles around our feet, the proprietor must have seen our stricken faces, looking like the last flat-earthers hearing about Magellan's voyage of circumnavigation. More gently, he said: 'Well, maybe they do it at home rather than out in public. But they all certainly drink, there's no doubt about that.'

He transacted some business at his till, saw that we were still standing there, and said, by way of coded closure: 'There are more toddy shops in the areas where the Communists are in power.'

This made little sense to me, but standing outside the toddy shop, Madhu interpreted it for us. 'He's talking about the biggest caste in Kerala, the Iravas, who have traditionally been toddy tappers,' he said. One of the proposed origins of the very word 'Irava' is the old Tamil word for toddy, 'iizham,' and some legend has it that the Iravas even brought the coconut palm from Sri Lanka to India.

In north Kerala, the Iravas have come to be known as the Thiyyas. 'The Thiyyas occupy a slightly higher position in the caste hierarchy, and they think that toddy tapping as a profession is beneath them,' Madhu said. There is, therefore, less tapping in the north; much of the toddy that is served near Kochi and Kozhikode is transported there from the districts of Alleppey or Palakkad. 'And there's a rule of thumb—a huge part of the Communist Party membership is made up of Iravas,' Madhu said. Even a body like the Sree Narayana Dharma Paripalana Yogam, a social reform organization working for the Irava community, steadily started, in the 1950s, to lose its members to the Communist movement, as Thomas Johnson Nossiter points out in his book *Communism in Kerala*. 'So the Iravas tap the toddy, and where the Communists dominate, they get licenses easily and set up their shops,' Madhu said. 'I've heard of officials in Irava organizations in Alleppey who own chains of toddy shops there.'

As Madhu spoke, and even later as I was looking up the histories of the Iravas, of Communism in Kerala, and of toddy shops, my mind's eye kept flicking back to that single whitewashed toddy shop outside Kottayam, that Wild West saloon transplanted out of its own space and time. It had looked so basic and peaceful, without a hint that it existed where it did because of statewide politicking and a centuries-old caste system. The confluence of politics, religion and society can wash over every single particle of life—even something as fundamental as the toddy shop, born out of the simplest of man's desires: to get off the road, out of the sun, and get a drink.

Fear and Loathing in Ahmedabad: Drinking in Prohibition Gujarat

Soumya Bhattacharya

In July 2009, 136 people died after drinking spurious liquor in Ahmedabad. A few days after the tragedy (the biggest disaster of its kind over there), I travelled to Gujarat to see how easy it was to get a drink in the Prohibition state. I wasn't looking for hooch—which is what had killed those people. I was looking to find how regular people, those who are social drinkers, manage what we in the rest of India take so much for granted: the pleasure of being able to have a drink with family or friends or even acquaintances or colleagues.

Rarely have I felt so grateful that I live in Mumbai. Well, that's not quite right. I'll try again. Rarely have I felt so grateful that I don't live in Gujarat. What follows is the story of my revelatory journey into the heart of officially teetotal darkness.

~

How odd it is, I think with a mixture of fear and loathing as the plane circles above Ahmedabad, a shining spittle of rain, like a glob of mercury, clinging to the window on my left, how odd, to not be able to go to a bar on the first evening of my visit to a new city and get a sense of the place at which I have arrived.

You don't go to bars in Ahmedabad—or anywhere else in Gujarat. There aren't any. There never have been, in the forty-nine years that Gujarat has been a state.

For someone like me, it is difficult to come to terms with this notion. Gujarat is a dry state. What's dry? How dry is dry? That's why

I am here. Just to see what it is like to be a drinker in a dry land; to see how, if one is so inclined, one gets around the dryness and manages to embrace the delight of alcohol; to carry out my own experiments with a certain kind of truth.

It is also a thought experiment, of making minor, immediate adjustments in my instinctive responses to things. On the short plane ride from Mumbai to Ahmedabad, I am teaching myself to temporarily obliterate from my core vocabulary phrases such as 'Let's meet for a drink'/'What will you have to drink?'/'The Sauvignon goes very well with the poached fish' phrases that are usually instinctive and, well, utterly normal to say out loud, I like to think.

Not so in Ahmedabad, I find. At a kebab-and-biryani festival at the hotel, I know what's missing: the beer. Mindful of where I am, I don't ask for one, of course. I can't bear aerated drinks. I have never in my life drunk so much mineral water as I do during my stay in Gujarat.

The 136 deaths are proof enough—if any were needed—that while you may not legally allow alcohol to be sold or served, you won't ever stop people from drinking it if they want to.

If they want to. If I want to. What should I do, then, if I want to have a drink? Like a participant in a big-money TV quiz show, I phone a friend. 'The bars are mobile. If you can't go to a bar, the bar will come to you.' I can hear the smirk. 'What on earth do you mean? You can't be talking about having booze home delivered.'

'Oh, we have that too, but that's not what I meant,' my friend said. 'Everybody drinks in cars here. Buy a can of cola, take a swig, mix in the rum and pass it around between friends. Even the soft drink sellers know. So they'll have colas ready on the counter at a certain time of the day for some, sodas for others. Drive around for an hour or so, and you're done.'

'That's disgusting,' I say. 'Where's the pleasure in that?'

'The pleasure is in the drinking. When in Rome etc. The choice is to turn teetotal,' my friend says, sounding grim.

That, I find out when I visit my friend at his home, is certainly not the only way in which you can drink in Gujarat. You can drink at someone's home (although it is of course illegal); you can have parties; you can—after a few drinks—pretend that you are not in Gujarat.

But there is always a slight edge of nervousness about these gatherings. In the room, like wispy cigarette smoke, is a sense of furtiveness. Danger can turn up at any time from any angle. A neighbour who is pissed off with you, for instance, might happen to hear drunken boisterousness (or music that is too loud or laughter that is deemed to be fuelled by alcohol) and tell on you. The police—swooping on the chance of a bribe or, failing that, plain harassment—would be at your door in a flash. Things would get ugly after that. This is hardly an uncommon occurrence in these parts. Many people in Ahmedabad narrate such stories to me.

At the end of the evening, we are all convivially drunk and full. I was particularly struck by something my friend said. 'When I go anywhere, you know, Delhi or Jamshedpur or Bangalore or wherever it is, I simply love the experience of walking into a booze shop, paying for the bottle and walking out with it in a plastic bag under my arm. It feels heavenly.' It is so divine a feeling in fact that my friend buys bottles for the sake of buying bottles. 'Sometimes, I will like the look of a 60 ml bottle and buy it, sometimes I will fancy the kind of bottle of wine that I know my bootlegger won't be able to get me and I'll buy that.' He doesn't dare bring any of the bottles back. All his trips, I assume, must pass in a kind of stupor.

My friend, like many other people I spoke to during my stay—and each of who had his own drinking story to tell—will remain unnamed. The police have got very strict since the tragedy. They have arrested 500 people. They want to be seen to be doing a lot. An amendment has been brought to the existing Prohibition law, and the death penalty suggested for those involved in the making or distribution of spurious liquor that leads to deaths.

The bootleggers—critical to the social fabric of the upper middle class in Gujarat—have gone underground. They will surface in a few weeks, everyone is sure. In the meantime, people have the stuff at home. Things change, things remain the same.

'Sometimes,' says someone I shall call a friend of a friend, 'we don't even feel we are living in a state with Prohibition.'

'Oh?' I ask. The gentleman smiles. 'Having a bootlegger is not enough. Having a reliable bootlegger is important.'

Otherwise, seals are tampered with, alcohol is diluted, toxic stuff gets in. I am told of how, only weeks ago, someone bought a bottle of whisky, and had the first sip to find a medicinal, alien taste overwhelm his palate. 'I had to throw it away. It wasn't my usual bootlegger. You need to be careful.'

Mere stealth won't do if you fancy a drink here. Eternal vigilance is the key.

Unsurprisingly, the bootlegger assumes a position of primacy in the life of the social drinker. The reliable bootlegger, well-dressed, polite, often with a respectable job (such as being in the income tax department, say) comes home swinging a briefcase. He has tea. Like a family friend, he chats. He sends cards at Christmas. If he is to be away from Ahmedabad on work, he will let his client know in advance so that stocks can be piled up. Or refer him to a similarly friendly and reliable co-bootlegger. He opens the case, and leaves you with what you want. It's pretty expensive. In 2009, a 750 ml bottle of Smirnoff vodka cost Rs 800—nearly double the price in Mumbai. And the prices vary according to the scarcity.

Thirty-seven-year-old Suresh Parmar was in the business of bootlegging for two years. He got out in 2005. He now runs a business of imported ladies' footwear. He comes to meet me at my hotel, wearing a blue half-sleeved shirt that is unbuttoned to his waist, a watch that is so heavy and chunky that it could pass for a potent weapon and with his feet shod in loafers.

Why did he get into this business? And why did he opt out? He tells me his long story.

'My auto-servicing-repairing business had collapsed and I was in debt. A client who owed me Rs 50,000 was into bootlegging. And got me in. He said he wouldn't give me the money but crates of booze. I sold the bottles to my friends and made a profit of Rs 2,000. I was in.

'You don't need marketing for this business. If, as supplier, I have the stuff, customers will come. Some bribe the police every month. I would pay Rs 50,000 to a lakh only if there was trouble. That is profitable; pay your way out of trouble, but no fixed hafta expense. The trucks would come with 400 crates to the state border. The main guy—the distributor—decided where and how the truck would be unloaded, and who would take the bottles. Twenty guys like me would pick up twenty-odd crates each into our cars. The distributor paid Rs 3,000 per crate to the guy sending it from across the border and sell it to me for Rs 3,300. A profit of Rs 300 per crate for him. There would be 20-25 deliveries in a month. So the distributor would make up to Rs 30 lakh a month. Of course, he had to give a lot to the police.

'I sold each crate at Rs 4,200. I wasn't a huge operator. I would sell 100 crates per month and make a profit of Rs 90,000. I was lucky I never got hauled in. It was useful because it gave me starting capital for my current business. I got out once I had that. It is dirty stuff. I'm a god-fearing man. I have a wife and two daughters and my conscience is clear.'

As in every business, supply-and-demand dictates prices. In July 2009, days after the illicit liquor tragedy, supplies are really scarce. It was like that in the run-up to the 2009 general elections as well. 'The politicians had asked for stuff to be hoarded for them,' I am told. 'Supplies dried up.'

Everyone is in on it. Everyone knows. And the travesty is perpetuated. A senior police official died recently from heavy drinking. The money some policemen get every month from bribes is more than their salaries. People go to posh clubs, nudge-nudge-wink-wink, the owner has a suite ready for them, and they sit there the whole day on a Sunday and drink behind closed doors.

But surely, they also miss the pleasure of drinking legally?

'Yes, of course,' someone tells me. 'There are three official watering holes for people in Gujarat. People in Surat drive to Daman. Those in Rajkot go to Diu. We, in Ahmedabad, head for Mount Abu.' Over there, it's almost impossible to find rooms in hotels just across the border. People sit in bars, or in shacks on the seafront, or in chairs in balconies, and assert their right to drink without being surreptitious.

Four hours to get to a bar. What a life.

Then there are health permits that allow you a quota of alcohol every month if you can prove that you need it as medicine. 'When I got mine two years ago,' someone with a mild blood pressure problem says, 'I had to spend Rs 20,000 in bribes.' The rate in 2009 is said to be Rs 40,000.

Palms are greased for everything. 'The police have a line with the kabadiwallahs. When you sell empty bottles, they find out where the bottles have come from. They turn up at your home, and ask for money. It is advisable to always have five or ten thousand rupees in cash at the ready. Paying people off is the only way.'

There is a reason why Prohibition stays on in Gujarat. Chunnabhai Vaidya, ninety-two, president of the Gujarat Lok Samity, an NGO that works for the uplift of the rural poor, tells me why—or at least tells me at length why he thinks so. 'Drinking alcohol is bad. It is against our tradition. Poor people force their wives to give them money for this and the women and children suffer. Because of Prohibition, Gujarat has industrial peace. There is no labour unrest. There are no strikes. Our women are safer on the roads here because of Prohibition. You can see them out in hundreds, on their own, late at night, during Navratri. We abide by Gandhian values. No drunkard threatens our society's peace. Can you say that for Delhi?'

But surely, I ask him, there is such a thing as drinking responsibly, such a thing as denying someone the joy of having a drink with friends? Vaidya flares up. 'How can you distinguish between responsible and irresponsible? If it is allowed for one, it has to be allowed for all. What is wrong with being a teetotaller? What does he lose in life?' Lots, I think, but Vaidya is not the person to whom I should say that.

Industry estimates say Rs 2,500 crore is lost every year to the state exchequer because of Prohibition. The state government is aware of it, although it fears a backlash from the women voters in Gujarat's rural hinterland (where hooch is consumed widely, but still not as widely as it would be if the state were to be wet) if it does anything about it. The government has proposed that the state's special economic zones will have no Prohibition. It is a hesitant start.

But one does get lucky in Gujarat. I did. Gliding along the magnificent National Expressway to Baroda, the wind whipping my face, I have the irresistible yearning to have a cold beer.

Two hours later, a very cold beer is thrust into my hands. We are at the home of Rahul Gajjar, a graphic designer, and he has a health permit to drink.

Before arriving at Gajjar's place, we have been to the department of fine arts of Baroda's Maharaja Sayajirao University, an old building ringed with eucalyptus trees. Jayanti Rabadia, who teaches there, tells me how he made a mural out of alcohol bottles. Another teacher talks of how some of the ex-students got busted some days ago. They were having a party. Someone—was it a neighbour? Was it some other ex-student not invited?—called the police, and there was a raid. The young men and women spent a night at the police station, were produced in court, and paid a fine of Rs 20 each to be released.

'It stops nothing,' Gajjar says. 'At farmhouses on the edge of the city, big booze parties are held over the weekends. Why, senior policemen and politicians turn up. I have been too.'

His father used to have lavish parties. 'The booze would come in Matador vans with a full police escort,' Gajjar says. Someone else talks about the 'wonderful evening' he had at the home of the deputy superintendent of police in Porbandar. 'He lived on the floor above the police station.'

Gajjar is a member of—hold your breath—Baroda's Alcoholics Anonymous society. I choke on my beer. An AA in a state that has Prohibition? 'Surat has a huge one. There is one in Ahmedabad. Ours has forty members.' Oh. Right.

I want very badly to have a legal drink before leaving Gujarat. (Whether at my friend's place or Gajjar's, I had been flouting the law; I didn't have a permit.) It's like a memento, like those kitschy miniatures of the Eiffel Tower you buy to show that you've been to Paris. I can't drive to Mount Abu or Daman or Diu. I can't get a health permit.

'Just get a visitor's permit,' my friend says. I go for my permit to a legal liquor store in the premises of a five-star hotel. I show proof of my identity, plane tickets, business card, and fill in a form as long and almost as convoluted as the one you do when you are applying for a US visa. It takes a very long time, but I finally have it: a license to drink in the state, within the confines of my hotel room, within the next week. Against it, I get a 750 ml bottle of vodka at almost twice the market rate in Mumbai. (Which is about as much as what a reliable bootlegger—had I had one—would have sold it to me for.)

Ibrahim Ranwala, who sits at the counter of the shop, elderly and balding, tells me with a gap-toothed smile: 'Now you can consume much.' I feel like a fuel-inefficient car. 'But only in your room. Or else,' he wags his finger, then crosses his arms and makes a clinking noise that mimes the metal gate of a prison cell closing.

I clutch my bottle and permit and run. Later in the evening in my hotel room, as I hear the familiar and reassuring sound of ice chiming in a glass, I remember Ranwala's words and begin to consume legally if not consume much. As I drink and smoke and read till late into the evening, I realize something. Even when one can make the activity legal, drinking in Gujarat is simply too much hard work. And where is the fun in that?

Booze, Bollywood, Bombay & I

Mayank Shekhar

'Nasha sharaab mein hota toh, naachti botal.'

—Lyricist Hasrat Jaipuri from the
soundtrack *Munimji* (1972)

Line stolen by: Prakash Mehra and Bappi Lahiri in the song *'Log
kehte hain mein sharaabi hoon'* in *Sharaabi* (1984)

Words mean: 'If booze was an intoxicant, the bottle would dance.'

Words imply: 'If books had any knowledge stored in them, they
would crack the exams by themselves.'

Well, I used to behave like a drunkard much before I had first sipped
booze. Stuff that your friends are too young, and your family is too
old to teach you—films inevitably will. I speak of a world before cable
television and the Internet; I was about five or six years old then.

You only had to be a half-indulgent uncle/aunty type to walk up
and gently request, 'Beta, kuch poem ya gaana sunao,' and I would
begin to stagger and sway with an imagined booze bottle in my hand,
singing aloud, *'Jaha char yar mil jaye wahi raat ho gulzar. Jaha char
yar...'*

I'm not sure what my neighbourhood uncle/aunty types thought of
me (or rather of my parents), but there was just no stopping beyond
this point, *'Khel risky tha, whisky ne kiya peda paar. Jaha char yar...'*
It's a ditty by Anjaan from the film *Sharaabi*. Amitabh Bachchan,
in all-white, sings it with five, as against four, friends in front of his

massive 'car-o-bar' (bar in the boot of his car). The song basically
concludes with the message that a loving wife (Smita Patil) can conquer
an alcoholic husband. Whatever that means.

The feedback I got for my own performance was that I was really
good at this, you know. And so when my mama, my maternal uncle,
was getting married, I had begun preparing steps for the grand brass-
band act before baraatis to the track, *'De daru, de daru. Oh mere bhaiya,
de daru'* from *Karma* (1986).

If I were to flashback to that moment, I really wouldn't know what
to make of this lafanga child in adult clothes—smart blue blazer and
formal grey pants—drunken tap-dancing, feverishly shaking and
perhaps lip-syncing, *'Peena hai toh muh se lagaakar botal peene de
daru.'* I can tell you this. Even at that age, I knew drinking was a fun
thing to do, not some social, health, cultural, economic, political,
psychopathic, linguistic malaise. And it was Bollywood, and not Bapu,
who had taught me this.

Watching the same pictures later though, it kinda became clear to
me that more often than not it was the villain who drank lots—ideally
in his 'aiyashi ka den', surrounded by gora guests and hot dancers.
Inspired by one of those scenes (heck, I'm just realizing how filmy I
used to be), I once raised my glass of water to my brother, and said,
'Let's have a drink'—slurring it in a leery way that only Prem Chopra
could.

Recall Kevin Arnold's elder brother from the TV show *The Wonder
Years*? Yeah that *was* my brother. He blackmailed me about revealing
this 'let's have a drink' line to my parents for at least a couple of years.
Whenever he needed to arm-twist me to get anything done, he'd pull
out the code word, 'SLO (Secret Leaked Out)' and I would quickly fall
in line (of course he held many other similarly catastrophic secrets).

So, sure, there was some shame in being seen as a drinker at age five
or six—at least before my parents. It's while growing up and travelling
a fair bit across east India, mostly Bihar in the '80s and early '90s, that
I began to appreciate how drinking, in most sanskari, shareef, izzatdar
homes and families, especially in public places, was a national taboo.
During weddings and even smaller social functions, the generous male

host ensured a separate arrangement, or intezaam, for drinkers, largely in order to separate them from civilized teetotallers.

The 'intezaam' usually meant a closed-door room, if not the secluded terrace, where bottles of whisky and soda were placed along with snacks for the evening in plastic trays with floral designs on them. The more responsible, elderly menfolk would on occasion slip into the room for a quick tipple as if to check on the arrangements. The family's designated drunks, veteran uncles usually (or the bridegroom's young male friends), would eventually step out of the prison at the end of the night—legs, wobbly; eyes, bloodshot; voice, very loud or very soft...Most of them would have their dinner, and obediently follow their wives to bed. Only the serious family-rejects would appear ready to pick a fight (verbal arguments mainly), calling to memory every injustice served upon them by fate, females, or history.

Being a genuine drunkard equalled being Devdas to some. It signified extreme melancholy and mild depression, at once associated with Sarat Chandra Chatterjee's eponymous hero from his 1917 novel. Few would have heard of Devdas, if K.L. Saigal (in 1936), Dilip Kumar (in 1955), Shah Rukh Khan (in 2002), and Abhay Deol (in 2009) hadn't reprised the same rich brat, alcoholic loser's role on the screen for each generation to identify with.

Devdas isn't the only on-screen Devdas. There have been several others in Bollywood. This central character though was possibly the Indian male himself in the '80s—drowning himself in Shatrughan Sinha's Bagpiper whisky, either alone, or surrounded by other lovelorn friends over a 'daru session', listening to gentle 'dard-bhare geet' about nazar (gaze), jigar (heart), sanam (beloved), aashiqui (romance), and various forms of ektarfa pyar, or one-sided, totally ignored and non-existent love.

There are thousands of sad, nasal songs—from K.L. Saigal to Kumar Sanu, Mukesh to Himesh—voicing this unrequited romance. Booze went well with brooding, I guess. Some of the best booze numbers, whether or not they feature daru in the lyrics or in the movie's frame, expectedly, are serious depressants.

But that's not the only kind of drinking we probably did in the '80s, or even the '70s. Of course not. Daru also denotes class and unlimited wealth and the after-party, following a deal struck between the cop, the smuggler and the neta…How else could you get rich being middle class in an economy growing at two per cent Hindu rate anyway? By passing the Bank PO (probationary officer) exam? And who *were* these rich people? Royal highnesses and princes? Maybe. Second or third generation Marwari sethjis? That's ghastly. CEOs? Of what—public sector companies?

Our access to more affluent, western societies and their sophisticated products was limited to start with. From the ideal position of the front stall of a cinema hall, Bollywood helped us reimagine the filthy rich: The aged man ('Loin' Ajit, quite often) in his massive mansion. Dressed in maroon silk brocade dressing gown. Walking down one of his twin spiral staircases. Cigar between his lips. Whisky in a thick cut-glass in his hand. Now that's what you call super-rich, the 'aiyaash'. You could spot other alcohol brands here and there at his home. But Vat 69 was suitably the world's finest nectar that money could buy. This was in the '70s.

By the late '80s, villain JK (Amrish Puri) in *Shehenshah* had graduated to Chivas Regal. Only on special occasions, when he would spot a white (fair-skinned) maiden, thousands of black dogs would begin racing in his heart, and he would drink Black Dog: *'Jab bhi mein kisi gori haseena ko dekhta hoon, toh mere dil mein sainkdon kaale kutte daudne lag jaate hai. Tab main Black Dog whisky peeta hoon.'* Now you couldn't argue with that, could you?

The janta class hero, Mithun types, on the other hand, walked, danced and chilled happily high in the local bar or theka swigging from brandless bottles of moonshine going, *'Julie, Julie, Johnny ka dil tujhpe aaya Julie….'* (My personal favourite from *Jeete Hain Shaan Se*, 1988).

The more genteel leading man sipped what looked like sunshine in a glass (whisky, of course), sometimes red wine, prancing around in a club or house party: *'Chhalkaye jam…Aapki aankhon ke naam…'* Either way, the 'daru song' is a proper genre of Hindi film music. The playlist could run into hundreds of tracks, going back at least six to seven decades.

~

It is only slightly astonishing when you consider that such blatant advertisements for alcohol consumption were being produced from a city, Bombay, that first came under the tyranny of Prohibition back in 1939. This is after the Congress party came to power in pre-independence provincial elections in 1937. Morarji Desai was Bombay's revenue and home minister.

The British lifted the draconian daru law once the desi government resigned en masse protesting Indian involvement in World War II. But then the Congress, this time with the piss-drinker Desai as chief minister, returned to rule Bombay under a sovereign, independent India. Desai re-imposed Prohibition in 1949. Top lawyer C.K. Daphtary (later attorney general of India) famously remarked, 'Now that we are a republic, and there is no pub in it, let us hope we will not become a relic.'

Did we see much reference to the realities of Prohibition in Bombay films of the '50s, for instance? Not that I can instantly recall. Are movies even meant to reflect realities? I never said so. Does a half-nude, dancin' hottie Helen entertaining suited, suave-looking guests with an 'item number' in the '50s and '60s sound like realism to you? Not exactly. But accounts of party districts of Bombay in the '60s (even Calcutta at the time) talk of properly licensed strip clubs, cabarets, and live pop and rock show venues with go-go girls.

This might even be unthinkable for Mumbai, fifty years hence, where innocuous 'dance-bars' with women moving to Bollywood songs in formal sarees were officially banned on 15 August 2005. Sure one can get a drink in Mumbai with much greater ease. But it is still, on paper, a city under Prohibition. The drinking laws are packed with so many riders and restrictions that it only takes one ACP Dhoble (equivalent of a local thanedar) wielding a hockey stick to show party people and bar owners across a sprawling metropolis their true place in a civil society.

To be fair to Mumbai, it is still the only Indian city with a proper dive-to-posh-pub culture. You could walk into a working man's bar alone, order a quarter bottle of liquor of your choice, share the table with five other strangers... Sometimes the stranger opposite you may push his plate to offer some of his boiled eggs. But mostly he leaves you alone. Even while in a crowd, you can be lost in your own world—as you would at the movies.

Nobody makes a big deal about getting a drink. When I moved to Mumbai in 2001, the bars used to remain open all night. Fourteen years later, like at all Indian metros, they are forced to shut around one a.m. But Mumbai being Bombay, the party only shifts underground.

Patrons in the '60s used to drink Coca Cola (slyly mixed with booze) at 'pubs' and nightclubs. 'Aunty bars' were speakeasies of Bombay during the Prohibition era, where Catholic aunties served moonshine at their homes that doubled up as drinking dens. There are speakeasy themed bars shining a light on 1920s America in Bombay—none that recreate its local version as similar tribute. So I don't know what the Goan 'aunty bars' were really like. I can only watch Helen aunty dancing before glum-looking, rustic darubaaz guests—'*Maangta hai toh aaja rasiya*' (*Inkaar*, 1978)—and guess that she's probably in a Disneyland or Bollywood version of an aunty bar.

~

We know that the Christian, coastal male is a drunkard. What, men, his religion permits the use of alcohol, or at least doesn't frown upon it. Even if you've never come across too many Makapaw boys and uncles in real life, you've met enough of their stereotypes in films. This is because they live in sizeable numbers in Bombay.

I work out of Chapel Road, a predominantly Christian colony in Bandra. Walk down its streets, and you might be able to spot fairly understated versions of Jack Braganza (Prem Nath in *Bobby*, 1976) or Morris (Om Prakash from *Julie*, 1975), or the most famous of them all, Anthony Gonsalves (Amitabh Bachchan in *Amar Akbar Anthony*, 1977)—who was incidentally named after Pyarelal's violin teacher.

So yeah, their English is better than the rest of India's. You hear a lot of retro western music blaring out of homes on Chapel Road. The men in boxer shorts and wife-beater vests sit with a drink with considerable ease in their front yard, which is the street itself. This happens in the evening. Even the Bible forbids drinking before sundown. But of course, you're unlikely to come across Michael D'Souza (Pran in *Majboor*, 1974) warning fellow residents with the song, '*Daaru ke botal mein tum kaiku pani dalta hai. Phir na kehna Michael daru peeke danga karta hai.*' I'm sorry but that accent is slightly flawed. As is the point of the song. The Michaels in my neighbourhood do no *danga* that I've heard of. For that you may have to travel further up to the north of India.

The female equivalent of the caricatured Christian in Bombay films was the vamp, anti-heroine type—Mona, Rosy, Lily... Usually Helen, Kalpana Iyer, Bindu... She symbolized the decadent margins of an urban society. She could be a drunkard. The audience wouldn't care. Is that really true? I'm not sure.

Whatever the reasons might be for a woman to booze up and break into a song or generally drown herself in self-loathing, there are far too many instances of Bollywood leading ladies, going far back into the early '60s, hitting the bottle, giving a rat's ass about what the front-bencher thought of her. Too many instances.

The most popular image perhaps is of the sozzled Meena Kumari singing in Geeta Dutt's voice, '*Naa jao saiyya*', in *Sahib Biwi Aur Ghulam* (1962). Both Dutt and Kumari by the way died of alcoholism. Then there's that lovely track '*Aao huzoor, tumko, sitaron mein le chaloon*' picturized on a drunk Babita (Kareena Kapoor's mother) in *Kismat* (1968). From the '70s onwards, leading ladies—Zeenat Aman, Parveen Babi, Tina Munim—were happy doing sensuous 'item numbers', earlier associated with vamps anyway. What's a glass of whiskey if you're already a 'vamp type' and the 'heroine material' too?

Still, you could hardly find top Bollywood heroes, let alone heroines, actively flaunting their drink in public. Same for most sporting icons or industrialists. Serious politicians equally take care. Even abroad, they raise a toast with apple juice for the press photograph. I've seen Rahul Gandhi drink (was it transparent gin or vodka in his glass? He couldn't be sipping on water with friends at Smoke House Grill in Delhi). Publicly I know he says he doesn't drink.

Here's what I'm getting at. Mahatma Gandhi, the father of the nation, was a passionate Prohibitionist. His children were expected to be teetotallers. Most middle-class Indian men in small towns prefer to drink at home, in more private corners. Their women probably serve them papads and pakodas. Tuesday is popularly a day for national abstinence. As are several Hindu seasons and festivals, often officially declared as 'dry days'. Given how much booze has openly flowed in Bollywood—north India's primary popular culture—it is rather odd that they were all directed at hypocritical audiences who saw drinking itself as taboo.

Bollywood has always been better, at any rate more liberal, than India. That we know. My wholly contestable theory is that this very permissive approach towards alcohol consumption has got something to do with the fact that from the '50s onwards the Hindi film industry began to be dominated by Punjabi producers and filmmakers, even stars. Punjabis, arguably the most naturally extroverted community in India, treat booze as very much part of their mass culture. They celebrate their whisky. They mix it freely with bhangra and butter chicken. There is no unnecessary shame attached to a legit social lubricant.

In fact Punjabis directed all the drunken moments I savoured from films while growing up. This can't be a coincidence: Prakash Mehra (*Sharaabi*), Subhash Ghai (*'De daru'*, *Karma*). And the finest of them all, where hero Anil Kapoor challenges villain Ranjeet to a drinking duel to impress heroine Madhuri. Ranjeet downs a full bottle of whisky bottoms-up, and passes out. Anil gets Madhuri. He jives with her thereafter to the track: *'Aap Ko Dekh Ke…'* That was a scene in the Punjabi Rakesh Roshan's *Kishen Kanhaiya* (1990).

It's important to mention here that the bottle of whisky in the drinking duel was Johnnie Walker Black Label, easily the aspirational state drink of Delhi-Punjab. I'll reserve India's national drink status for Old Monk. Nobody does Vat 69 anymore. Not in films. I guess nobody has it at home either.

What the young drink in India, I suspect, has always been influenced by desi pop-culture, or Bollywood to be precise. In the post-liberalized India, the first time we saw cans of chilled beer was when Shah Rukh Khan came down to a pind in Punjab to set up Stroh's beer factory in *Dilwale Dulhaniya Le Jayenge* (DDLJ, 1995). It was the finest product placement ever. Almost instantly thereafter,

I noticed everyone around me holding cans of Stroh's beer at school/ college parties in Delhi.

Punjabi Yash Chopra, patron saint of urban cool, produced DDLJ. In *Dil Toh Paagal Hai* (1997), he introduced two memorable concepts: the special 'amawas ki raat ka Valentine's Day' (Valentine's Day on a blue moon night), and tequila. Yash Chopra was sixty-five then. His movie was aimed at teenyboppers. It was a massive hit. Again I could see school/college kids, even adults at TGIF (Thank God It's Friday, the newly opened American chain in Delhi) sprinkling salt on the back of their palms—between their thumb and index finger—holding a fat slice of lemon in the other hand, knocking back shot after shot of tequila.

You could gradually tell beer was becoming the drink of choice at Indian bars and clubs. How many whiskies could you possibly down before screwing up the next day? Even the goons, Kallu Mama & Co., heroes of *Satya* (1998), guzzled Kingfisher beers. Tequila is much loved still if you're a teenager (because you can handle it), or an investment banker (because you've had a screwed up week). Of course there are far too many options available on bar shelves now. The tongue-twister wine list alone boggles my mind (I still only care for two kinds—red and white!). To drink or not to drink is no more a national 'dharam sankat'. It's a done thing.

Bollywood hoots this from rooftops in its own inimitable ways. Heroine Sadhana in *Inteqaam* (1968) would apologetically reason, *'Kaise rahoo chup ki maine pi hi kya hai, hosh abhi tak hai baaki....* (How do I keep quiet, when I'm still so sober).' The heroine (Mallika Sherawat) in *Ugly Pagli* (2008) has no qualms announcing, *'Mein tully, mein tully, mein tully ho gayi'* (I'm hammered, I'm hammered, I'm hammered). By 2014, *'Hungama ho gaya'*, a song about double standards, daru and debauchery, originally from *Anhonee* (1973), featuring the 'badnaam' Bindu, had turned into a statement on women's lib with Kangana Ranaut in *Queen*.

The leading man doesn't seem far behind. Dilip Kumar in *Leader* (1964) would gently urge, *'Mujhe duniya wallon, sharaabi na samjho. Mein peeta nahin hoon. Pilayi gayi hai* (Oh world, don't mistake me for a drunkard. I don't drink. I've been made to).' Cut to a 'nanga' Akshay

Kumar gyrating to the Honey Singh song in *The Shaukeens* (2014), admitting rather boastfully, '*Mein* alcoholic *hoon. Mein* alcoholic *hoon. Haan haan, mein* alcoholic *hoon.*'

The customary 'daru song' is usually set in a beach or poolside among bikinis, or at the discotheque, packed with pretty young things in little dresses. It's the 'party song'. The track is meant to be cranked up at actual nightclubs with suitably tipsy young men and women vertically expressing their horizontal desires. But most posh discotheques in metropolitan India simply refuse to play Bollywood.

And there are hardly any nightclubs in small towns. I presume you're supposed to blast these 'dhinchak' daru/party numbers through car speakers, wheels in full speed, while the night is forever young—half the booze is inside the driver and his friends' systems, there is always one for the road. This is how the Punjabis I know drink in their hometowns. And they know how to hold their drink.

~

Which brings me to a significantly existentialist question. WTF was I doing staggering, slurring, hiccupping at age five, apparently pretending to be drunk? I've been a drinker for all my adult life. I can't remember behaving that way ever. Nobody I know sways uncontrollably like that when purportedly drunk either. Of course I learnt those kindergarten moves from Bollywood. And those in Bollywood must have learnt it from others in Bollywood. We often associated exaggerations with any kind of acting in Bollywood ('Pitch *thoda upar*,' as director Sooraj Barjatya would instruct his actors).

Be that as it may, I humbly submit that the original template for a strangely knocked out drunken performance, all so common in Hindi films, may well have been Johnny Walker. Mr Walker was born in the early 1920s as Badruddin Kazi. Actor Balraj Sahni, who was at the time scripting Guru Dutt's *Baazi* (1951), first spotted Kazi doing an improvised drunken act to amuse bystanders (on a film set, or a bus; it's not clear. Kazi used to work as a bus conductor while trying his luck in films). Sahni recommended Kazi to Guru Dutt. Much impressed, Dutt gave him a part in *Baazi* and also the screen name Johnny Walker, for brand-recall. So much for setting a precedent for the perfect drunken routine in films, Johnny Walker never touched alcohol all his life. This is a fact.

Film buffs in Andheri—ever so generous with Bollywood trivia (some of it even made up)—tell me Keshto Mukherjee and Jagdeep, the other two stock drunkards from the movies, were also teetotallers. This is hard to verify. At any rate, by the time Amitabh Bachchan played the eponymous *Sharaabi* (1984), he had already given up drinking. Which is also obviously true for when he delivered the terrific *'gandi naali ke keede'* drunken monologue in *Hum* (1991).

Bachchan has been singled out over decades in Bollywood for his unwavering self-discipline. It's unlikely that he entertained the excesses of alcohol anyway. Bachchan's father, the poet Harivansha Rai, had immortalized his society's liberal values through the metaphor of a bar in *Madhushala* (1935)—inspired by Omar Khayyam's *Rubaiyat*. The words of *Madhushala* have traditionally served as a totem for drinkers to justify their own love for booze. Bachchan Sr was himself a teetotaller.

But superstars deserve their tipple. It would be hard to survive the insanity and pressures of their day-job otherwise. *'Haan haan mein alcoholic hoon'* Akshay Kumar, however, has never touched booze, or so he claims. This isn't to suggest that you must be a drunkard in order to crack a drunk character. That's like saying you need to be dead at least once to play a dead man on screen. But personal experiences with severe highs and lows of alcohol ought to help with genuinely portraying a boozard, right?

My favourite drunken scene, unsurprisingly, was delivered by the good drinker Om Puri playing Inspector Anant Welankar in *Ardh Satya* (1983). All that Inspector Welankar does while being drunk on duty is he quietly, equally self-consciously, walks back to his police station. The gait is slow and tentative. He tightens his palm into a clenched fist and shoves it into his pocket, as if firmly holding himself to the ground beneath his feet. In his head, he's flying. The scene lasts for hardly a second or two. You can immediately sense Om has nailed it still. But that was the art-house *Ardh Satya*. Those aren't the kind of pictures that inspire you when you're five or six, no? Thank god.

Permit Room: Drinking in Hindi Cinema

Sidharth Bhatia

In popular Hindi cinema, a bottle of liquor is almost always loaded with symbolism. Depending on the context in which it is placed, drinking can signify evil, moral depravity or a slide into a personal hell. It can also be used evoke laughter, since it makes the drinker do funny and stupid things. If the on-screen character lifting that glass to the mouth is a woman, the viewer gets a frisson of excitement, because it is almost certain she is a good girl gone astray. Rarely is drinking casual, a lifestyle choice with no subtext or in-your-face moralizing. Whenever a bottle is picked up and poured into a glass (usually in close up), the viewer knows there is a message in it.

So when, in *Vicky Donor*, the two ladies, Mrs Arora and Bijji, sit down after a difficult day for an evening drink or three, it was immediately seen as a breakthrough moment. Mrs Arora is Bijji's daughter-in-law and theirs is a relationship based on mutual bickering and bitching, but come evening, and the whisky comes out. The small-scale war continues, but now it is a bit more good-natured and the candid confessions are lubricated with alcohol.

Never before were women from middle-class backgrounds shown drinking and that too so informally, with no moral baggage associated with it. There have been occasions when sophisticated, upper-class women have held a glass, usually in a party scene, like in *Raat Aur Din*, a tale of a woman (Nargis) and her family dealing with her schizophrenia, or in *Waqt*, where a Rani Sahiba, soon to be a victim of a robbery, elegantly puts down her wine glass when invited to dance.

Hindi filmmakers loved doing those club and party songs where posh people gathered to listen to jazz, rock and roll, pop and whatever else may have been the craze of the moment. Set designers came up with outlandish Arabesque or Oriental themes, costumiers let their imaginations run wild and music directors looked all over the world for inspiration. But, shorn of these details, it was much the same each time: dancing on the floor, waiters flitting about and in the background, expressionless, uniformly dull and standing immobile, junior artists holding a glass in hand. Whether it was a party or a night club, a bar was a must-have, with its array of colourful bottles, most prominent of them being that one brand that Hindi filmi villains simply loved—Vat 69.

But while the extras in the background could imbibe, the virtuous heroine couldn't and if she did, it could only mean she had been provoked or had fallen into bad company. A classic example is *Intequaam*, about a simple girl (Sadhna) who is accused of stealing a valuable piece of jewellery by the father of her boyfriend. Thrown into jail, she comes out vowing revenge and humiliates their family publicly, by knocking back drink upon drink and swaying to '*Kaise rahoon chupke maine pee li, chahe hosh abhi tak hai baki, aur zara si de de saqi.*' The obliging 'saqi' is Helen, a cabaret dancer, who too, not unsurprisingly, has her own glass of wine. (The song is also famous for being a rare LataMangeshkar number—she normally left such songs to her more adventurous sister Asha.)

The girl-gone-bad trope was big in the 1960s, as more and more films set among the upper crust were made. The 1950s were all about the proletariat, the downtrodden or the seedy underworld, but come the 1960s, and with black and white giving way to glorious Eastman colour, the movies became more glamourous, more frothy and more frivolous, often reflecting the lifestyles of the upper classes. The one exception was *Sahib Biwi Aur Ghulam*, which was released in 1962 but had a strong 1950s feel to it; for one thing it was made in black and white, but the story, set among the decaying zamindari system, was decidedly old-fashioned. Meena Kumari was brilliant as the neglected Chhoti Bahu who, to entice her wayward husband, takes to drink, gradually sliding into an alcoholic stupor, only to be further rejected by her husband who finds her morals unworthy of a woman of her class. *Sahib Biwi Aur Ghulam* is of course a classic, raised to great heights by the performers, the music and the subtlety of the story itself and is atypical of what was to come in the rest of the decade.

With the advent of colour and keeping pace with an India shedding its colonial hang-ups and embracing fun and frivolity, Bombay producers of the 1960s discovered the vales of Kashmir and not soon after, the mountains of Switzerland and the cobbled stone streets of Paris. Now stories were not about indigent poets or taxi drivers but about rich scions with a lot of jaidad to their name. Their lifestyles included much socializing and club-going and naturally alcohol played a big role in it. The hero was more often than not a model youth, with no vices except perhaps flirting and stalking, but all those around him, whether the elders, friends and obviously the villain, drank with abandon. The messaging was fairly obvious—drinking per se was not a problem, but it was not meant for anyone wanting to lead a pure, virtuous life.

The conflation of alcohol and alcoholism is an old trick in Hindi cinema, drawn no doubt from the country's social value system. Indians don't, or are not supposed to, drink just for enjoyment. Drinking is against Indian culture and brought into the country by foreign invaders. There may be references to somras in Indian mythology, but that was a pleasure reserved for the gods; mere mortals were supposed to lead a pious life. Whenever humans strayed, they paid a heavy price for it.

An early film, *Brandy ki Botal* (1939—also made simultaneously in Marathi), scripted by the witty Marathi writer Acharya Atre, told the story of a man who sets out to find a bottle of brandy and comes across all kinds of characters, among them regular drinkers. That was the period of films with a social reformist agenda. Widow remarriage, communal harmony, women's education—Shantaram and others were committed to using the medium to propagate such causes. Occasionally, a sub-text about the evils of colonialism used to be slipped in.

In the Fearless Nadia series, produced by the Wadia brothers, who made it a point to slip in a social homily or two, the bad guys were usually shown sitting around in bars. Nadia herself, playing a wayward twin in *Muqabla,* is given to drinking and is shown as a girl of 'easy virtue' though in the end she redeems herself by saving her sister's life. In Hindi films then and for a long time after, death was the only redemption for someone gone astray.

In the 1950s, when a breed of young directors—Raj Kapoor, Guru Dutt, Raj Khosla, Vijay Anand—started making urban-centric films, it was almost *de rigeur* to have a scene in a low-rent bar, complete with dancing girl and gamblers. Drinking, however, had to be shown mostly by implication—Bombay, where these films were conceived and made, was under strict Prohibition and censors frowned at even screen representations of alcohol. This continued, in one way or the other, till much later—in a cabaret scene in *Jewel Thief* (1967), the hero, Dev Anand, walks down the stairs to a basement level night club and props himself up at the bar, where a sign clearly announces, 'For Permit Holders Only.'

Not that there was no drinking, but it was portrayed either as comedy—the innumerable drunken scenes by Johnny Walker or as tragedy, of which the most well known example is *Devdas,* based on the 1917 novel by Sharat Chandra Chattopadhyay.

Several versions of *Devdas* in different languages have been made. From the 1930s to the early noughties, the film, with its maudlin and defeatist theme, has found favour not just with directors but also audiences—almost all versions have been hits. There are many ways to interpret the novel, which the author himself was not happy with. Though it is not a direct commentary or critique of the more stifling conventions of the time, it draws upon the social mores of the period in which it is based. Devdas is a zamindar who just cannot find it in him to break the shackles of his class and marry the girl he loves. He runs away and takes refuge in drink. In Calcutta, he is introduced to the city's richest and most beautiful prostitute Chandramukhi, but insults her because of her profession. Both, the noble and golden-hearted Chandramukhi, and his childhood sweetheart, Paro, are props to the weak-willed Devdas, whose broken heart is at the centre of the story. Despite the degradation thanks to his alcoholism, the notion of taking to drink because of lost love acquired a glamourous patina among lovelorn Indian youth. Dilip Kumar at least brought enormous depth to the role and the scenes showing him in a gutter would be a warning to anyone considering drinking too much alcohol; in Sanjay Leela Bhansali's modern take, the dazzling sets, sarees and actors pushed the drinking part into the background. This version was not about boozing, which was more or less seen as a fun activity—it was about song and dance by the two female leads.

The ravages of alcoholism, not just on the drinker but also on his loved ones, were explored in some more detail in a small and long forgotten film, *Sharabi* (1964). Dev Anand, as a reformed alcoholic, tries to put his life back in order but soon relapses, which leads to a broken engagement and alienation from his mother. Twenty years later, a film by the same name, loosely based on the Dudley Moore comedy *Arthur*, had Amitabh Bachchan as the poor little rich boy who takes to drink because his father is a cold, distant businessman. This was no study of alcoholism, just another vehicle for the reigning superstar of the day.

Bachchan's best 'drinking' role is obviously in *Amar Akbar Anthony*, where he plays the bootlegger Anthony who runs a fully licensed bar for country liquor and spends his profits on good deeds. Manmohan Desai based the character on a real-life maker of the moonshine which passed as liquor during the height of Prohibition in Bombay. Countless such stills operated in the dark lanes of the city and the produce found its way to the typical 'aunty's bars' found all over. Though *Amar Akbar Anthony* was made in the late 1970s and the bar Anthony runs is legal, it echoes those downmarket joints, where the grog was cheap and the ambience decidedly sleazy.

But Desai does not waste time setting anything more than one fight scene in the bar. Instead, he exploited Bachchan's comedic talents for the much heralded mirror scene, in which a drunken Bachchan, badly beaten up by the tough bodyguard of his heart-throb, berates himself for drinking too much. Idiot, he tells his reflection in the mirror, I told you not to drink too much—see the net result, you got bashed up. It is an acting *tour de force* which probably does more to warn the punters about the dangers of over-drinking than any abstinence lectures would. That is not its main purpose of course; once again, liquor is a good device to serve up some comedy.

Booze began to make a more regular appearance in Hindi films in the 1970s, corresponding with changes in the law in Bombay. Prohibition rules were relaxed in the early part of the decade and it was now common to see bottles of beer and whisky on the screen. The dons preferred the choicest Scotch (pronounced skaatch) and the flunkeys drank beer, sitting around in their trunks at swimming pools and trying to hold their gut in. But the drinkers were still the bad guys, the comedians or character actors with names like Braganza and Michael. The hero, even if he had shades of grey, remained aloof from the temptation.

~

Drunken villains and comedians are no longer a staple of new Hindi cinema. Contemporary strains and themes—the Karan Joharesque universe of stylish people in foreign lands with their designer clothes and colour coordinated emotions and the moffusil chic of Anurag Kashyap and his cohorts—rarely need the crutch of liquor to tell their stories. In the small towns, the vice of choice is violence, not country liquor. In the cities and in foreign lands, where our characters go at the drop of a hat, the emphasis is on song, dance and romance or on blowing up cars. The buff heroes of today don't drink, busy as they are in the gym.

Their place has been taken by the girls who knock back tequila shots, which is shorthand for fun-loving, modern and liberated. From the virginal heroine of the 1960s and after, who has a momentary lapse of reason but eventually gets back on track to the new breed of shorts-wearing, cleavage-showing party chick who climbs on to tables has been quite a ride. It signals the emergence of a new breed of women, confident and in control of their lives, who can match every drinker in the bar, shot for shot. A perfect companion for the New Age Man, one would think.

But the New Age Man, while enjoying the company (and the bed) of this wild child, is happily still living in the 1960s, when his girlfriend, soon after their engagement, switched from dresses to sarees and covered her head when she met his parents. He is not ready to bring the new Indian woman home; she is fine as is in the bar.

In the 2012 film *Cocktail*, the hero, Saif Ali Khan, loves going clubbing with Deepika Padukone (called Veronica in the film) and even sleeps with her, but then quietly explains to her that he is actually in love with her demure and bashful friend Diana Penty (Meera) or, as he tells his mother, 'an ideal Indian girl.' Meera does her bit to fulfill those expectations. Veronica is kind and understanding about the whole thing. After all, Saif does not want to come home to a wife and have her join him for a drink in the evening.

The *Vicky Donor* moment thus is an exception and one that is not likely to become a rule anytime soon. Casual drinking, among men and women, is a fact of modern Indian life, but our filmmakers have either not caught up with it or don't want to think about it. For them, liquor is a device to signal moral corruption, which can occasionally be laughed at, but can never be treated as just another part of quotidian existence. For all our claims to modernity, that is a line we have never been able to cross.

Whisky Nation

Sandip Roy

'As a boy he'd been terribly scared and contemptuous of drunks, horses and Englishmen.'

—Kaliprasanna Sinha, *The Observant Owl*,
Translation by Swarup Roy

The first alcoholic drink I had was at home in Calcutta. It was most likely some New Year's Eve. The brightly coloured liqueur mini-bottles were opened with great ceremony by my parents. My sister and I were given little thimblefuls of bright orange Cointreau or perhaps Bailey's Irish Cream or emerald-green crème de menthe. Then we all watched the rather staid New Year's Eve programme on Doordarshan, then the only TV channel available—comedy sketches, balloons and the ever jolly Usha Uthup. By 12:10 a.m. we were all in bed.

New Year's had a certain ritual to it. Someone would burst firecrackers out there in the neighbourhood. We could hear the mournful bellow of foghorns from steamers docked on the Hooghly river. We knew that out on Park Street revellers were probably giddily emptying out on to the streets, blowing on shiny foil-wrapped trumpets and wearing silly sparkly paper hats. But as we rinsed out our little liqueur glasses we didn't particularly care. The nights were chilly. The prospect of crawling under a quilt seemed quite appealing. The Cointreau gave it just that little festive fillip. The next day was New Year's. We would likely go out for Chinese.

We didn't drink whisky. That would have been just too adult and too much like real alcohol. The liqueurs had three things in their favour—they were sweet, brightly coloured and foreign. That also made them perfect for a rare treat—a playful New Year's Eve special.

In middle class pre-liberalization India pleasures had to be rationed out and that included alcohol. Once as college students we went out for a big drinks and dinner celebration. Unfortunately we unwittingly chose drinks from the Imported section of the menu. By the time we realized what we had done it was too late. We had our drinks, emptied our wallets and came home for rice and dal and large helpings of humble pie.

The rites of adulthood (or more accurately manhood) were pretty clearly marked in alcohol. Beer in high school. Rum and coke (or rather Thums Up) in college. And finally whisky. Vodka—what was that? Gin—that's what ladies sipped at Calcutta Club. Wine was vinegar.

Whisky, however, was king. Whisky was the serious stuff. Of course none of us knew that we were drinking what Sanjeev Bhattacharya describes in *Business Today* as 'a molasses-based drink which brazenly defies the definition of whisky as a grain-based product—and therefore isn't whisky at all. (In fact, it's closer to rum, not that you'd ever call India a Rum Nation.)' We have Vijay Mallya, the King of the original Good Times to thank for that piece of nomenclature. Mallya has been fiercely defending Indian whisky's right to be called whisky to protect what comes out of his UB Group. (We're talking of the pre-Diageo days here, of course.)

But we kept drinking it. We drank whisky because the British gave it to us along with cricket. We drank it because Amitabh Bachchan slugged it down in *Deewar* while he contemplated the curvaceous charms of Parveen Babi. But mostly we drank it because it was there.

And as we drank it, we found which slot we fit into in whisky's own caste system.

There were the whisky drinkers who had uncle-aunty-abroad who could always be relied on to bring back a bottle of duty-free Johnnie Walker Black Label and a carton of Dunhills. 'Always take back Johnnie Walker,' my aunt in England advised me when I was living in America. 'That's the only kind of whisky they appreciate in India.' We had not yet discovered the alternate status value (or the spellings) of Glenfiddich and Laphraoiag.

Then there were the whisky drinkers who went every evening to the Calcutta Clubs and Bengal Clubs where liquour was illogically cheap given that clientele was among the city's wealthiest. The whisky was served by ancient uniformed waiters and ordered not by name but by abbreviation. BP in those starchy circles meant Blenders Pride, not blood pressure.

There were the closet drinkers at home whose empty bottles of shame were weighed in broad daylight by the kabadiwallah every month. But Indians being Indians we couldn't throw away the freebies even if they were badges of ill-repute. So we all used the Royal Reserve coasters and branded glasses while grandmothers turned the fancier (read imported) whisky bottles into flower vases.

And then there were those who drank Indian whisky in shady smoky bars. They were the whisky riff-raff, the ones who hooted and whistled when Amrish Puri growled about Black Dog in an item number.

The crown for the highest per capita alcohol consumption goes to Kerala—over 8 litres per person per year according to the BBC. The Kerala State Beverages Corporation was the monopoly that sells the alcohol. But Kerala has now gone dry which means we are left with the Punjabis, who are a Patiala peg apart in the Indian imagination when it comes to whisky. As Shivani Vora writes in *India Ink*, growing up in a Punjabi family meant 'drinking whisky is a ritual as sacrosanct as a religious ceremony.' Her childhood memories are of 'watching my father, my dadaji, and all the uncles from my parents' social circle sip a glass pre-dinner while nibbling on salted nuts.'

My childhood memories are not quite so convivial. My father, a well-bred Bengali gentleman, was a social drinker at best. He sipped on his whisky with his friends when they had their periodic no-children parties but rarely went beyond a glass. Despite that when I think of whisky now I think of aged fathers and their middle-aged children finally joined in quiet ritual. A friend talks about the simple joys of sharing a glass of Scotch at home in the evening with her father, a man in his late eighties. The writer Vikram Seth has written that when he got a £250,000 advance for *A Suitable Boy* he promised his father a lifetime supply of whisky. It's a promise he keeps diligently. It was all very dignified and touching but it gave whisky more of an avuncular charm than a forbidden allure. It was a grown-up drink, almost sedate in its amber propriety.

That image of whisky was in keeping with the stories we heard about the state's patrician Communist chief minister Jyoti Basu who wore starched white dhoti-panjabis but didn't let ideology or attire get in the way of his fondness for Jeffrey Archer novels and Scotch. Whisky on the rocks or with a little soda was a very bhadrolok drink, a gentlemanly drink, one that might be offered to a partner of the firm. Or a visiting journalist, as Ian Buruma recalls in the *New York Review of Books* while describing a meeting with Aveek Sarkar, the head of the Ananda Bazar Patrika media empire: 'We met in his office, housed in an old building in the centre of a commercial district where beggars and rickshawallahs dodged in and out of the hopeless traffic jams, while entire families, the children naked, the adults in flimsy clothes, washed themselves by burst waterpipes. Aveek was dressed in a dhoti and smoked Montecristo cigars. He offered me a fine Scotch whisky and talked about Bengali poetry. Every Bengali is a poet, he said.'

Then Sarkar took him to meet Satyajit Ray. But naturally.

There was another image of whisky—a darker one, far less bhadralok, steeped in irresponsibility and indulgence. This was whisky that was more recklessly adult rather than responsibly grown-up. I remember the bachelor uncle sitting at home on a shiny Rexine sofa drinking his Royal Reserve by himself. 'Another one? Your eyes are already red,' his sister's voice would be tight with disapproval. We would always hear the family story of some aunt married to a rich drunk. 'He'd come home from work every night so drunk the driver would have to help him to the door. I have heard she would stand on the balcony quietly looking down at him. It was such a sad life. She was so beautiful. Such a grand ICS family. No children either.' Another uncle in North Kolkata said he was glad his father dropped dead when he was just a boy. 'Otherwise we would be penniless. He would have spent it all on whisky and women. Every time he went to a courtesan's house he left his new shawl there.'

The nineteenth-century satirist Kaliprasanna Sinha had many tart portraits of such drunken babus lolling around in drunken excess in his famous book *Hootum Pyanchar Naksha* translated as *The Observant Owl* by Swarup Roy. He writes that while the drunken 'low-born sods' were carted off to the police station and given a good hiding and made to pay a fine of four annas, the drunken babus were a class unto themselves. The way they behaved would make anyone 'develop a deep loathing for well-to-do Bengalis.' Like Ghosh Babu of Thuntuneah: 'On another occasion, Ghosh Babu of Thuntuneah hosted (the play) *Vidyasundar* at his house. The babu was blind drunk. Reclining on a bolster, he was watching the jatra and snoring away loudly! He lay in a drunken stupor the whole night. He woke up at dawn at the shouts of the guards in the execution ground scene. But not seeing Krishna in the scene, the babu got steamed up. "Get Krishna! Get Krishna!" he bellowed. Others tried to reason with him: "Huzoor! There's no Krishna in *Vidyasundar*", but the babu wouldn't listen. Finally, he burst into tears (accusing Krishna of denying darshan to one of his ardent devotees!)'

In the novelist Nabarun Bhattacharya's famous tragicomic book *Herbert* fantastic flying creatures called Fyatarus hover over the decaying and debauched city of talking crows and crematoriums. One is named Madan, one is named Purandar Bhat and the other, their leader, is DS named after Director's Special whisky.

Bhattacharya's uncle (and his father's great friend) was the filmmaker Ritwik Ghatak. Ghatak was an alcoholic who started with branded liquor and ended with country booze that rotted his liver and even consigned him to an asylum. He looked like an old broken man when he died but he was only fifty-one. In his 1974 film *Jukti Takko Aar Gappo*, Nilkantha, the washed-up intellectual played by Ghatak himself, lies in an alcoholic stupor while his wife removes everything from his phonograph to his books from around him, afraid that he will otherwise sell them for another drink. The raw intensity of Ghatak, with a burn as intense as that cheap whisky scared me as much as the refined baritone of Satyajit Ray, as smooth as a smoky single malt, soothed me.

Caught between these two archetypes I remained an outcast in the whisky caste system. But in a sense, staying away from whisky also prevented me from ever having a real coming of age in Kolkata. My alcohol experience remained adolescent, not adult. I knew of shady bars with little dishes of peanuts, where men got into drunken fights over nothing at all but they made me uneasy. Instead I discovered bars and nightlife in the United States. I learned to drink California wine and Cosmopolitans and microbrews.

It was only after returning to India that I got reacquainted with whisky. Everyone was still drinking it. But something had changed. The mood had shifted.

As Bhattacharya writes in *Business Today*, 'The whisky graph first started to spike when Manmohan Singh reformed the trade tariffs in the 1990s, a time when duties on imported Scotch were so severe that only the uppermost crust could enjoy it.'

Drinking became more affordable, more commonplace and more varied. Whisky lost its Mona Darling connotation. Hindi villains post Ajit and Prem Chopra stopped flaunting that iconic green Vat 69 bottle as proof of their lecherous intentions. All of that was closed economy daydreaming.

In the more open economy our horizons expanded. In post-liberalization India getting smashed has never been easier. The average age for drinking dipped ever lower. Once alcohol was both expensive and not freely available. A friend remembered how she and her friends would dip their cigarettes into the dregs of their alcohol in the belief that they could eke out an extra high from the fumes of the boozy cigarette. There was no need for such desperate measures any more.

We didn't have to depend on London Aunty and California Uncle either. We could afford to experiment with that dragonfruit-infused vodka from abroad instead of sticking to the tried and true old standards for that treasured two-litre allowance. We learned that vodka had other advantages. At a famous drinking hole in Kolkata, with antiquated unwritten rules for women drinking alone, the waiter told a group of women they couldn't have whisky on the rocks because it looked like hard liquor. Vodka with orange juice however could pass the respectability test.

Indian publishing houses brought out books like *The Tulleeho Book of Cocktails* with recipes with names like Anarkali and Instant Karma. Department stores sold stainless steel cocktail shakers and ice buckets with tongs. Wine got better and more acceptable. The popularity graphs of drinks long ignored were on the rise. Indian wine still struggles to be taken seriously but there are some fifty domestic wineries now. An industry report says wine consumption is expected to increase by 73 per cent in 2017. And no corner of India is exempt not even the most hallowed stomping grounds of whisky—the Punjab. *India Today* spotted wine boutiques and wine clubs even in the Punjab. In the new India, Honey Singh, a Punjabi rapper no less, sings about how *char botal vodka* is *kaam mera roz ka.*

Thank goodness, Khushwant Singh, the grand old raconteur, didn't live to see this. The sardar who till the end enjoyed his muchhe-gilli-ho peg (moustache-soaking whisky) would probably have not survived the news.

The story of whisky's fortunes in this new India is mixed. It all depends on who you ask. 2013 was not good for India as the Whisky Nation—the largest guzzler of whisky in the world according to *India Ink*. Growth in whisky and brandy consumption declined and overall spirit sales were down by two per cent. Some blamed it on the sluggish economy and high taxes. Some pointed to the rise of wine. Others said it was the busy election cycle. Voting days are dry and the Election Commission has been especially watchful. But the International Wine and Spirits Research worried that year on year growth in whisky sales, in fact, have been going down every year since 2010. That's a dip in the growth though, not in actual sales.

So we shouldn't get too carried away. Whisky in India is in no danger of going the way of the Ambassador car. It's still a solid 57 per cent of the strong spirits market according to the annual report from Drinks International.

Not a single Indian institution made it into the top 200 of The Times Higher Education World Reputation rankings in 2014 but Drinks International names seven Indian brands in its list of the top ten fastest growing whiskies in the world. Officer's Choice is the largest

selling whisky brand now at 23.8 million cases ousting McDowell's
No. 1 from the top spot. The Johnnie Walker my aunt used to make
me carry back from 'foreign' is at No. 3. Drinks International says
there are seventeen millionaire brands in India aka brands that sell
more than a million cases each annually. The biggest attraction isn't
the taste. It's simply the price. 'On an average the cheapest whisky
globally would be fifteen dollars, whereas in India an expensive whisky
would be around that price,' Deepak Roy, executive vice chairman
and MD, Allied Blenders & Distillers (ABD) tells *The Times of India*.
And the market still has room to grow.

The number of Indians who drink is still relatively low—about
32 per cent according to a Nimhans study. Of that less than 13 per
cent drink daily. But what's striking is how we drink. The standard
international unit of alcohol is about 30 ml of spirit. In India, the
Nimhans study found, the usual drink poured at home is anywhere
between 60 ml and 270 ml. We drink to get drunk—a country on the
binge of an alcoholic breakdown. The genteel tradition of one chhota
peg everyday is fast being drowned out in a culture that worships
excess in every sphere. We have mixed the American frat house cool
of getting hammered with the English miner's serious drinking after
a hard week's work to create a dangerous cocktail. There's nothing
subtle or even refined about it.

Perhaps that is why in India today there's an attempt to target the
creamy layer of whisky consumers to bring back a whiff of exclusivity.
Pernod Ricard India sends invitations to journalists inviting them on
junkets to Scotland to 'extend your knowledge of Scottish whiskies,
sample topnotch malts and blends and absorb breathtaking scenery.'
Business Today describes whisky tastings at perfumeries helping people
'pick out the vanilla and geranium, the aubergine, lemon peels.' Five
star hotels have been doing high-end dinners with whisky pairings.
McDowell's even has DietMate which it calls the world's first ever
diet whisky.

It's enough to give an old-school whisky drinker an instant
hangover.

But luckily for the diehard drinker some traditions defy makeovers.

Alcohol is still sold in many places in cities like Kolkata in cage-like hole-in-the-wall shops with iron grids. The babu drinking his arrack out of a bottle bearing the label of Presidency Medical Hall, caricatured in Kaliprasanna Sinha's sketches would feel right at home there. In those days it was common for chemist shops to have an under the table booze business. Now that layer of pretence has been shed but it still remains a walk of shame.

The buyers throng outside on the sidewalk in a raucous disorderly group where auto-drivers rub shoulders with business executives. The bottle is passed through the bars in the cage wrapped in newsprint like some kind of contraband. And when the respectable middle-aged Indian man shoves that little bottle of Officers' Choice into his briefcase with a surreptitious glance around him and calls his friend on the phone to say cryptically 'Yes, got it', you know that whisky still occupies a special place in our imagination.

BLACK KNIGHTS AND RUMMY DAYS
Bhaichand Patel

Someone once said that life should not be a journey to the grave or the crematorium with the intention of arriving safely in a well-preserved body; it should be an exciting joy ride with a glass of whisky or wine in hand, body thoroughly used up, totally worn out and screaming, 'Wow! What a ride!'

That sounds like good advice to me so long as the body does not get thoroughly used up at too early an age. Conventional wisdom, of course, is that drinking alcohol in moderation is good for you and can prolong life. Excessive drinking, on the other hand, will take its toll.

I had my first drink in a pub behind Selfridges in London. You carry such memories to the grave, like your first kiss. It was gin and I was a student. It was the swinging '60s but the bartenders in British pubs gave a dirty look if you ordered anything more complicated than a gin and tonic. Their idea of a Bloody Mary was tomato juice poured out of a bottle over vodka. If you requested ice cubes, you were considered a difficult customer. How things have changed! These days some of the best cocktails are mixed in trendy establishments in London's West End. Be warned, they don't come cheap.

A few years later, when I embarked on a misguided career as a lawyer in Bombay, I was penniless. The only booze I could afford was rum. The naval base in Colaba provided sailors with rations of rum at eight rupees a bottle. I would buy a bottle from my bootlegger, who also happened to be my chemist, for twenty-five rupees.

Bombay was under Prohibition in those days, a legacy of a former chief minister, Morarji Desai, whose taste in drinks ran in another direction; he had the habit of drinking his own urine for medicinal purposes. Even at the princely price of twenty-five rupees, the rum often came adulterated. But I had no choice. There was nothing else available in that price range, except for hooch made in the slums—and one could risk one's life drinking it.

I have had a soft corner for rum ever since. Hercules was not bad-tasting for that kind of money. I haven't seen a bottle in years but I am told it is still available in certain parts of the country. A few years later I upscaled to Old Monk, another dark rum, that I bought from a licensed liquor shop. Since I was a foreign national I was entitled to a government-issued permit that allowed me to buy six bottles of hard liquor a month and a dozen bottles of beer.

Besides Old Monk I also bought Black Knight whisky at more or less the same price, around fifty rupees a bottle, not a small sum of money for someone with my income in those days. Both Old Monk and Black Knight came from Mohan Meakin's distillery in Solan, a small town in the Himalayas on the road to Simla. The company was a direct descendant of a British-owned company, Dyer Brewery, that was started by Edward Dyer in the late 1820s in nearby Kasauli. This enterprising Englishman brought his brewing and distilling equipment from Britain to Calcutta and then took it up the Ganges by boat as far as he could go. He then transported it in bullock carts all the way to the Himalayas.

Kasauli was initially selected as the location for its fine spring water, needed for both a decent beer as well as whisky. Mr Dyer was determined to produce whisky that was as good as Scotch. I am not sure he succeeded. Later he moved to nearby Solan where he found more space for his expanding operation. In the beginning his customers were mainly British troops stationed in India but there was soon a growing demand for his beer and whisky from the local population. The company was acquired by N.N. Mohan after Independence and his descendants still run it today.

Mohan Meakin's Golden Eagle beer was easily the best-selling beer thirty or forty years ago. Sadly, it is no longer in the market. The company's Solan No. 1 was mainly targeted at the military canteens while its Black Knight whisky found its way into the liquor shops. If there was a difference in taste between the two brands I couldn't detect it. Today the sales are way down. You will have a hard time finding a bottle of either brand in Delhi. Other brands like Blenders Pride and Royal Challenge have overtaken them.

Mohan Meakin also produce Old Monk which continues to be the best locally-produced rum in the country. It is part of our heritage. Its devotees are very possessive about it. It was a good rum fifty years ago when I first tasted it and it is a good rum today. Some claim that it is as good as the dark rums from the Caribbean, Myers's Rum from Jamaica for example, but I wouldn't go that far.

Old Monk still comes in a distinctive bottle, fat and short, which its devotees love. A few years back, Mohan Meakin decided to give the bottle a more conventional shape with disastrous results. There was a time when Old Monk had the rum market pretty much sewn up. There were other brands also, of course, but none came close in quality or popularity. About eight million bottles were sold annually. Today the sales are a quarter of that and they continue to decline.

What went wrong? First, a large percentage of its sales have been recently overtaken by McDowell's No. 1. This is partly due to aggressive marketing on the part of the newcomer. The brand is owned by one of the world's largest wine and spirits company, Diageo. It has deep pockets.

Then, with the easing of import restrictions in recent years, several foreign interlopers have entered the Indian rum market. Among them is the Bacardi brand which comes in white, dark and gold rums. Take your choice. Bacardi began life in Cuba in 1862. The tin-roofed shed in which it was first distilled housed a colony of bats. That's why the bat trademark appears on every bottle. It is the world's best-selling rum by a wide margin. When Fidel Castro seized the distillery in Cuba after the revolution the company moved its operations to a friendlier base in Puerto Rico.

Before you knew it, Bacardi was distilling and bottling it in India itself, in Karnataka. Old Monk, or any dark rum for that matter, is essentially a man's drink though I have a number of women friends whose drink of choice is Old Monk. I hope I am not accused of being sexist when I say that most women tend to drift towards wine, if it is offered, or one of the white spirits which they like diluted, preferably as a cocktail.

This is where Bacardi had an advantage. There were few bars around in the days when the sales of Old Monk were at their peak. Men bought a bottle, took it home, mixed it with coke or soda, added some ice cubes and drank it before the food was on the table. Those salwar kameez, Doordarshan days are gone. Nowadays, restaurants and bars in hotels or malls are filled with young women, with or without male friends, and occasionally even alone. Parents prefer not to know what goes on in these places. They will order wine by the bottle or cocktails that are vodka-based, gin-based or rum-based. Mojito, a white rum cocktail with crushed mint leaves floating in it, became a very popular drink among women as well as men. There were other rum cocktails like daiquiri and piña colada. All of them required white rum. Old Monk and other dark rums became passé, they were no good for cocktails. Dark rums were something parents drank at home while watching television. Not cool.

Old Monk still remains popular with a certain class of people, painters, journalists and those struggling in the performing arts. Many of them drink it because they like the taste, others because they can't afford Scotch. Old Monk tastes great sitting on plastic chairs in a barsaati in Delhi or on a beach in Mumbai with close friends, late at night, with smoke from something illegal floating in the air. It is more a Press Club of India drink than an Oberoi Hotel drink. Always was.

Rum is one of the oldest spirits in the world and, unlike gin, vodka or whisky, it is unmistakably a tropical spirit—just about every country that grows sugar cane, its staple ingredient, makes rum. When the cane is crushed it turns to cane juice. This is boiled down and part of it becomes the crystallized sugar you buy in shops. The rest is a thick, sweetish by-product known as molasses. This is fermented with yeast and then distilled to separate the alcohol from the solid wastes. The result is a clear, colourless liquid which is about 80 per cent alcohol. White or light rum is basically this product diluted down to 40 per cent alcohol. The dark and gold rums have a richer, heavier flavour. They get their colour from ageing in oak casks but some producers cheat by adding caramel to the white rum.

Rum is also the most versatile of liquors. You can drink it cold or you can drink it hot. You can mix it with just about anything—coke, tonic water, any fruit juice. You can add it to pudding or pour it over ice cream. You can even set it alight over gulab jamuns as some of our society matrons do. Most people drink it with coke. I like mine with soda and just a dash of lime cordial. It also goes well with ginger ale.

A popular rum cocktail is Planter's Punch, the credit for which is given to Frank Myers who opened a distillery in the late nineteenth century in his plantation in Jamaica. There are wide variations to the recipe. Anything vaguely tropical can be added to Planter's Punch: orange juice, Angostura bitters, even a sprinkling of red pepper powder. Garnishes range from nothing to those ridiculous paper umbrellas. Tourist traps will serve them to you in coconut shells instead of glasses. I found myself in Fiji with one that had a hibiscus flower sticking out of it. In 1930, Alec Waugh, brother of Evelyn and author of *Island in the Sun,* described the art of mixing rum punch as 'quarter of a finger's height of sugar, two fingers high of rum, the paring of a lime, the rattling of ice.'

The high quality brands, like 21-year-old Appleton Estate and Mount Gay Extra Old, should be treated like fine cognac and drunk neat. Don't waste them on your piña coladas and punches. The Mount Gay distillery in Barbados traces its origins to 1703, making it the world's oldest rum brand. That island with a population of 265,000 consumes more than 200,000 cases of rum every year.

Beneath rum's benign image lurk tales of depravity. It was the drink of the pirates and shady adventurers as well as the slaves in the West Indies. But let me tell you something wonderful about rum in the Indian context. It is the only genuine spirit produced in our country. Almost all Indian gin, vodka and whisky are fakes. Rum is distilled from molasses. Genuine whisky on the other hand, is made from grain, mainly barley, but other grains like wheat and rye are acceptable. While Scotland is the biggest producer, it can be made anywhere in the world. A number of countries make fine whisky.

That does not happen in India. Our whisky producers cheat by using neutral, tasteless alcohol extracted from molasses to which they add flavours and colours and, occasionally, a bit of genuine whisky imported in bulk. Indian whisky is a closer relative to rum than genuine whisky. This is also true of Indian vodka, gin and brandy. They are all distilled from molasses. More than 90 per cent of Indian whisky is not whisky at all. It is rum that has been given the flavour of whisky.

So why does Indian whisky taste more like real whisky than rum? Good question. Let's start at the lower end with bottles you buy for around a hundred rupees. This is alcohol to which colour and flavourings are added: caramel to give it the whisky colour; essence and tinctures to make it taste something like whisky. This concoction is not remotely whisky.

One step up the ladder is alcohol to which, in addition to all of the above, a small amount of locally produced malt whisky is added. In India malt whisky is produced from barley that is grown mostly in the border area between Haryana and Rajasthan.

Then you have whiskies like Shaw Wallace's Royal Challenge that sell for around Rs 400 a bottle. They contain some imported Scotch and Indian malts. The labelling of these brands is deceptive and one cannot really tell what's in the bottle. For example, the label of Royal Challenge, one of the largest-selling Indian brands, states: 'A blend of Scotch and matured Indian malts.' It does not say: 'A blend of *only* Scotch and matured Indian malts.' It does not tell you that the bulk is something else: molasses alcohol.

So why don't our distilleries switch from molasses to grain? It is a question of cost. Molasses is a waste product and cheap. Grain is expensive. And who wants to go through the process of ageing in oak barrels for four years or more? We are good at cutting corners. It makes Indian distillers mad that most countries, including the European Union, will not allow the import of their product labelled as whisky since it is not whisky.

Like most Indians, I have a soft corner for Scotch. These days I can afford it. It need not be single malt as long as it is genuine whisky. Scotch whisky has always been around and India probably consumes more bottles of it than any other country. It is said that India drinks more Scotch than is produced in Scotland. That's because a considerable number of bottles sold by bootleggers are fake! In fact, Indians are the largest consumer of whisky in the world, 40 per cent more than the United States, the second-largest consumer. It is the drink of choice of most people in this country who drink alcohol. No other spirit or brew comes even close to its popularity. Most Indians will drink anything that is labelled whisky but it is Scotch that we love with a passion.

Scotch comes exclusively from Scotland. No other whisky has the right to be called Scotch. It tastes great. It must be the water from the Scottish Highlands. How else do you explain that no country outside Scotland has been able to replicate Scotch? Some whiskies from Ireland, Canada and the United States are quite good. So is the Suntory brand from Japan. But they all pale when you compare them to Scotch. They don't give you the same satisfaction. And Indians, certainly, refuse to touch any of them.

Malt whisky in Scotland is made exclusively from barley. The process has remained unchanged for hundreds of years. Records of production go back to 1494. The oldest existing distilleries date from the 1700s. When whisky production began, the notion of brands was unknown and whisky was sold by the barrel to merchants who dispensed it in whatever container was available. Johnnie Walker was one such merchant and George Ballantine another. The Chivas brothers were partners in another shop. John Dewar started his business in 1806 and he was the first to sell branded whisky in bottles.

Besides whisky, I also like a good gin and tonic on weekends. Nothing gives me more pleasure than an ice-filled glass of Pimm's before lunch in the heat of summer. Or a hot buttered rum by my fireplace on a cold winter evening. I enjoy my tipple and I can say in all honesty that I mix cocktails better than most bartenders I have known in our country. They tend to be too generous with the sweeteners, not so generous when it comes to adding spirits and liqueurs.

I have not lived in one place very long. A nomadic life has its disadvantages but it has given me an opportunity to mingle with people from different cultures and backgrounds and try out their food and drink. I had my first shot of tequila, with a piece of lime in one hand and a pinch of salt on the back of the other, in Acapulco. Walter the barman in the delegates' lounge at the UN in New York taught me how to mix a great Bloody Mary. The best beer I have tasted was in the town of Ceske Budejovice in the Czech Republic. I hate those little paper umbrellas that they put in glasses of tropical cocktails but I would not say no to one when I am lying on a beach in the South Pacific. I like to go with the flow.

Let me leave you here with a thought. I enjoy a good whisky and a good rum. I also like fine wines. But some of my most memorable evenings have been spent drinking feni on Delhi's rooftops or what we call barsaatis. At that point in our lives that was all my friends and I could afford. When you are entertaining, you should always remember that it is the generosity of your spirit, the mix and the mood of the people you invite that will ensure the success or failure of the evening. Serve what you can afford. If a guest complains, don't invite that person again.

WHEN NIGHTS TURN INTO DECADES

Kanika Gahlaut

I wake up these mornings and, coffee and iPad in hand, cat at my feet, I sit in my little garden room, anticipating the arrival of the butterflies.

Once the plants have been watered, the early birds have made their noise and are done with it and the dew is gone, they begin to arrive from over the boundary wall.

The castor butterfly, feeding on the forest of wild castor plants growing in the no man's land behind my house, is among the first visitors. It glides lazily if effortlessly, as if there's enough castor for its machinery to never be short on oil. Its wings have an exquisite brown on brown self pattern, resembling pencil shavings.

If it's a particularly sunny day, the lime butterfly, an astonishingly large member of the swallowtail family, with a strong flight, will come in to circle around the mandarin orange tree my mother planted thirty years ago, when we moved here. And if I'm really lucky, I may even get to watch the common jay butterfly, or the great egg fly, with iridescent blue and purple wings, stop by and rest on the line of false Asoka trees at the boundary wall.

Butterflies have flight paths. Or there are some invisible super highways out there, between grass and sky, a sophisticated system of travel, with the butterfly species sticking to lanes by and large. They'll hop over from across the boundary, either alone or dancing in twos or even threes, then make their way around the greenery that outlines the glass, hovering over a shrub of choice, then pass under the green archway, before gliding out to the backyard of the next house.

You may be wondering what butterfly flight paths have to do

with, well, the subject of this anthology. My friend PKM may have
had a coronary while reading this, seeing blank pages where my essay
should have been.

Well, the point is this—I no longer drink. I am forty. After twenty
years of drinking—qualification enough to land me a piece in this
anthology—I find myself going further and further away from the
bottle. The birds and the butterflies have always been here, I just never
saw them in my drinking years. I was too busy—busy tripping into
the house past midnight, hoping no one would notice the swaying
walk or the car parked wrong, to crash on the bed, head spinning.
The morning after also followed a predictable route—wake up with
pounding head, rush to work, swear never to do this again, until the
next time.

I drink sometimes. I'll open a bottle of beer and have it sitting
out on the grass on a cloudy day. Or I'll meet an old friend or two,
and we'll have a piss up. But now the alcohol is coincidental to the
friendship, not the other way round.

I was having one such sangria pitcher lunch with a younger
girlfriend the other day. We met for lunch at Khan Market's
Smokehouse Deli soon after her return from her honeymoon. I
mentioned the anthology, and the irony of being asked to write for
it when I barely drink anymore. 'But you've had enough experience,'
she shrugged in return.

So then this is it.

For sociological purposes, and in order to present my credentials
in the field of drinking—a rich and diverse adventure that has seen
me hopping from after party to bar in my hectic days as a Chatterati
reporter, to the less flashy but angst-ridden binges in makeshift carobars
and press clubs with members of my journalistic tribe, to clandestine
rooftop drinking in Rohtak at a cousin's wedding, to the champagne-
popping world of fashion to which I got a backstage pass at another
point in my career—my intention is to give to you a sketch of various
types of drinking in India.

While I have stated my current relationship with alcohol upfront
(note to Ed: every anthology needs a rebel), let it by no means be

construed as a vote against alcohol. And now that we're stating positions, let me elaborate—I may not be judgemental about drinking, but don't expect me to glamourize it here either.

My feelings towards alcohol are, well, a cocktail. For the most part, it's an exhausting, meaningless and pointless exercise that arises as a coping mechanism to human anxiety, pain, loneliness, insecurities and emotional fear.

On the other hand, in defence of the many pained, anxious, lonely, emotionally paralyzed people who continue to seek alcohol as a means out of the tunnel, these are natural reactions to the act of living. Anybody who hasn't felt such emotions acutely enough at some point in their life to want to somehow alleviate the symptoms, even if briefly, is, perhaps, less than human.

There are types of drinkers. The binge drinkers. They let go. And then next morning, they are in control again.

The sliding drinkers—you see them fall slowly and steadily into the arms of the seductive booze, unable to come up again, the intellect slowly wasting away.

The hangers on: drinking for them is not the purpose. They feed off the energy of other drinkers, going with the flow.

The hangers on will hang out with the performer, who at least has the courtesy to make an arse of himself, while the rest of the table will escape censure simply because the performer is behaving so badly.

And so on.

But while some writers make the case that alcohol provides rare insights into character and the human condition, for most of us, the problem arises with documenting it.

Often, you come back from a binge with the notion that you nailed something vital about the characteristics of the person you were drinking with, but the next morning you can't put your finger on exactly what it was that gave them away.

Or you're sitting with a glass of red wine after a normal day, and then the one glass becomes three, and suddenly you have a flash of insight about a work problem or character flaw in your boyfriend, and you are convinced that acting decisively and immediately is the only answer—and you do. You call the boyfriend and 'break up' with him. Or you text the boss and tell him you're quitting, only to, in some survival instinct that swims to the fore, change the text to 'not coming into work tomorrow' and press send. Phew.

And so on.

You're getting my point—drinking has its misses as much as its hits.

But having said that, to be a participant in and a witness to periodic and sustained binges through one's life does put one in a unique position of being exposed to, and humbled by, both the boringness and specialness of human frailties in an intense slow-motion theatrical performance that, even though it amounts in the end to nothing but a hazy blur in memory, leaves you with a sense that a window of perception opened up somewhere and altered possibilies forever.

Happy families are all alike, unhappy families are unique in their own way said Leo Tolstoy and, with due apologies, I'll say for alcoholism: drunks are all alike, it is the symptoms that are unique in their own way.

Age, or more specifically, age related circumstances are likely to be a factor in attitudes to drinking, and for many the urge for the bottle diminishes with the need for company. Relationships, break ups, marriages, children, divorces, career successes, career failures are all stresses that require us to be battling with people for dominance—once you are at an age when the mad dust of making it has settled, and your future, for better or for worse, is no longer a blank hole but something tangible that you built over the years, and now that you can see where the road leads, you may not need the alcohol-fuelled quick fix as often.

One's attitude to alcohol also depends on your relationship with it: did you make it your lover, drowning in its charms, unable to pull yourself out? Or did you treat it as an equal, seeing it for what it is? Each alcohol seeker's journey depends on the road he or she has chosen.

In the Chatterati world of which I was an accidental inhabitant, when the liberalization-fuelled Page 3 phenomenon in Delhi coincided with the early days of my career in journalism, these heady relationships with the bottle were just going on display in the public domain.

Budding socialites got drunk, smooched for the cameras, then, in a sober state in their south Delhi homes, waged war against newspapers for printing the pictures and ruining their relationship with the potential business baroness mother-in-law. Models danced semi-naked on bar tops till the cops were called. These were days that culminated, most memorably, at the end of the 1990s, in a drugs and alcohol-fuelled shooting at an illegal bar, in which a model was shot dead.

While the pros and cons of this culture of excess are much fodder for spicy newspaper features—not to mention books from Scott Fitzgerald's *The Great Gatsby* to Mohsin Hamid's *Mothsmoke*, a wonderful take on the effortlessly rich in Pakistan—there is always a sheen of glamour around these stories, as if these individuals are merely exhibiting free choice and, somewhere, ready to pay the price for it.

In homes in neighbouring areas—for instance the village near west Delhi from which my father's family hails—villages which have had to suddenly deal with urbanization, and the social problems it brings, alcohol is every family's dirty secret. It is still a choice, perhaps, but not an educated choice.

Alcohol is not a manifestation of empowerment here—as it is for the gay boys who climbed atop a bar and gyrated to music at a Rohit Bal after party—but a tool of fear.

It is the fear we felt as children when we heard that the head of a family in the village, in an alcoholic rage, shot dead his entire family before turning the gun on himself.

Or the fear that led my uncles to come to our home, a decade later, and remove all the licensed guns—the pride of my ex-army father who had severe alcohol problems—from their caskets and take them away from our home forever, so that they no longer posed the threat of being used against us by their owner.

In such homes, the alcohol becomes the cue. Children can, if they wish, turn it from trigger into ally. They enter the house. They smell the whisky. Their brain starts mapping the room for escape routes. Cause and effect are lessons learnt early. These are homes where alcohol precedes random violence.

But while I roamed both these worlds where alcohol runs as a subtext in the story, one was only a professional curiosity, and the other, a mere accident of birth. In India's many parallel realities that exist together, these worlds were already around and, for all practical purposes, will continue to exist.

What is as much a symbol of our times as a byproduct of liberalization's children—I began college in 1991, the year of economic reforms, and entered the Indian economy a couple of years later—is the pubbing culture that mushroomed in our earning years.

While Khan Market once only had Chonas, the hangout college students considered the ultimate in luxury—we entered an economy— as lawyers and journalists, bankers and architects, physiotherapists and HR professionals—where we could, unbelievably for those of us who grew up in the Krishi Darshan days of Doordarshan, channel our inner Ally McBeal and head to the bar after work.

From Thank God it's Friday to Djinns and Ricks, to now the numerous new breweries in Gurgaon, old gems like the UCH and the crazy days of Turquoise Cottage, in the graffiti-filled basements, and of course, the cat-friendly, sweaty Press Club, the city has been witness to two decades of nocturnal excesses of a growing number of men and women that made up the cliche India Shining.

Our drinking epitomized, in a way, our lifestyle: the work hard and play hard generation that was the hope of the Indian economy, we bought Marutis on EMIs and drove from one bar to another after work. We dated in bars. We went to bars when we broke up. We moped in bars. We celebrated a promotion with Margaritas. We got onto the floor and dragged strangers with us. We got back home—heaven knew how—only to get into bed and, inexplicably, weep. Only to drag ourselves to work because we had that assignment to turn in.

Here, alcohol represented freedom. For a whole new generation of women, the easy access to alcohol has been like crossing the final bastion to being equal with men: the right to waste shitloads of money on LITs in one evening. Or to bunk work to drink martinis with a colleague and heap abuses on the patriarchal system at the work place. Or to go to a friend's house for an afternoon of drinking, sneer covertly at the pseudo intellectualism of the company present, and leave because the music is too pretentious.

While alcohol was certainly not what empowered us, with the ability it has to exaggerate a moment, it made us feel empowered (though I'll admit that as far as feelings induced by alcohol go, nothing beats that old bastard, nausea). Equal pay may be still some way ahead, but the ability to buy one's own drinks and then proceed to act whichever way we like under its influence, is in a way an equalizer.

If excess—and bingeing—are liberating, then these are acts of emancipation and solidarity and free will that we could not even imagine even in our growing years, before the landscape suddenly changed in the mid '90s. It allowed us a certain respite from our daily lives that men in popular culture have always seemed entitled to but women, even till our mothers' times, did not have. It allowed us, also, to break away, as much for ourselves as for the world, from traditional womanly attributes and expected social behaviour—an inebriated, incoherent, messy woman is not a charming sight, and we learnt to not only be in touch with it, but assert our right to it.

As we sped down the empty highway on our way home in our dinky little cars, pondering the mysteries of existence while simultaneously keeping the peripheral vision on alert for dodgy encounters on the capital's unsafe streets, had he seen us, the great Ghalib—former resident of Delhi and friend to alcoholics everywhere—would have approved and perhaps even penned a couplet or two in honour of the emerging new breed of boozards.

This is not the culture we were born to, or the life we envied from afar, or the lifestyle we hoped to marry into. This was a whole new lifestyle we created and—as women's safety increasingly becomes a political issue—it is clear that there is no going back on it.

It is, finally, this new tribe of entrants into the great Indian Middle Class, and the force of their sheer numbers, that makes them at once consumers as well as co-conspirators in the India story.

We owned these nights. We worked hard. We played hard.

The nights suddenly turned into decades.

Yes, the butterflies were here all the time—there is just no way in hell I could have had any time for them.

Disclosure: The butterfly-watching is often accompanied with lighting up a wee one: it helps the joints. Besides, butterfly spotting requires immense patience and some calming of the nerves helps.

EPILOGUE: SOME PATHOLOGIES

Amit Chaudhuri

I was born with a defect—but, then again, I don't know if I was born with it or acquired it. Can you acquire a defect? Maybe I'm looking for a different word. It's not a defect in the sense that my heart murmur, discovered when I was two and a half, was one. The cause of the murmur was attended to when I was thirty-six years old, and, until then, caused me no distress—it was mainly distressful to my family. This other defect I mention wasn't actually noticed until I was an adult, and, even then, people saw it less as a defect than as perversity. I'm talking about the fact that I don't drink. This isn't a stance I've taken on behalf of a world-view or an ideology. That would have been forgivable. No, I don't drink because I feel no craving for drink. This is seen by the people I encounter socially not only to be inexplicable but suspect. For, to deliberately reject pleasure is sinister. As D.H. Lawrence said of 'people who are genuinely repelled by the simplest and most natural stirring of sexual feeling...they nearly always enjoy some unsimple and unnatural form of sex excitement, secretly.' Over the years, I've realized that this absence, in my brain, of whatever lobe it is that instructs you that you're missing the taste of alcohol is probably a mysterious pathology. Once you're discovered, you are looked upon as the last surviving human being might be by the new colonies of body snatchers: with hostility and accusation. They nod and smile when you refuse the glass, but the eyes say, '*What?* You *look* just like one of us.'

This isn't to say I don't drink. I began drinking beer when I was sixteen years old because it seemed to go well with playing the guitar and being a young man. Opening the can with an inaugural pop gave much satisfaction; I poured, and admired the surplus of froth on the top; I liked the mild bitter cold taste. After five sips, I grew bored of the increasing tepidity. Finishing a glass was hard work, requiring diligence and commitment. If alcohol is an acquired taste, I didn't have the patience or respect to undergo the socialization necessary to my acquiring it. The love of drink either had to come naturally or not at all. Also, to my misfortune, the taste had a faint resemblance, for me, to medicine. But the polite drinking I was introduced to as a student in Oxford, I enjoyed—wine, port—though, strangely, perhaps crassly, I enjoyed other things (like eating an egg and cress sandwich) even more. I discovered I liked German Riesling. My taste had nothing to do with refinement or understanding. In relation to Riesling or port, I was like the person who confesses his favourite raga is *Kedar* while admitting to knowing nothing about classical music. Also, like the person who loves *Kedar* but gets progressively bored of it after fifteen minutes, my capacity for Riesling was half a wine glass. After that, I reached saturation point and had to force myself. Not only did I not have loyalty to the concept of drinking, I lacked, as cricketers say, temperament.

A dislike of drink could be the result of a particular kind of socialization; but an indifference to it must have its source elsewhere. That source must be deeper; or biological. Anyway, I was brought up by parents who imposed almost nothing on me. So, to explain my drinking habits, I—like at least a few alcoholics—need to look away from my milieu and to my DNA. I have to consider my father—not as my instructor or exemplar, but as an author of my genetic make-up. My father didn't drink. He also didn't smoke. Neither my mother nor I found this odd; we found it amusing. He rose very high on the corporate ladder; as a result, my parents went to a lot of parties. The familiar story about my father's drinking strategy was this: that he got himself a glass of whisky and for the rest of the evening replenished it with soda or water. A couple of times, I saw him return from a party frazzled and slightly ill, my mother oddly unworried: my father had smoked a cigar, and it had disagreed with him. Why he never took to drink or cigarettes he never explained to us. This silence is connected, in my mind, to two things. The first is his innocence—I can't think of another word to describe his dissimulation, concealing the fact that he was both of the corporate world and not of it. The second is that he was actually a deeply private man. He was friendly and transparent, so I didn't become aware of this until towards the end of his life, when it occurred to me that most of the family stories I'd heard, even about my father, had been told to me by my mother (she'd known my father since they were children). It's not that my father was inarticulate; it's as if he either doubted if he could express himself on this subject, or was waiting for the right moment to speak. The business of his general abstention from cigarettes and alcohol reminds me that there's much I don't know about my father.

Another confession: I don't smoke. You might presume that I was stepping into my father's shoes unconsciously. I don't think so. In reality, I contrived in fundamental ways *not* to step into his shoes. I'll mention two instances. The first was the absence in myself of any ambition to replicate my father's corporate life: the company house and furniture, the company car, the job security (so important in the 1970s). The second had to do with a minor rebellion that my father didn't even notice. He, a man without affectations, ate with cutlery. It was a habit he'd picked up in his years in London. I remember doing the same as a child, then becoming mildly impatient at the sight of a man eating with a fork and a spoon, until, at the age of ten, I switched to eating at home with my fingers. The dining experience suddenly improved, and I stuck to fingers with meals at home. So I think my relationship to drinking and smoking extends my father's legacy not through conscious resolve on my part, but via genetic inheritance.

I should introduce another element here to contextualize my non-smoking and largely non-drinking ways. It's to do with resistance. I recall going after school with a small group of friends to a space behind the New Empire cinema in Bombay. Somebody had named this derelict space the 'adda'. The main purpose of the brief, triumphant, slightly panic-stricken congregation was to smoke. The smoking was completed in a desperate rush, as if the smokers were inhaling snakebite antidote. As hurriedly, they procured and sucked on Halls' lozenges later, to disguise the smoke-breath from their parents. The entire undignified proceedings were enveloped in the haze and ingenuousness of rebellion. I politely refused to partake of the experience, and sat and talked with them till they finished. My opting out had to do with an innate sense of superiority that I should have been well rid of, but wasn't. It emerged from a high-faluting conviction that rebellion couldn't be earned cheaply. I may have made my friends a little uncomfortable, not because they felt I'd judged them, but because I'd elected to be a witness. There are few things more disorienting than to have an observer among you. The greatest sin is not the sin of having a bad habit, or of high-handedly deciding which habits are bad and which good, but the transgression of not joining in.

The pressure I've felt, then (mainly in India), is not the pressure faced by a non-drinker, but a non-joiner. The situation is easier in, say, Britain. Drinking is a longstanding social ritual there, and it's up to you as to whether or not you wish to subscribe to it. In India, it still carries with it an improbable tinge of wrongness, of secret rebellion, of grown-upness—to drink is to be part of a freemasonry or, more appropriately for present-day India, a coterie. To not drink is to place yourself on the outside; the outside being a zone without status or definition. Which is why, I suppose, my father had to pretend, filling his glass with water all evening. I haven't been able to quite shake off some of the puritanism of my early youth—which wasn't a puritanism against alcohol, but against causes and coteries. I was too intolerant towards cozy ideas that alcohol could be a sort of substitute for individuality, imaginativeness, and angularity; that, even if you had little of these qualities, simply drinking or smoking would provide you with some kind of credentials. There's a charm in this notion— this concept of performance—that I've perhaps noticed too late. My stance has left me a bit lonely, and lacking in the experience of the camaraderie of drunkenness, and its gift of oblivion. But, as I hinted earlier, I've known other, more powerful pleasures.

Notes on Contributors

Sumanta Banerjee has been a journalist by profession for nearly half a century. Currently based in Hyderabad, he writes political commentaries on current events in India and is engaged in research on popular culture and social history of nineteenth-century Bengal. His published works include *In the Wake of Naxalbari* (1980); *The Parlour and the Streets: Elite and Popular Culture in Nineteenth Century Calcutta* (1989), and *The Wicked City: Crime and Punishment in Colonial Calcutta* (2009).

Gautam Bhatia graduated in Fine Arts and went on to get a Masters degree in architecture. A Delhi-based architect, he has received several awards for his drawings and buildings and has also written extensively on architecture. Besides a biography on Laurie Baker, he is the author of *Punjabi Baroque, Silent Spaces* and *Malaria Dreams*—a trilogy that focuses on the cultural and social aspects of buildings. His most recent book *Lie: A Traditional Tale of Modern India* was published in 2010. Bhatia is currently working on *Below the Horizon – Ideas for the City*.

Sidharth Bhatia is a journalist and the founder editor of the online site www.thewire.in. He enjoys old Hindi and Hollywood films, rock music and loves to walk in his beloved Mumbai.

Soumya Bhattacharya's books about how cricket defines India, *You Must Like Cricket?* and *All That You Can't Leave Behind*, have been published to international acclaim. His novel, *If I Could Tell You*, was a finalist for the Hindu Prize for Fiction 2010. He is also the author of the fatherhood memoir, *Dad's the Word*, and, most recently, *After Tendulkar: The New Stars of Indian Cricket*. His writing has appeared in the *New York Times*, *Granta*, the *Guardian*, the *Independent*, the *New Statesman* and the *Sydney Morning Herald*, among a host of publications across the world. He is the editor of the *Hindustan Times*, Mumbai.

Amit Chaudhuri is the author of six novels, the latest of which is *Odysseus Abroad*, one work of non-fiction and a number of books of literary criticism. Among the many prizes he has won for his fiction are the Commonwealth Literature Prize, the Betty Trask Prize, the Los Angeles Times Book Prize, the Infosys Prize and the Sahitya Akademi Award. He is also a highly respected critic, a fellow of the Royal Society of Literature, and Professor of Contemporary Literature at the University of East Anglia. Amit Chaudhuri lives in Kolkata and Norwich, and is also an acclaimed musician.

Siddharth Chowdhury was born in Patna in 1974 and is the author of *Diksha at St Martin's* (Srishti, 2002), *Patna Roughcut* (Picador, 2005), *Day Scholar* (Picador, 2010), shortlisted for the 2009 Man Asian Literary Prize and longlisted for the 2012 DSC Prize for South Asian Literature, and *The Patna Manual of Style* (Aleph, 2015), shortlisted for the Hindu Prize for Fiction 2015.

Kanika Gahlaut is a journalist and writer. She lives in Gurgaon, Haryana.

Anjum Hasan is the author of the novels *The Cosmopolitans, Neti, Neti* and *Lunatic in My Head*, the short story collection, *Difficult Pleasures*, and the collection of poems, *Street on the Hill*. She is books editor at *Caravan* magazine and lives in Bangalore.

Indrajit Hazra is a writer and journalist. He is the author of the novels, *The Burnt Forehead of Max Saul* (2000), *The Garden of Earthly Delights* (2003), and *The Bioscope Man* (2008). His *Grand Delusions: A Short Biography of Kolkata* was published in 2013. He writes the fortnightly column Red Herring for *The Economic Times* and is an occasional contributor for *The Times of India*. He lives in Delhi and has no fondness for single malts, preferring the company of Jameson Irish whiskey.

Pavankumar Jain was a bilingual writer who wrote in both Gujarati and English. Born in 1947, he was educated at St Xavier's College, Bombay, and was in the first batch of students to pass out of the National Institute of Design, Ahmedabad, in 1974. His first book *Desh Pardesh Ni Loka Kathao* (Folk Tales from Around the World), published in 1997, won the Kala Gurjari Puraskar. This was followed by a collection of poems *Pasath Kavyo* (2012), which was the runner-up for the Gujarati Sahitya Academy Prize, and a short story collection *Taitris Vartao,* published posthumously in 2015. His second book was also published in 2015. His poems have been translated into Hindi, Marathi, Malayalam and English. Jain also wrote and translated under various pseudonyms: Roshan Ali, Naseera Ansari and Ivan Stephen Dedalus. Between 1967 and 1971, he edited the little magazine *Tornado.* He died in 2013.

Adil Jussawalla was born in Bombay in 1940. He is the author of four books of poems. His third, *Trying to Say Goodbye,* recently won the Sahitya Akademi Award for an outstanding work of literature in English. He also edited the anthology *New Writing in India* (1974). *Maps for a Mortal Moon* (2013) has some of his prose selected and edited by Jerry Pinto. *I Dreamt a Horse Fell from the Sky,* a selection of his poems, fiction and non-fiction, was published by Hachette in 2015. As for his drinking, he'd like it to be known that he gave up alcohol in March 1999 and, though not everyone may want to believe him, hasn't gone back to it.

Abhinav Kumar belongs to the 1996 batch of IPS. In his nineteen years of service, primarily in the state of Uttarakhand, he has served as police chief of four districts. He has also served as ADC to the Governor, Uttarakhand, and Additional Secretary, CM, Uttarakhand, and PS to a Union Minster. Since July 2014 he has been with the Indo-Tibet Border Patrol (ITBP). He is a recipient of the Police Medal for Meritorious Services. He is a regular contributor to the *Indian Express.* Unusually for a police officer, he has a B.A. (Hons.) and an M.A. in Philosophy and Economics from Oxford University.

Anup Kutty is a guitarist, music producer/curator and restaurateur based in New Delhi. He has worked for *The Pioneer, The Times of India* and *Caravan,* and was the youngest editor for *Maxim* magazine globally. He has written on music for *Rolling Stone* (India) and the *Indian Express.* He is a founder-member of Delhi-based rock band Menwhopause and performs frequently with poet Jeet Thayil's music project, Still Dirty. He has recorded an album in a cave with American singer-songwriter Joseph Arthur, and is currently producing an EP for YouTube's Hindi rap sensation, Faadu. He also organizes the Ziro Festival of Music in Arunachal Pradesh and runs The Toddy Shop, a Kerala cuisine restaurant, with his mother and friends. They don't serve cows there.

Vijay Nambisan has worked and written for journals in many parts of India. His poems have been widely published. His books include *Bihar is in the Eye of the Beholder, Language as an Ethic* and *Two Measures of Bhakti.* His first collection of poems since 1992, *First Infinities,* was published in 2015. He has been five times to treatment/rehabilitation centres for alcoholism.

Bhaichand Patel has lived in Fiji, London, New York, Caracas, Cairo, Jerusalem, Manila, Mumbai and New Delhi. Spirits and wines have always been his travelling companions. A graduate of the London School of Economics, Bhaichand has served before the bar as a barrister and behind the bar as a bartender. He is the author of four books including the best-selling *Happy Hours: The Penguin Book of Cocktails.*

Sandip Roy is a writer and journalist currently living in Kolkata after many years in San Francisco. His first novel, *Don't Let Him Know,* is set in both Cals—California and Calcutta—and has been longlisted for the DSC Prize for South Asian Literature among other awards. As a journalist, his work has appeared in the *New York Times,* the *Guardian*, the *San Francisco Chronicle* and *The Times of India.* He has been a senior editor at Firstpost and is currently a contributing editor at Huffington Post. He is a commentator on National Public Radio and the BBC and his radio dispatch from Kolkata airs on public radio in the San Francisco Bay Area every week. His work has appeared in various anthologies like *Out!, Story-wallah* and *Contours of the Heart.* He has a weakness for kitchen appliances, boutique hotels and exotic cocktails.

Arunabh Saikia is a Delhi-based journalist. Like most desis, he sticks to whisky during the summer and rum in the winters. But unlike most desis, he does drink beer in the winters.

Aditya Sinha is a journalist living on the outskirts of Delhi. He was editor-in-chief of *The New Indian Express,* based in Chennai, and of *DNA,* based in Mumbai. His latest published book is *Kashmir: The Vajpayee Years,* co-written with ex-RAW chief, A.S. Dulat.

Mayank Shekhar is a writer, broadcaster and film critic. He runs TheW14.com, and practically lives on beer and Mumbai's polluted air.

Manohar Shetty has published seven books of poems, including *Domestic Creatures* (Oxford University Press). His new books are *Living Room* (HarperCollins) and *Morning Light* (Copper Coin). Several anthologies feature his work, notably *The Oxford-India Anthology of Twelve Modern Indian Poets* (ed. Arvind Krishna Mehrotra, OUP) and anthologies edited by Eunice de Souza, Vilas Sarang and Jeet Thayil. He has edited *Ferry Crossing: Short Stories from Goa* (Penguin India) and *Goa Travels: Being the Accounts of Travellers to Goa from the 16th to the 20th Century* (Rupa). He has lived in Goa since 1985.

Jairaj Singh is a New Delhi-based writer and journalist. He is the editor of DailyO, India Today's opinion website.

Samanth Subramanian is an award-winning journalist and the author of two books, *Following Fish: Travels Around the Indian Coast* and *This Divided Island: Stories from the Sri Lankan War*. His journalism has appeared in the *New Yorker*, the *New York Times*, the *Guardian*, *Granta*, the *Wall Street Journal*, *Intelligent Life* and *Caravan*, among others. *Following Fish* won the Shakti Bhatt First Book Prize in 2010. *This Divided Island* won the Crossword Non-fiction Prize in 2015 and was shortlisted for the Samuel Johnson Non-fiction Prize the same year. A graduate of Columbia University's School of International and Public Affairs, Samanth lives and works in New Delhi

Mayank Tewari is a screen-writer.

Jeet Thayil was born in Mamalasserie, Kerala, and educated in Mumbai, Hong Kong and New York. His four poetry collections include *English* and *These Errors Are Correct*, which won the 2013 Sahitya Akademi Award for poetry. He is the editor of *The Bloodaxe Book of Contemporary Indian Poets* and is a visiting professor of poetry at the University of Goa. As a musician and songwriter, he is one half of the contemporary music project Sridhar/Thayil. His Delhi-based band is Still Dirty. Jeet Thayil's novel *Narcopolis* won the 2012 DSC Prize for South Asian Literature, and was shortlisted for five other prizes, including the Man Booker prize, the Man Asian Literature Prize and the Commonwealth Prize.

Zac O'Yeah is the author of popular comic thrillers *Hari, a Hero for Hire* (2015) described by bestselling novelist Ashok Banker as 'one of the best crime novels set in India written by anyone', *Mr Majestic! The Tout of Bengaluru* (2013) and *Once Upon a Time in Scandinavistan* (2010), plus ten other books. His books have been translated into several languages and he has also translated Indian literature into Swedish. As a veteran travel writer, he is a frequent contributor to *National Geographic Traveller* magazine. He is also a columnist with *The Hindu BusinessLine* and an influential literary critic. He is a Bangalorean and bent on staying one, and is a familiar face in almost every seedy bar in town. Download his updates from www.zacoyeah.com